BUSH LEAGUE

IF THEY WERE GOOD ENOUGH...
THEY'D BE IN THE NFL?

BRUNO BRANCO

This book is dedicated to anyone that has ever felt the sting of rejection...

Always continue striving to be the best that you can be!

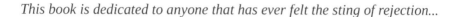

*A special thanks to my beautiful wife Elisa and our two boys;
Tyson and Cristiano.*

*Your unwavering support and understanding is what allowed me to dedicate
thousands of hours to this project, and what ultimately allowed this book
and PSC as a whole to exist.*

Thank you for your immense patience and understanding!

I love you guys!

About Pro Stats Canada

Pro Stats Canada analyzes players' statistical production to produce player ratings and rankings, primarily in the Canadian Football League (CFL).

Our rating system is founded upon measuring a player's statistical production and comparing it against the production of other players within the same position group, over the same period of time. While we understand that the numbers may not tell the whole story about a player's talent and contribution to the game, the numbers also "don't lie" as the saying goes. Generally speaking, the best players on the field produce statistically. The system can be used to rate a player's performance over a single game, week, season, or even a protracted period of time such as a decade.

The system works by assigning numerical ratings out of 100.0 to each player for each particular metric/category being evaluated. The leader in each particular metric 'sets the bar' and is assigned a perfect rating, with each subsequent player being assigned a rating proportional to the leader based on their production. These ratings are then adjusted for positional factors, and a final rating is then generated. In other words, it is not necessarily the overall number achieved in a particular metric which is relevant for attributing a rating but how a player's output compares to others in the same position group over the same period of time.

We hope you enjoy this book and we look forward to continuing to expand our coverage and bringing additional exposure and interest to the world-class athletes that play the game of football in the CFL and beyond!

Sincerely,

Bruno Branco

Founder
Pro Stats Canada

Success occurs when
opportunity meets
preparation.

- Zig Ziglar

CONTENTS

FOREWORD

"If they were good enough, they'd be in the NFL!"

This one singular phrase has become the mantra of the CFL hater. It is repeated fervently around the water cooler in offices across the country, it is written in ALL CAPS in online forums, and it is tweeted, retweeted, and posted on Facebook walls around North America and around the world. Using it in conversation grants its user the immediate appearance of being knowledgeable. Using it also solidifies the user's superiority in the argument in a manner that cannot be contested. It is the one phrase that will always end any discussion or debate about the quality of professional football in Canada or anywhere outside the NFL, and it is a complete fallacy!

Before we begin, let's get the obvious out of the way: I am a fan of the Canadian Football League. I would definitely not have dedicated countless hours to compiling and analyzing statistics, creating my own comparative performance evaluation algorithm, creating and editing info graphics, and engaging in endless discussion and debate about the league if I weren't. But more important than understanding that I do in fact have a great love and appreciation for the Canadian version of gridiron football, more important is the question of why.

I grew up in Toronto during the 80's and 90's where as a first generation Canadian, I really had no idea what the Toronto Argonauts and the Canadian Football League were all about. I had heard of the team, but in all honesty like most children that grew up during that time in the GTA, I had no real knowledge, understanding, appreciation of, or connection to Canadian football; a fact that is painfully apparent today looking out over the CFL landscape.

Although the CFL has a rich and storied 100 plus year history, the past few decades have seen the league drop down to an afterthought in a few of the largest cities in Canada where baseball, basketball, and even soccer have all grown in popularity and have now surpassed a league that was once one of the hottest tickets in town. Even among those that consider themselves football fans, one of the league's most notable problems has been its perception as an "inferior" football league. Despite numerous initiatives and campaigns over the years, the league has not been able to shake its minor league image. In fact, although the league features some world-class athletes playing a highly entertaining brand of football, at times it seems like no professional league in the world has been the object of such scorn as the CFL has in the panorama of Canadian sports.

Anyone that has ever spent any amount of time online discussing football has no doubt heard the arguments CFL haters like to make. You may have even made some of these arguments yourself! *"Bush league football", "Only 9 teams", "An American high school team could beat a CFL team", "There's no talent in the CFL", "It's unwatchable".* While the hate behind these kinds of comments is certainly real, fortunately there isn't much actual substance to these frivolous arguments, at least not to anyone who's willing to objectively assess the matter. That is precisely the mission I aimed to accomplish with this project.

In this book you will read references to a person I call "Dave; the NFL ONLY fan". While I'm sure there may be some people actually named 'Dave' that fit this mold, the title is intended as a moniker for generic CFL haters. Individuals that call themselves fans of the game of football, yet only swear by the NFL and its *"infinitely superior product and players"*. Despite having no actual knowledge of the Canadian game, its players, or basically anything about the league, "Dave; the NFL ONLY fan", who ironically is most often actually Canadian, is a person who vehemently opposes the existence of the CFL and the Canadian game. Armed with the CFL hater's mantra, "Daves" around the country do their best to spread their opinions with ardent fervour, always ready and willing to tell everyone about how much they hate CFL football, and the myriad reasons why. My hope is that at least a few of them will be able to read this book objectively and open their minds to the reality the book intends to convey.

This book will analyze, in detail, the statistical production of 20 players who have played in both the CFL and NFL, in addition to a couple of other bonus comparisons. There are hundreds of other players that could have been profiled; legendary players like Warren Moon, Doug Flutie, Jeff Garcia, Raghib Ismail and others, however I decided to only feature players that had played in either league within the last 5-10 years. In lieu of having inter-league play, I believe the most accurate way to evaluate the level of competition of one league relative to another would be to evaluate the performance of players that have had comparable playing time in both leagues and contrast the results. Essentially, this would compare a player to himself, making the exercise as close to "apples to apples" as is possible with two leagues that play by different rules with different sized fields.

In this book I will be comparing players' statistical production from both leagues, Pro Stats Canada Ratings from both leagues, and Pro Football Focus overall grades for NFL playing time. While we are on the subject, do yourself a favour and check out PFF and their excellent NFL content. I will also be drawing parallels to other established players in each league that the profiled player compares to from a production standpoint.

In addition to the statistical and numerical analysis which is purely objective, I will be featuring quotes from players and coaches who have had significant playing and coaching time in both leagues to find out what the actual experts think about the level of play in either league, and what they believe the main differences are between the CFL and NFL. After all, who better to compare and contrast the differences between them than players and coaches with first hand knowledge of the inner workings of both leagues.

I believe the statistical analysis, coupled with the quotes and reasoning of dozens of players and coaches over the years will help to properly paint the picture. When we look at all of the above factors in conjunction, we can begin to develop a deeper understanding of how high the level of play in the CFL actually is relative to its southern counterpart. As a matter of fact, while this book is specifically about the CFL, the principles of this book could also apply, in varying degrees, to other alternative football leagues that pop up around the world such as the XFL, USFL, X-League, LFA, ELF, etc. It is very easy for people to compare other secondary leagues to the NFL and immediately state that since the NFL is far richer, it is obviously far better. In truth, simply equating the difference in talent and quality of play between leagues with the size difference in their bank accounts is a very lazy viewpoint that I believe does not paint an accurate picture of the calibre of players found outside the NFL.

Why do I love CFL football? Well, besides the fact that it is a highly entertaining brand of football, it is a league of second chances. It is a league full of players who have been overlooked, written-off, or discriminated against because of a few pounds, a few tenths of a second, a few inches in height, or having previously played at the "wrong" school. It is the ultimate underdog league, and as such is full of fierce competitors that will do anything to prove they are as good as they know they are! This book makes an argument in favour of the elite talent that is found in the Canadian Football League, and uses data analysis and first hand testimony to support that argument. I hope you enjoy reading this book as much as I have enjoyed writing it. Without further ado, let's get to it!

"PEOPLE IN AMERICA HAVE NO CLUE WHAT GOES ON UP THERE (IN THE CFL), OR ABOUT THE QUALITY OF FOOTBALL WE HAD. THAT'S WHAT MADE THE EXPERIENCE FOR ME. MOST OF THE GUYS WERE NFL CALIBRE TALENT, BUT WERE UNDERSIZED OR JUST DIDN'T FIT THE MOLD IN ONE WAY OR ANOTHER."[1]

DOUG FLUTIE

NFL PRO BOWL QUARTERBACK
6X CFL ALL STAR
3X GREY CUP CHAMPION
INDUCTED TO THE CANADIAN FOOTBALL HALL OF FAME

INTRODUCTION:

WHAT ARE PRODUCTION RATINGS AND PFF GRADES?

Throughout this book, you will be exposed to dozens of comparisons that utilize production ratings to compare players. Whether it is comparing their athleticism, their on-field statistical production, or any other type of comparison, a Pro Stats Canada production rating (PSC rating for short) is essentially a single grade assigned to an overall body of metrics.

The rating system arranges players into the following 6 categories based on a normal distribution bell curve model.

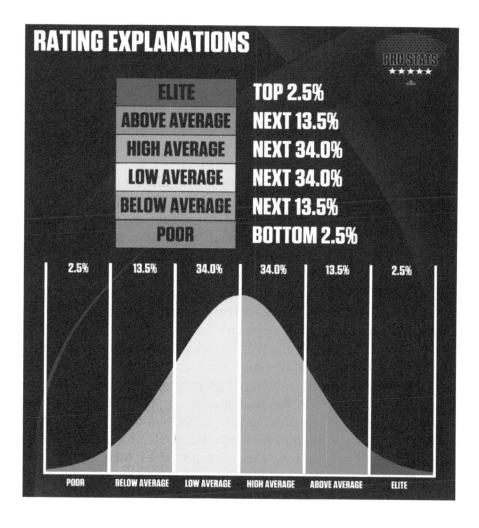

I will begin by briefly explaining the logic behind the PSC rating system. The system is founded upon measuring a player's statistical production or other specific metrics and comparing them against the production or metrics of other players within the same position group, over the same period of time. The system is completely numbers based. As such, there is no room for subjectivity in the ratings. While we can understand that the numbers may not tell the whole story about a player's talent and contribution to the game, the numbers also "don't lie" as the saying goes. Generally speaking, the best players on the field are statistically productive.

The system works by assigning numerical ratings out of 100.0 to each player for each particular metric being evaluated. The leader in each metric 'sets the bar' and is assigned a perfect rating with each subsequent player being assigned a rating proportional to the leader based on their production. The system is comparative, so it is not able to assign a production rating to a single player in isolation, it can only compare 2 or more players. The reason for this is simple, with very few exceptions, there are no objective standards of "perfection" as it relates to the metrics being evaluated in football. As such, the highest statistical output achieved within a particular position group becomes the standard over the evaluated period of time.

For example, defensive back A makes 6 interceptions on the season. The number of interceptions they made in isolation is completely useless for assigning a production rating unless there was an objective standard established for "interceptions per season" that could be regarded as "perfection", which of course there isn't. If we were to compare defensive back A's 6 interceptions with all the other defensive backs over that season we could then see how defensive back A's production compared to that of his peers. If defensive back B and defensive back C had made 4 and 5 interceptions respectively, then defensive back A's rating for interceptions made would set the standard for that particular period of time. Defensive back A would receive a rating of 100.0 for that metric, and defensive back B and defensive back C would receive ratings proportional to the standard of 6 interceptions which was set for that season. If that comparison is then opened up to multiple seasons where defensive back D had made 7 interceptions in a single season, defensive back D's production would then set a new standard over a new expanded period of time, at which point defensive backs A, B, and C would then receive ratings proportional to the newly established standard of 7 interceptions over the period. Any additional production over and above the number that contributed to the perfect rating does not result in additional rating points for the achieving player, but rather will contribute to distancing that player from all others for that same metric.

In this example, any player making 7 interceptions or above would have achieved the perfect rating of 100.0. If defensive back D had made 9 interceptions in this example, their rating would remain unchanged at 100.0 however the other players' ratings would be impacted negatively as it would widen the gap between the top performer and everyone else.

The system does not have a limit to the amount of metrics that can be added to a comparison, neither are there any limits on the amount of players that can be compared at any one time. The only limitation resides in having to keep the parameters the same for everyone. Any adjustments or factors applied to a particular position group must be applied uniformly to all players within that group.

The ratings for each production category are calculated and are then adjusted for certain positional factors; not all plays are rated equally. Generally speaking, the bigger plays on the field are rewarded with higher ratings. For example, a defensive end who makes 7 tackles might have led the league at his position, however another defensive end that only made 3 tackles, but made 1 tackle for loss and 2 sacks would be credited with having made bigger, more disruptive plays, thus achieving a higher overall rating when all is said and done.

Each position on the field has certain metrics associated to it but as mentioned above, not all plays are rated equally. Think of it this way, in a perfect world where each position executed the perfect play, what would that look like? What would be the "perfect outcome" for each position on the football field for every play? What is the end goal of their position? This is the mindset behind how the metrics are evaluated at PSC and the reason why certain metrics are ultimately rated higher than others. While it is nice to see a quarterback throw for hundreds of yards per game, ultimately those numbers do not put points on the board as passing yards are only a means to an end, they do not win football games in and of themselves. A quarterback's ultimate goal is to throw touchdown passes, followed closely by not turning the ball over.

Observe the following practical example:

QB-A – 9 completions, 15 attempts, 60% completion rate, 180 yards, 4 touchdowns, 0 interceptions, 141.7 quarterback rating – **95.6**

QB-B – 35 completions, 50 attempts, 70% completion rate, 350 yards, 1 touchdown, 1 interception, 87.9 quarterback rating – **83.8**

QB-C – 25 completions, 40 attempts, 62.5% completion rate, 550 yards, 0 touchdowns, 2 interceptions, 85.4 quarterback rating – **80.8**

In this example, QB-C passed for the most yards but actually ended up with the lowest PSC rating. Despite throwing for an impressive 550 passing yards, QB-C threw no touchdown passes and turned the ball over twice, which ultimately resulted in their QBR being the lowest in the group.

The same way a quarterback would ultimately want to throw touchdown passes every play, a defensive back would want to intercept the ball and return it for a touchdown every single play if they could. In lieu of that, it would benefit the team more to have the DB knock down a pass than allow a catch and have to make a tackle. A defensive end would choose to sack the quarterback, make a tackle for a big loss, or force a fumble every play if they could. Each position on the football field makes certain plays that provide more value to the team than others, and PSC's algorithm takes that into consideration when calculating production ratings. In short, a PSC rating essentially depicts how a player compared to the most productive player in their respective league at their respective position, over a given period of time.

How to interpret inter-league PSC Rating Comparisons

In this book I will be profiling 20 players who transitioned between the CFL and NFL. A player may have ranked as the 5th most productive at their position in the CFL and 20th most productive in the NFL. If we compare their ordinal ranking at face value we would be led to the conclusion that the player was much better in the CFL than in the NFL due to their much higher ranking, however this is not actually the case.

The reason for this is the CFL player is being compared to a much smaller group of players. Remember, the CFL has only 414 active players at any given time (9 teams times 46 players), while the NFL has 1,696 (32 teams times 53 players); which is more than 4 times greater. A player that ranked 5th in the CFL out of 20 players would be rated high average, but similarly a player that ranked 20th in the NFL out of 80 players would be rated high average as well. We must pay greater attention to the ranking category and PSC rating than the ordinal ranking a player ends up with.

For further clarification, if player A achieved a season production rating of 55.9, slotting into the high average category in the CFL, and subsequently achieved a production rating of 57.8 slotting into the high average category in the NFL, it would mean that he was actually closer to the top performer in the NFL than he was to the top performer in the CFL. He may have been ranked 5th in the CFL, and 20th in the NFL, however this number is relative because it is proportional to the total number of players in each league per position.

While PSC ratings are based on statistical game metrics, the references made to PFF overall grades are a completely different type of evaluation. A brief explanation of PFF grades can be found on their website, and reads as follows:

"Each player is given a grade of -2 to +2 in 0.5 increments on a given play with 0 generally being the average or "expected" grade. There are a few exceptions as each position group has different rules, but those are the basics. The zero grade is important as most plays feature many players doing their job at a reasonable, or expected, level, so not every player on every play needs to earn a positive or a negative.

At one end of the scale you have a catastrophic game-ending interception or pick-six from a quarterback, and at the other a perfect deep bomb into a tight window in a critical game situation.

Each position has its own grading rubric so our analysts know how to put a grade on the various expectations for a quarterback on a 10-yard pass beyond the sticks or what the range of grades might look like for a frontside offensive tackle down blocking on a "power" play.

There is then an adjustment made to the "raw" grades to adjust for what the player is "expected" to earn given his situation on the field. For instance, a player's grade may be adjusted down slightly if he plays in a situation that is historically more favourable while a player in more unfavourable circumstances may get an adjustment the other way. We collect over 200 fields of data on each play, and that data helps to determine what the baseline, or expectation, is for each player on every play. Each grade goes into a specific "facet" of play in order to properly assess each player's skillset. The facets include passing, rushing, receiving, pass blocking, run blocking, pass-rushing, run defense and coverage. Special teamers also have their own facets of kicking, punting, returning and general special teams play. Facets are important in order to have a clear view of where a player's strengths and weaknesses lie."[2]

When writing this book I attempted to use as much data as was available for each particular player comparison. The logic behind using multiple forms of evaluation was simple, the more evidence the better! There are those that do not believe in analytics regardless of type, and there are those that will have doubts about one style of evaluation over another. In this sense, the more variety of evidence I can present, the more robust an argument I can make.

Below I will be explaining some additional terms that I use at PSC, some of which may not be included in the comparisons of this book but are nevertheless important to know if you follow PSC's social media channels. They are: weekly production ratings, single game production ratings, season production ratings, and positional rates of production (P.R.O.P.).

Weekly Production Ratings

This rating is how a particular player's statistical production measures up in comparison to other players in the same position group during a particular game week by basically taking week by week snapshots. While this rating accurately reflects a player's comparative production during a single week, it is by far the smallest sample size used by any PSC rating, and only includes data from that game week. Nothing a player has done prior in the season has any impact on the rating. As such, a small variance between players can actually result in what appears to be a large difference in their ratings. For example, weekly CFL receiver production ratings are obtained by comparing, on average 50-60 individual performances. If one player achieves a metric no other player does, depending on the metric, the rating will appear to credit that player disproportionately to the detriment of others.

Single Game Production Ratings

A single game production rating differs from a weekly production rating as the sample size being evaluated is drastically larger. In contrast to the weekly production ratings, the single game production rating is obtained by comparing all player performances for an entire season. Essentially, every single player performance is compared to every other player performance from the same position group, using data from every game of the season. Although PSC calculates single game production ratings season to season, it is technically possible to expand a single game comparison to include multiple seasons.

For further clarity, a player may have achieved a weekly production rating of 95.7 ending as the most productive player at their position that particular game week. However, when the comparison is ultimately expanded to every single game of the season, that same performance could very likely receive a completely different, potentially much lower PSC rating. The reason for this is because it is now being compared to every other performance that season, some which could have been much more productive.

Season Production Ratings

A season production rating encompasses the entire body of work completed by a particular player over the course of an entire season. It is not a cumulative sum of each single game rating, nor does it have much to do with the weekly production ratings. This rating is ultimately the most accurate reflection of a player's quality of play. Players with consistent production normally achieve higher season production ratings than players who go through many peaks and valleys. In addition to the entire body of work completed by each player, a season production rating also includes credit for each player's Positional Rate of Production for the various metrics evaluated.

Positional Rate of Production (P.R.O.P.)

A player's P.R.O.P. is a measurement of the pace at which a player executes. For example, breaking down total tackles, rushing yards, or touchdowns measured on a per game basis. The higher the P.R.O.P. in a certain metric, the higher that player's potential is. While having a high P.R.O.P. indicates a high potential in a specific area, depending on the sample size it may or may not correlate to a high production rating. For example, a player that makes one catch for 25 yards with one touchdown has a P.R.O.P. of 25 yards per catch average, and 1.00 touchdowns per game. Over a one game span this would not necessarily indicate much, however if a player managed to play an entire 18 game season and made 60 catches, maintaining a P.R.O.P. of 25 yards per catch average with 1.00 touchdowns per game, they would end their season with 1,500 receiving yards and 18 touchdowns which would be a phenomenal season. The larger the sample size, the more accurately P.R.O.P. reflects elite play.

As I mentioned in the beginning of this chapter, while a player's statistical production isn't everything, the best players on the field will produce statistically. Have you ever seen a player considered an elite pass rusher that did not have any sacks or tackles for loss? How about an elite quarterback with no passing touchdowns? The truth is, with very few exceptions, statistical production accompanies elite play, whether it is NCAA, CFL, NFL or anywhere else.

After all this you may be thinking, why even bother with all this analysis? Because I believe being objective and having objective standards is the key to any comparison. With a CFL vs NFL comparison where the perception is already so skewed in favour of the NFL, objectivity becomes even more important. If a CFL player makes an NFL roster and ends up with a higher PSC rating and PFF grade than notable NFL players, it becomes very difficult to disparage them as elite athletes and players.

Objectivity vs Subjectivity

There are many things in life that cannot be objectively measured. For example, if someone claimed that the Ford Mustang is "the most beautiful car in the world", there would be no actual way to prove the statement true or false. Beauty cannot be objectively quantified so the statement is completely subjective and based solely on the belief or perception of the person making it. The person could go on to state that because of that, they love Ford Mustangs and hate Dodge Challengers. In this instance, they are essentially voicing their subjective opinion about the two vehicles. The story completely changes however if that person then made a statement claiming that one vehicle was much faster than the other, as speed is measurable. If both cars were taken to the track and tested similarly, then regardless of what the person felt, it would be conclusively proven that both vehicles were equally quick.

At the end of the day I use the analytics in an attempt to bring objective clarity to a subject that is unfortunately very often infused with vitriol. Haters can (and likely will) still hate the CFL, however they will no longer be able to claim there is "no talent" in the CFL when it can be objectively proven that there is.

SECTION 1 – A TALE OF TWO COMPANIES

Try to imagine a company everyone in your field aspires to work for. We will call this fictional employer "Ingens". Ingens has a reputation of being the best in the business. They have state-of-the-art facilities, the highest wages in the industry, and full benefits and retirement plans for every employee. Ingens is a world renown company in their field. As a destination of choice for highly educated and skilled individuals, Ingens is also highly selective with regards to available employment opportunities; preferring candidates that graduated from Ivy League schools over everyone else. Although in truth, many of their finest employees graduated from non Ivy League institutions, some from community colleges and a small handful with no post-secondary education at all, Ivy League graduates make up the largest percentage of their workforce. Ingens actively recruits from the Ivy League investing thousands of dollars a year to scout and recruit the best available candidates from those preferred schools. To anyone that works in your field, Ingens is the gold standard. As a result, every year they receive thousands of job applications.

You graduated summa cum laude from a highly respected university. While you may not have a Harvard or Yale diploma in hand, you certainly do not consider your education second rate as you have worked hard to study your field! You have done the required internships and demonstrated your proficiency in the subject matter by acing numerous exams and industry certifications along the way. As a highly qualified graduate, you obviously aspire to work for Ingens.

You were not recruited by the company, but upon graduating you decided to put in an application, and much to your delight you were chosen for the next phase of their selection process! You prepare for the interview, buy a new suit, and continually practice your greetings and dialogue in the mirror. The big day finally comes. Upon leaving the interview you feel great about your chances. You were able to clearly articulate your worth, highlight your knowledge, and make a great first impression. You were able to meet with various different department heads of the company and you believe you managed to impress them all.

Some time later, Ingens begins the process of calling back all the successful applicants to congratulate them, have them sign an offer of full-time employment, and advise them of dates for training beginning in a few weeks. You patiently wait for that call, but unfortunately it does not come. The next few weeks are painful as you ponder what went wrong.

'What could I have done differently that would have helped me stand out from the competition? My qualifications were just as good as the other candidates I saw!' you think to yourself. Just then your phone rings. It is one of the department managers from Ingens on the other end! She tells you that even though you did not get an offer for full-time employment, they would like to make you an offer for a part-time position! You are thrilled! You immediately accept and prepare yourself to attend the company's paid training program scheduled to start in a few days.

As you walk into the facilities on your first day you are confident. You think to yourself *'I am going to finally show these people what they almost missed out on'.* As the orientation and subsequent training begins, you quickly realize how far behind everyone you are! During the past few weeks while you have been trying to figure out what your next steps were going to be, those that received their offers of employment weeks ago, the first group hires, have been preparing themselves for training. They have been hard at work studying the procedures manual, familiarizing themselves with the facilities, and getting to know the other employees; both new and veteran. While there are a couple of new hires that obviously stand out as exceptional candidates, demonstrating advanced skill and knowledge right out of the gate, the majority of your new colleagues are quality candidates just like yourself. You certainly do not feel out of place among them. Based on what you see early on, you know that you are just as capable as pretty much everyone present.

The next few days you work as hard as you can to play catch up and find yourself making progress. You may have started behind the 8 ball, but you are slowly gaining ground. You gain confidence as you get more and more familiar with the company's procedures and policies. Ingens culminates their training program with a series of practical scenarios performed over the course of 4 days. The practicals do not involve only new hires, but also company veterans. You become excited at the prospect of finally getting to work alongside some of the best professionals in the industry.

As the practicals begin, day one is composed of mainly watching the full-time veteran employees, with only a small handful of new hires allowed to participate in the scenarios. Day two comes and goes with much of the same. As day three begins, you begin to wonder why you have not yet been given an opportunity. Day three sees mostly new employees, but practically all of them were in the first group of hires with only one or two part-time employees actually allowed to participate. By the end of day three, you start to become concerned. You have yet to participate in any of the scenarios and are beginning to notice that certain new hires are being given chance after chance, while others are sitting off to the side relegated to watching. As the fourth and final day begins, you approach your manager to inquire about your opportunity and you are assured you will finally be getting in on the action. However, by the time your name is called the veteran employees are no longer participating, and the group one hires are also no longer involved. The scenarios you are participating in only involve people who were in the second part-time group of hires. You complete your scenario to perfection, doing everything that was asked of you exactly as per procedure.

At the close of day four everyone is congratulated for a job well done and is advised to go home for a few days of some well deserved rest before work begins in earnest the following week. A few hours later as you are relaxing at home reflecting on your day your phone rings. Your department manager is on the other end asking you to attend the office tomorrow morning at 9am, and to bring your company manuals with you.

After a practically sleepless night, you do as you were requested and attend the office. Your manager greets you at the door and ushers you into a meeting room near the entrance. After taking your manuals back, your manager advises you that unfortunately the company is going to have to let you go. When you ask what you did wrong you are advised that although you did everything that was requested of you, the company decided that you did not quite fit into their plans for the time being. Your manager assures you that you are a quality candidate that has a bright future in the field, but unfortunately they just do not have an open position for you anymore. You are advised that they will keep your number handy, and if anything changes they will notify you immediately. A brief handshake later, well wishes are exchanged and you are directed to leave the premises.

As you walk away from the facilities watching your dream job slowly disappear from view, questions begin flooding your mind. *'Why didn't they give me the same opportunities they gave some of the others? Why did they even waste time hiring me in the first place if they had no intention of giving me a fair chance? I am just as qualified and just as capable as most of the other new employees, why did they choose them over me?'*

Ingens is truly a juggernaut in the field, and as such has a large following on all forms of social media. When you happen to check their Twitter account, you observe your department has made a small posting regarding having parted ways with you and numerous other employees. Upon reading Ingens' post your phone rings, and on the other end is a representative of a company called "Parvus". While the name sort of rings a bell you do not really know too much about Parvus besides the fact that it is headquartered in another country. The Parvus representative tells you that their recruiting department has been following your progress for quite some time. They even know about a few of your major projects in university! The Parvus representative advises you that they are interested in offering you a position with their company. You are not quite sure what to make of the opportunity as you do not really know too much about the company or even the country it is in for that matter. You really had your heart set on working for Ingens and working with the best of the best, making top dollar. You take a few moments to reflect on your options. You can either take the job from Parvus, start actually working in the field, gain some additional experience and make some money, or you can stay unemployed and patiently wait for another opportunity with Ingens to come around again, if it ever does. After some consideration you decide to accept the position. After all, what do you have to lose?

You eventually find your way to Parvus' employee orientation. You can immediately notice the large gap in finances that exists between Ingens and Parvus. The facilities at Parvus are decent, but modest; much smaller than Ingens. The company as a whole is minuscule by comparison. At orientation you are surprised to recognize a few faces from the training program at Ingens.

The processes and procedures at Parvus are a bit different than those you learned in school and at Ingens, but they are familiar enough that you feel you can transition without much fuss. The procedures manual at this company is not as thick as the one you had to learn at Ingens, but it is quite similar in content. As you learn more about your new employer and its employees, you are surprised to find that many of your new colleagues are former Ingens employees! The more you speak with them, the more you realize how many have actually spent time with Ingens both as part-time as well as full-time employees. Their levels of skill and experience are exactly the same as the employees you met at Ingens. As you learn the stories of your new colleagues, you learn that much like yourself they were one day called into the office and promptly told their services were no longer needed; just like that. Some after having been with the company a short time, and others after having spent years and becoming seasoned Ingens veterans.

As orientation and training progress, you make headway in learning the new procedures and policies. Like Ingens, Parvus also has practical scenarios for final evaluations. You fly through the 2 days of practicals and ace everything thrown your way. At the end of it all, you are rewarded with a full-time position! The money is significantly less than you would be making as a full-time employee at Ingens, but it is a starting point, and one that you are grateful for.

Once you finally begin working full-time, you are astonished with the level of professionalism you see at Parvus. While you notice that there are a couple of employees here who most likely would not be able to handle the pressure of working for Ingens, the majority of your new colleagues are excellent at their craft, and are no different than the employees you observed while at Ingens. Sure, you make a lot less money and do not get the recognition you would if you were at Ingens, but you are pleasantly surprised with the high level the employees here operate at.

If you have not already guessed by now, this analogous short story represents the journey undertaken by the typical CFL player. The CFL is quite obviously Parvus; a smaller, much more modest organization than the juggernaut, Ingens, which is the National Football League.

It is a well known fact that the NFL tends to favour players who played collegiately at big time college programs. The Ivy league schools in the story refer to college football programs like: Alabama, LSU, Florida State, Ohio State, USC and the like. By and large, the NFL is populated with graduates from programs like these from the so-called "Power Five". Even if there are players from other smaller schools who have a high enough potential to play at the NFL level, they are often discriminated against for having played against what is deemed "inferior competition".

Think of it this way, if player 1 and player 2 both come to training camp and demonstrate they are equally fast, strong, and smart, all other things being equal, the player from the big school will most likely remain on the roster to the detriment of the smaller school player simply because of where they played in college. As a result of this strong bias in favour of certain schools, the overwhelming majority of college football players are overlooked coming out of college. The majority of players in the NCAA pyramid (D1 FBS, FCS, D2, D3) are not regularly and actively scouted because at the end of the day, even NFL teams do not have unlimited scouting resources and need to get the best return on their investment.

Teams are not normally going to invest thousands of dollars to scout a small school for one or two players, when they can invest the same amount to potentially scout hundreds of players from multiple teams in a single conference. Getting fish from a hatchery provides a much better return on investment than fishing from a boat in a large lake. I do not blame NFL teams for this fact, it makes good financial sense. Continuing with the metaphor, while the hatchery can provide you with a large number of good quality, well bred fish, although far fewer and far between, lake fishing can land you some truly amazing specimens; diamonds in the rough if you will. While some exceptional smaller school players may even earn a short stint in the NFL during the off-season up to and possibly including training camp, most undrafted players are cut mercilessly before ever getting a real chance to prove their worth. Of course any reasonable person would aspire to work for the biggest company that pays the most money, but more often than not, hundreds to thousands of highly talented players that with a little time and opportunity could be stars, find themselves on the outside looking in; for myriad reasons.

The similarities between the CFL and NFL are greater than their differences, not the least of which is the high level of play these players are capable of; anyone that watches the film can see it. Unfortunately, because the dollars are far fewer in the CFL, the league is often looked down on as being second rate, ignored by many and even hated by some for the mere fact of being smaller than its giant neighbour to the south. The expression "good things come in small packages" most definitely applies to the CFL. Despite the haters and naysayers, the CFL is a quality product played by high level athletes. The reality is, sometimes people just need a little more time and investment before they can really begin to shine, and this is what the CFL does best!

"THE SPEED IS EXACTLY THE SAME. IT'S THE SAME THING I'VE DEALT WITH THE PAST 12 YEARS IN THE NFL, THERE'S REALLY NO DIFFERENCE. ESPECIALLY THE COMPETITION LEVEL, IT HAS BEEN AN EYE OPENER, NOT ONLY AT MINI CAMP, BUT COMING OUT HERE TODAY (CFL TRAINING CAMP), IT'S AN EYE OPENER AGAIN. THE LEVEL OF COMPETITION IS REALLY NO DIFFERENT, INCLUDING THE SPEED OF THE GAME...SO THIS IS NOTHING TO TAKE AS A JOKE, WITH ME BEING ON BOTH SIDES OF THE FENCES NOW, THIS IS THE REAL DEAL UP HERE AS WELL." [3]

"SO I GO TO THE CFL AND I'M THINKING 'OK, THIS IS GOING TO BE A BREEZE.' I GET THERE, FIRST PRACTICE I'M LIKE...'WHOA, THESE DUDES ARE GOOD!' EVERY WEEK...I'M LOOKING AT THE LANDSCAPE LIKE, 'WHY ARE YOU NOT DOWN THERE (NFL)?' THE NUMBERS! THERE'S ONLY SO MANY PEOPLE AND CERTAIN OPPORTUNITIES. THE CFL WAS REALLY VERY SURPRISING BECAUSE EVERYBODY WAS GOOD. THEY WERE GOOD ENOUGH TO BE DOWN HERE PLAYING IN THE NFL." [4]

CHAD JOHNSON
"OCHOCINCO"

6X PRO BOWL WIDE RECEIVER

SECTION 2 - PROFILE OF A CFL HATER

Personally, I have never understood the hate. While I can definitely understand a person not liking a certain sport or league, most people in that position are simply indifferent to said sport or league. Do not read the article, change the channel, do not buy a ticket. It is really that simple. For example, I am not a fan of PGA golf, NBA Basketball, ATP Tennis, Curling and so many other games and sports. As a result of my strong dislike for these sports, I do not watch them. What I do not do is criticize those who do watch them. After all, why would my opinion about a sport that I do not care for and honestly do not know too much about matter to someone who is passionate about that sport? What would I gain from trying to convince fans of PGA golf that their sport sucks? Similarly, I do not go out of my way to comment on these organization's social media posts and I do not start arguments with fans of these sports about how little I appreciate their "garbage" sports, and how terrible the athletes that play those sports are.

It is a situation that is completely illogical to me. I get that some people do not like the CFL, quite frankly that is fine as there are millions who do! Being an NFL only fan is also fine! As is being only a fan of college football! Or all 3! Or NONE! That is the beauty of personal choice and preference. The arguments and criticisms against the CFL are highly passionate, almost as if the hater has somehow been wronged by the league. It is almost as if the mere existence of the CFL is in and of itself offensive to them, and they believe the world will only be able to truly achieve peace once the CFL has been forever eradicated from the sporting world.

The dismissal of the CFL by some is a phenomenon that is difficult to understand, and not seen to this degree in other sports. Good-natured ribbing is seen between fans of different teams from different leagues all over the world. While it is common to see fans of one league believing their favourite league is better than another league, we just do not see outright passionate hate for other leagues that we see being directed toward the CFL.

MLB fans might not watch the Japanese or Korean professional baseball leagues, but I do not see and hear insults being hurled eastward. Similarly NHL fans do not criticize or bad mouth the KHL, Swedish Elite League, AHL, OHL, or any other number of "lower tier" hockey leagues, despite most NHL fans believing the NHL is the top league in the world. NBA may be the highest level of basketball in the world, but the relationship between NBA fans and the Euro leagues are not hateful or dismissive in nature, at

18

worst they are indifferent. Even in the highly competitive world of soccer, while English Premier League fans are confident of their league's overall superiority in the pyramid, they cannot outright dismiss La Liga, Serie A, Bundesliga, Ligue 1, heck they cannot even dismiss the Portuguese Primeira Liga or Dutch Eredivisie because they understand that even those other leagues have some pretty amazing athletes competing there as well. We see athletes transition from the Portuguese "Big 3" or from Holland's Ajax Amsterdam into the bigger leagues all the time. Talent can literally be found anywhere if you are looking for it.

Those that are fans of only the NFL and that subscribe to this ideology of hating everything CFL related believe that CFL players simply are not good enough to play in the NFL. They believe CFL athletes are far inferior to those athletes that ply their trade south of the border on the grandest stage and are therefore terrible and not worth watching. In fairness, the casual fan that observes the glitz, glamour, and spectacle of the NFL can easily get lost in the sheer magnitude of that league, which as far as sports leagues go, literally has no equals. The NFL stands alone at the top of the world sports pyramid as the most profitable professional sports league on planet earth. According to Statista.com in 2021 the NFL generated an absolutely colossal 17.2 billion USD in revenue.[5] That is a whopping 7.6 billion dollars more than second place Major League Baseball.

The CFL hater is a special kind of individual as their mind seems to only work in straight lines. An example of hater logic is illustrated below.

1. The talent gap between the NFL and CFL is as enormous as their financial gap; The worst NFL player is still better than a CFL All Star.

> a) This idea is just asinine. The profiled players in this book will absolutely destroy this point. While it is no doubt true that the NFL completely dwarfs the CFL in terms of financial clout, if one actually analyzes the data we find that the talent gap and the financial gap are not at all comparable. To expand on this point, while it is easy to get blown away by the NFL's mega dollar contracts such as Pat Mahomes' 10 year $450 million deal, if we look at the league financial records as a whole (www.overthecap.com/contracts) we find that 1,049 players (over 40% of the league) make less than 1 million dollars per season in annual salary (average of $857,973 per year), with only $23,659 guaranteed! As a matter of fact, a total of 899 players (36% of the league) have a total of $0 guaranteed. As you can imagine, without guarantees a player can be cut from one minute to

the next with virtually nothing to show for their time spent in the NFL. Do not get me wrong, $500,000-$999,999 a year is definitely life changing money any way you slice it, but the popular belief that every player in the NFL makes tens of millions of dollars a year is just not true.

2. The fact that a player gets cut from an NFL roster is "ipso facto" proof that they are not talented enough to play in the NFL.

b) There are myriad reasons why players get cut! Salary cap considerations, incompatibility with the system the team runs, internal politics, running into issues with team rules or criminality, not having the "right measurables" are just a few of the many reasons. Not to mention there is a very small number of professional roster spots available relative to the amount of amateur talent that is produced each and every year. It is quite frankly impossible to hold onto every player who has the potential to play at the professional level.

3. The NFL is nothing but the best of the best.

c) While there is no doubt that the NFL contains the most elite football players in the world, this upper echelon of players are not an accurate representation of the entire NFL population. One can accurately say that J.J. Watt, Khalil Mack and Aaron Donald have been among the best pass rushers on the planet, but to say that all pass rushers in the NFL are equivalent to them would be a gross exaggeration. To the people that say they "only watch the best of the best", I ask: Do you also not watch the bottom 3/4 of the NFL? In truth, they do NOT belong to the "best of the best". Or do you consider them to be the best of the best, simply by virtue of being on an NFL roster?

The biased and narrow viewpoints of CFL haters are based on the principle that the world works in absolutes. If one honestly believes that the worst NFL players are better than even the best CFL players simply by virtue of being in the NFL, then that person has demonstrated a complete ignorance of the game of football, and even worse, an ignorance of how the world works. Everything in life exists on a spectrum or bell curve, but unfortunately most CFL haters subscribe to a very limited way of thinking and are blinded by their feelings.

Some time ago I began making a series of posts on PSC's social media channels called "Head to Head". The aim of the posts was to compare CFL players with notable NFL players from an athleticism standpoint. Many people hold the belief that the NFL is full of elite athletes, while simultaneously believing CFL players are basically equivalent to high school kids. Although being bigger, faster, and stronger isn't everything in football as you can well imagine, it is fundamental in that it represents the base upon which elite football players are built. At the very least, the posts allow people to be exposed to the fact that there are some serious athletes playing in the CFL.

In this particular example, I had created a post which compared Montreal Alouettes wide receiver Eugene Lewis with LA Rams wide receiver Cooper Kupp from an athleticism standpoint. You can see the posts below for yourself.

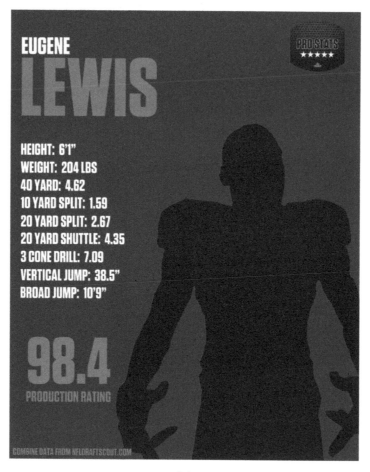

COOPER **KUPP**

HEIGHT: 6'2"
WEIGHT: 204 LBS
40 YARD: 4.59
10 YARD SPLIT: 1.61
20 YARD SPLIT: 2.63
20 YARD SHUTTLE: 4.08
3 CONE DRILL: 6.75
VERTICAL JUMP: 31.0"
BROAD JUMP: 9'7"

96.5
PRODUCTION RATING

COMBINE DATA FROM NFLDRAFTSCOUT.COM

After analyzing and rating all their combine metrics side by side, the final result was:

Eugene Lewis – PSC Rating of 98.4
Cooper Kupp – PSC Rating of 96.5

Please note that there isn't anything insulting or contentious about this comparison! The numbers speak for themselves. As athletes, these two players are **VERY** comparable. Geno is clearly and demonstrably just as big, just a hair slower, a little bit less agile, yet far more explosive than Cooper. This post simply illustrated these facts. And yet, it managed to trigger some sensitivities!

The following is an actual conversation chain which took place between myself and a typical CFL hater regarding the post:

Hater: *"the fact your [SIC] actually comparing the @NFL best receiver to anyone in the @CFL shows your [SIC] completely clueless. Geno isn't even good enough to make the nfl let alone be compared to an all star receiver. Your [SIC] a joke! p"*

PSC: *"Please enlighten us! The post is about athleticism. Please show us where we went wrong."*

Hater: *"Geno is not even athletically good enough to even make the NFL!"*

PSC: *"Once again, please show us where we went wrong!"*

Hater: *"Haha i just did. How can you actually compare a guy who's not even athletically good enough to make the best league in the world!"*

PSC: *"Athletically, Geno is just as big, just as fast, and just as strong. Perhaps you're using some other metrics we're not aware of. If so, what are those metrics, and how do these two stack up?"*

Hater: *"Ya I'm using the best league in the world. This guy couldn't even make it out of a minicamp in the nfl!...Your [SIC] totally clueless. He can't even make the league haha. Compare him to another cfl reciever [SIC] for a fair contest!*

PSC: *"Facts are facts my man. Guess numbers aren't your forte. All good!"*

Hater: *"I'm totally all about #'s my friend. His NFL #s across the board are all ZERO!!! 0 receptions. 0 yards. 0 touchdowns. Yet your [SIC] comparing him to a guy who has133 receptions 1734 yards 14TDs this year alone and the season isn't over! #zero"*

PSC: *"Interesting. We didn't post a single thing about stats. The post is about ATHLETICISM: Speed, agility, strength etc. If proving these two athletes are comparable athletically hurts your feelings, please feel free to block us! Enjoy "real" football tomorrow."*

Hater: *"You keep forgetting the main fact and only fact that matters is that he's not athletically good enough to make the nfl! So therefore they're not athletically equal! You didn't post a thing about stats? Every # in your tweet is a stat smart guy! My stats matter!"*

So here we have in full view, the logic (or lack thereof) often used by haters. Despite being confronted with the bare bones facts, they are completely and utterly blinded by their love of the NFL shield! Regardless of whether a player plays in the NFL, CFL, NCAA or some random league in Bolivia, a 4.6 40 yard dash is a 4.6 40 yard dash! A vertical jump of 38.5" is a vertical jump of 38.5"! It is really not that hard to see if we're looking at the situation without a massive bias.

Does that mean that both players are equally good at football? No. Neither did I ever say such a thing! People are just unable to separate one thing from the other. They make assumptions, and then vehemently defend their position; but their position is not actually being attacked. Upon being confronted with the irrefutable evidence that Geno Lewis and Cooper Kupp are virtually identical elite athletes, the evidence is rejected in favour of the haters mantra **"If they were good enough, they'd be in the NFL"**.

In my opinion, the strong beliefs of the CFL haters are spurred on by their love of, and sheer blind faith in the NFL. Blind faith that every good player gets in the door. Blind faith that every player that is not afforded an opportunity is conclusively not talented enough to play in the NFL. These types of blind faith declarations just end up making them look foolish to anyone who knows anything about football. It boggles my mind how anyone can say that one player is more athletic than another player when they are demonstrated to be equally big, equally strong, and equally fast. Against all logic and reason, the hater is able to believe that an NFL player who runs a 4.6 second 40 yard dash is somehow much faster than a CFL player who also runs a 4.6 second 40 yard dash. To the haters, there is only one criterion that matters: currently being in the NFL.

In addition to their blind faith, haters also have a very skewed understanding of the concept of "talent". They are very quick to scoff at the "talent level" in the CFL, and constantly assert that NFL players are "way more talented". But ask the hater a simple question, and their argument crumbles to bits. That question is; *How do you define talent?* The sound of crickets will be deafening as you wait for a logical answer. For a group of people that use the word so liberally, they really don't seem to have any idea what they actually mean when they say it.

How does one measure "talent"? What does "talent" look like? How can someone assert that one player is "more talented" than another player with absolutely no objective metrics being involved? Do they mean a player's physical abilities? Obviously not. Most CFL players are highly gifted athletes, that demonstrate those gifts with excellent pro day and Combine performances. Do they mean production in college? Obviously not, as many CFL players were absolute studs in college having played in and performed well in some of the biggest games of the NCAA/USports calendar. Do they mean a player's ability to be productive on a professional football field? Obviously not, as many CFL players are highly productive in their respective positions, some having done it in both the NFL as well as the CFL. Do they mean consistent play with few mistakes? Obviously not, as many of the CFL's best are dominant players who display great consistency.

So what do they mean by talent? The truth is, the hater's definition of talent means: playing on an NFL field, by NFL rules, on an NFL team, making NFL money. That's it. That's the whole definition. Unfortunately, it seems that most haters are not reachable because their arguments are based on feelings instead of facts. They are unable to see beyond their NFL bias and would rather believe what they feel about the CFL, than listen to people who have actually been involved in both leagues, or rely on evidence based ratings or grades of a player's actual performance or play in either league.

Haters are also masters of moving the goal posts. If a CFL player played at a top college, the argument against them would be **"Well, they weren't drafted into the NFL"**. If they had been a later round NFL draft pick the argument would then change to **"Well, they weren't a first rounder"**. If they had been a first round NFL draft pick, the argument would then change to **"Well, they couldn't stick in the NFL"**. If they had been productive in the NFL for a season the argument would then change to **"Well, they only had 1 good season"**. If they had been a productive player for multiple seasons the argument would then change to **"Well, they were never a Pro Bowler"**. If they had been a Pro Bowler the argument would then change to, **"Well, they're obviously washed up. If they were good enough, they'd still be in the NFL"**. No matter what the circumstances of the player, the hater will ALWAYS find a reason to disparage them. As we have already seen, haters measure talent by one criterion, and one criterion only; _currently being in the NFL_.

When performing an objective case study as this book intends to do, "Dave; the NFL ONLY fan" would expect to see the following types of results. The elite CFL players would perform around the bottom half of the NFL, with the good CFL players basically only good enough to be on the practice squad or play some special teams. By contrast, Dave would expect to see undrafted players with significant NFL experience among the best players in the CFL and he would also expect to see high NFL draft picks absolutely dominating the CFL. After all, high NFL draft picks are products of some of the best college football programs in the game. Surely an NFL player drafted from any SEC or Big TEN school would absolutely destroy the "lowly" CFL competition, would they not? I mean, if Dave believes that a good high school team could beat a CFL team, then surely a player that was on the roster at Alabama or Florida State would be able to decimate the CFL.

CFL linebacker Micah Awe was interviewed and provided an interesting perspective on the matter. Micah played collegiate football at Texas Tech, as a 2 year team mate of Patrick Mahomes. Texas Tech is an NCAA division I FBS school that competes in the Big 12 conference. Micah spent some time with the Tampa Bay Buccaneers in the NFL and was responsible for a sack in the 2016 NFL preseason that ended up breaking the ribs of 1st round QB Carson Wentz.[6]

During the interview, Micah was promoting a new application he helped develop called "PurpleShift", which he created to allow direct comparison of players' athleticism. In an interview on the Rod Pedersen show, Micah used the app to directly compare his athleticism to 4x Pro Bowl Running back Alvin Kamara.[7] With the app he objectively demonstrated that his athleticism was on par or above Kamara's in a couple of benchmark combine tests. Despite the objective proof of Micah's elite athleticism, "Dave; the NFL ONLY fan" would no doubt still have arguments to make against the quality of Micah's play because he played in the CFL. Dave might think to say:

"You didn't play high level college football".

Micah's response would be: *I played at Texas Tech with Patrick Mahomes against top competition in the BIG 12.*

Then Dave would say **"Well, maybe. But I doubt you played against any elite players, who have you tackled?"**

Micah would answer:

"*Let's start with Chris Carson; Oklahoma State. Joe Mixon; Oklahoma. Leonard Fournette; LSU. Tyreek Hill; Oklahoma State. I've tackled all these guys.*"

Then Dave would say **"Well, maybe. But I doubt you made many tackles. Anyone can get lucky."**

Micah would answer:

"I had 127 tackles which led the Big 12 in tackles my senior year, and I was top 15 in tackles in the whole entire country."

At that point, Dave would be running out of arguments.

Micah could go on to say: *"I realized when I came up to Canada that there are good players here and there's that thought that CFL players can't play with the NFL and that they don't have the same talent but they do."*[8]

Poor Dave. His world is slowly beginning to crumble around him. How could this be? Dave's long held beliefs about the low quality of CFL football have now been contradicted by information from a source that actually played at a high level in the NCAA, experienced the level of play in the NFL, and played at a high level in the CFL. This information brings into question Dave's views and beliefs about the CFL. To counter this terrible feeling of cognitive dissonance, Dave will begin to rationalize and will act out by rejecting the new information, and acting to persuade others that the new information is untrue.

Dave does not actually have any reasonable counterpoints to make. Dave also has no contradictory evidence to present. So instead, Dave will likely resort to fallacious arguments. Dave may attempt to discredit Micah himself with an Ad Hominem argument such as *"Who is Micah Awe anyways? He couldn't make it in the NFL. I'm supposed to believe that an 'NFL reject' in the CFL has the same talent as an NFL player? He'd be in the NFL if he did."* Dave might also make attempts to devalue the points Micah made by using a Strawman argument against them, saying something like *"That's cute. The 'thousandaires' in the CFL are just as athletic and talented as the millionaires in the NFL. They're 'good enough' for the NFL, but choosing to play in Canada for a fraction of the money. Sure."* In the end rather than watch the film, analyze Micah's actual production, or listen to Micah's honest assessment of the quality of play in the CFL, to restore his mental balance Dave would ultimately end with the CFL hater's mantra:

"If you were good enough, you'd be in the NFL!"

Dave 1, logical argument 0. Needless to say, the haters do not like facts or truth. Dave wants to believe what Dave wants to believe. Unfortunately not I, or Micah, or an angel straight from the 7th heaven of Canton, Ohio can convince Dave of the truth he does not want to be convinced of.

"I THINK WHAT HE'S (CHAD 'OCHOCINCO' JOHNSON) LEARNING IS THAT...MAN, THERE'S SOME TALENT IN THE CANADIAN FOOTBALL LEAGUE, YOU KNOW, AND I THINK HE'S GETTING HIS EYES OPENED TO THE FACT THAT, AS MUCH AS HE PLAYED IN THE NATIONAL FOOTBALL LEAGUE, AND YES, THOSE ARE SUPPOSED TO BE THE BEST OF THE BEST, THERE ARE A LOT OF REALLY GOOD FOOTBALL PLAYERS IN CANADA, PLAYERS THAT COULD PLAY IN THE NATIONAL FOOTBALL LEAGUE IF GIVEN THE RIGHT OPPORTUNITY.[9]

JEFF GARCIA

4X PRO BOWL QUARTERBACK
4X CFL ALL-STAR
GREY CUP CHAMPION

SECTION 3 – THE PRO BOWL TRANSPLANTATION

What do you think "Dave; the NFL ONLY fan" would say if we told him we were going to take an NFL running back and transplant him to the CFL for a season in the prime of his career? I am not talking about just any run of the mill NFL RB, whom to Dave would already be a huge upgrade over whatever "scrubs" were playing in the CFL. I am talking about an elite player; an All-Pro calibre player who during his past 6 seasons had **AVERAGED** 14 games played, 293 carries, 1,183 rushing yards and 8 touchdowns.

For a little perspective on these numbers, observe that over the past 6 seasons (2017-2022 inclusive) Ezekiel Elliot has averaged 14 games played, 214 carries, 1,105 rushing yards and 9 touchdowns. What do you think Dave would say if we told him Ezekiel Elliot was going to be the starting running back for the Saskatchewan Roughriders next season? I'll save you the trouble of guessing and tell you exactly what Dave would think. There would be no doubt in his mind that Zeke would absolutely destroy the CFL. He would destroy every rushing record there was to destroy, rush for 2500+ yards, score 30+ touchdowns, drop the mic when he was done and head back to the NFL victoriously, leaving nothing but scorched earth and demoralized defenders in CFL stadiums from coast to coast.

Interestingly enough, this scenario is not a hypothetical one as this exact scenario took place during the 2006 season when Ricky Williams signed with the CFL's Toronto Argonauts. When he signed in the CFL Ricky was 29 years of age, and up until that point in his career had been averaging the production recorded above. He had missed the 2004 season due to an unexpected retirement, but had resumed his NFL career in 2005 where he rushed for 743 yards at 4.4 yards per carry with 6 touchdowns.

The results of the Ricky Williams experiment were absolutely fascinating as it was one of the few, if not the only time in recent football history that an elite and proven NFL player, still pretty much in the prime of his career had the opportunity to play in the CFL. As history would have it, the experiment did not yield the results "Dave; the NFL ONLY fan" unquestionably expected to see play out on the field. When the dust had settled at the end of the 2006 CFL season Williams had turned in the following performance:

Games Played: 11
Carries: 109
Carries/Game: 9.9
Yards: 526
Yards/Game: 47.8
YPC Average: 4.8
Long: 35
TD: 2
TD/Game: 0.18
10+ yard runs: 12
10+/Gm: 1.09
20+ yard runs: 3
20+/Gm: 0.27

Do not get me wrong, he performed well during his time in the CFL, ending up top 10 in the league! He was the leading rusher on his team that season, but truth be told, was hardly the "destroyer of worlds" that many expected him to be. Of course as always, "Dave; the NFL ONLY fan" would likely have had an excellent and highly scientific explanation for Williams' lack of performance in the CFL: *He was obviously washed up.* Maybe Dave has a point. Between the NFL retirement in 2004 and the unimpressive production during his last NFL season after coming back out of retirement, Williams might just have been past his prime when he came north. At 29 years of age maybe he was in fact over the hill, well past his prime. Surely there was no way that an ACTUAL NFL All-Pro could come to the CFL and not dominate, right?

Unfortunately for Dave, there was just one small problem with the "washed up" hypothesis; Williams returned to the NFL the very next season, and ended up playing 65 more games over the following 5 years. During that period he rushed for 2,912 yards on 674 carries at 4.3 yards per carry and scored 19 more touchdowns! In fact, during the 2009 season, three full years after his CFL stint and at the age of 32, he rushed for his 5th 1000+ yard season. That season he played in all 16 games, rushed for 1,121 yards on 241 carries, with a yards per carry average of 4.7 and an impressive 11 touchdowns. He would eventually conclude his illustrious NFL career with 2,431 carries for 10,009 yards with a 4.1 yards per carry average, and 66 rushing touchdowns. His career yardage left him only 598 yards short of joining the top 25 most productive NFL running backs of all-time.

The argument that Ricky Williams may have been "washed up" when he arrived in the CFL could no longer hold water based on his production during the rest of his NFL career. So what else could "Dave; the NFL ONLY fan" argue?

Dave might think to say:

"How can ANYONE rush for good production if their offensive line is bush league? Of course he couldn't dominate. No one in that scenario could!"

This makes some sense does it not? Assuming Dave is correct and the CFL is in fact completely inferior to the NFL, then it stands to reason that the o-line that blocked for Ricky would definitely be subpar, potentially making it much more difficult to gain yards. However, in that scenario that would mean that everyone else was subpar as well. The defensive line and linebacking core that Ricky had to plow through would also be made up of subpar players. If that were the case, everything would technically be proportional! Leaving Ricky, a supposedly far superior player, as a man among boys. In other words, an inferior o-line would be blocking inferior defensive linemen, who were backed by inferior linebackers and defensive backs, which should not have had a negative effect on Ricky at all. For an example of this principle in action, I highly recommend watching this video which depicts a literal "man among boys" scenario with NFL running back Marshawn Lynch playing against high school kids during a suspension from the NFL.[10]

If Ricky Williams was in fact such a vastly superior athlete, who had dominated against the most elite football talent on the planet in the NFL, "Dave; the NFL ONLY fan" would imagine his performance in the CFL would look much like the Marshawn Lynch video above. At the very least he would be the best running back in the league and definitely the best back on his team that season. It shouldn't have even been close! The truth of the matter is, it just did not turn out as expected.

During the 2006 season there were 3 running backs who carried the ball at least 50 times for the Toronto Argonauts: Ricky Williams, John Avery, and Jeff Johnson. All 3 were in the same backfield, and all three had to run from behind the very same offensive line, under the very same offensive system and blocking schemes drawn up by the very same offensive coordinator and head coach, against the same competition. As such, comparing these three players is as close to "apples to apples" as a comparison can get.

Keep in mind that Ricky Williams was a graduate of the University of Texas at Austin, who had been a 1st round NFL draft pick in 1999 (5th overall). As of the beginning of his CFL career he had already won the following accolades and awards:

31

Pro Bowl 2002
First-team All-Pro 2002
NFL rushing yards leader 2002
Heisman Trophy 1998
Walter Camp Award 1998
Maxwell Award 1998
AP Player of the Year 1998
The Sporting News Player of the Year 1998
2× Doak Walker Award 1997, 1998
2× Unanimous All-America 1997, 1998
2× Big 12 Offensive Player of the Year 1997, 1998
3× First-team All-Big 12 1996–1998

Williams was only 4 seasons removed from rushing for 1,853 yards and 16 touchdowns in the NFL, a performance that at the time of writing this book STILL stands as one of the top 15 NFL rushing seasons of all-time.

John Avery curiously enough, had also been an NFL first round draft pick in 1998 (29th overall). However, unlike the highly respected Williams, he was largely considered one of the biggest NFL draft busts of all-time.[11],[12] He had appeared in 16 games his rookie season with the Miami Dolphins and was only able to gain 503 yards on 143 carries at 3.5 yards per carry with 2 touchdowns. His rookie season saw him used primarily as a kick returner. Despite having been a first round pick, the Dolphins traded him to the Denver Broncos the very next season, and after only his second year of professional football, he was deemed "not talented enough" to play in the NFL and the Broncos cut him. He spent 1 season in the original XFL before coming north for 1 season with the Eskimos. He turned a productive season in Edmonton into another NFL opportunity with the Vikings, but was ultimately released without making an impact. He then returned to the CFL to close out his career playing 4 seasons with the Argonauts.

Jeff Johnson was an undrafted Canadian player out of York University in Canadian Inter-University Sport (CIS). He was a highly successful and decorated college football player who had won the following awards and recognition:

Peter Gorman Trophy - CIS rookie of the year (1996)
Norm Marshall Trophy - OUA rookie of the year (1996)
3x OUA first-team all-star selection (1996, 1997, 1999)
2x CIS second-team all-Canadian (1997, 1999)

The following are the statistics for each of the three primary running backs on the 2006 Toronto Argonauts roster:

Ricky Williams	John Avery	Jeff Johnson
Games Played: 11	Games Played: 7	Games Played: 11
Carries: 109	Carries: 82	Carries: 54
Carries/Game: 9.9	Carries/Game: 11.7	Carries/Game: 4.9
Yards: 526	Yards: 432	Yards: 227
Yards/Game: 47.8	Yards/Game: 61.7	Yards/Game: 20.6
YPC Average: 4.8	YPC Average: 5.3	YPC Average: 4.2
Long: 35	Long: 23	Long: 33
TD: 2	TD: 2	TD: 2
TD/Game: 0.18	TD/Game: 0.29	TD/Game: 0.18
Car/TD: 54.5	Car/TD: 41.0	Car/TD: 27.0
10+ yard runs: 12	10+ yard runs: 15	10+ yard runs: 4
10+/Gm: 1.09	10+/Gm: 2.14	10+/Gm: 0.36
20+ yard runs: 3	20+ yard runs: 1	20+ yard runs: 1
20+/Gm: 0.27	20+/Gm: 0.14	20+/Gm: 0.09
PSC Rating: 85.6	**PSC Rating: 81.3**	**PSC Rating: 58.3**

Jeff Johnson was overall the least productive of all three on the team with a PSC rating of 58.3. Although in fairness, Johnson was not called upon to be the every down back, so it is not surprising to see these results. Despite his overall production being lower than the other two backs, his longest rush of 33 yards was only 2 yards shy of Williams' 35, his touchdown per game ratio was equal to Williams', and he had the best carries per touchdown ratio of all three; scoring a touchdown every 27 carries.

The competition between Ricky Williams and John Avery was much closer than one would have expected between an NFL All-Pro and an NFL "draft bust". Williams came out on top with a slightly higher PSC rating of 85.6 compared to Avery's 81.3. It is interesting to note that despite playing 4 less games, Avery only ended up 94 yards behind Williams for the team lead. Avery's yards per game average was higher, as was his yards per carry average. In addition, Avery had a better carries per touchdown ratio of 41.0, vs Williams' 54.5. All three backs scored 2 touchdowns each, however Avery's 0.29 touchdowns per game ratio was best among the 3.

If we extend the comparison to include the other top running backs in the CFL that season we find that Williams was not able to top the league in any relevant metric, not even if broken down on a per game basis. I applied my PSC rating system to the top 10 running backs in the CFL for the 2006 season and obtained the following results:

1	Charles Roberts	97.6
2	Joffrey Reynolds	97.1
3	Robert Edwards	82.8
4	Joe Smith	75.1
5	Kenton Keith	73.5
6	Troy Davis	71.1
7	John Avery*	47.0
8	**Ricky Williams**	**46.0**
9	Corey Holmes	40.5
10	Josh Ranek	30.8

*For an explanation of why John Avery ranked higher than Ricky Williams when the comparison was expanded see endnote.[13]

During his time in the CFL Ricky stated:

"As far as talent...the talent here is comparable to the NFL, it's just consistency. From what I saw out there, these guys can run, these guys can hit, these guys know what they're doing. Football is football. There are a couple of differences in the game but for the most part it's just terminology."[14]

There can be no doubt that Ricky Williams was in fact an elite player. His NFL career basically ended as nearly hall of fame worthy. So his lack of production in the CFL is not in any way an indictment of his talent and abilities on a football field, but rather it is a testament to the quality of players that play in the Canadian Football League. Ricky Williams was quickly alerted to the fact that the CFL is full of elite football talent. A few years ago when Terrell Owens was rumoured to be considering attempting a comeback at football in the CFL after having been retired for a few years, CFL wide receiver S.J. Green went on record saying the following: "*Just don't disrespect the league, don't come up here thinking this is some bushwick league, or something you can just come out of retirement 7-8 years down the road and not come into this league respecting the players and the work that everybody has put into it, because there are players that can play good football, and if you do come up here half stepping, somebody will put you in your place.*"[15]

Ricky Williams would most likely agree.

"THE LEAGUE (CFL) IS A LOT FASTER AND HARDER-HITTING THAN PEOPLE THINK. THE GAME IS A LOT MORE COMPLEX WITH MORE TALENTED PLAYERS THAN WHAT HE (JOHNNY MANZIEL) FACED IN COLLEGE."[16]

WARREN MOON

9X PRO BOWL QUARTERBACK
INDUCTED TO THE PRO FOOTBALL HALL OF FAME
CFL ALL-STAR
5X GREY CUP CHAMPION
INDUCTED TO THE CANADIAN FOOTBALL HALL OF FAME

SECTION 4 – COMPETITION FACTOR: THE SOCCER PARALLEL

Competition brings out the best in athletes. We see this principle in action all the time, most notably in inter-league play in professional soccer competitions. In the soccer world, the English Premier League is the most popular and wealthiest professional soccer league in the world. Outside of the Premier League, only a few clubs like Real Madrid, Bayern Munich, Barcelona, and Paris St. Germain can rival the Premier League clubs' world-class players, facilities, and staff. However, each and every year we see small teams, from small leagues, in small countries, with comparatively minuscule budgets that manage to compete against these juggernauts of world soccer, oftentimes drawing and sometimes even defeating them. For example, during the past couple of UEFA Champions League seasons we have seen the following results which illustrate this principle:

Maccabi Haifa - 2
37th ranked league
Israeli Ligat ha'Al
Squad Value: 24.9 Million Euros

Juventus - 0
4th ranked league
Italian Serie A
Squad Value 442.3 Million Euros

Sheriff Tiraspol - 2
73rd ranked league
Moldovan Super Liga
Squad Value: 19.1 Million Euros

Real Madrid - 1
2nd ranked league
Spanish La Liga
Squad Value: 780.0 Million Euros

Antwerp FC - 1
11th ranked league
Belgian Jupiler Pro League
Squad Value: 52.7 Million Euros

Tottenham Hotspur FC -0
1st ranked league
English Premier League
Squad Value: 738.6 Million Euros

There will be those that read the above facts and scoff at them. They will say things like "a 1-0 victory does not mean anything". "If they played each other 10 times, the big team would win 9", or a whole slew of other excuses for why these games ended the way they did. The truth is, if financial value is the primary and MOST IMPORTANT indicator of quality and talent, then these results should not be possible. Realistically, there should be NO WAY a team with a roster worth 780 MILLION Euros loses to a team valued at 40 times less, which for those keeping track at home means Real Madrid was worth 760.9 million Euros MORE than their competition! They did not lose against a team from a league ranked 2nd or even 3rd in the world, but a league then ranked 73rd in the world. Yet it happened. The financial disparity in the above mentioned examples is absolutely enormous; a disparity one would normally equate to a "men against boys" type of scenario.

The interesting thing about this principle is that there are those that would concede that while this is in fact possible in world soccer, it would never be possible in gridiron football, but let's explore this possibility a bit further.

The world soccer system is highly developed, and as such almost every participating country on the globe not only has a professional league, but many have multiple tiers of leagues within their own countries to form an absolutely enormous pyramid. Arguably, the best soccer in the world is found on the European continent, as such I applied my PSC Rating system to rate eligible[17] top tier soccer leagues in Europe based on financial criteria, and discovered the following results.

Depicted below are the top 10 European leagues by average team market value[18]

Tier 1
1st place   English Premier League - 100.0
Drop of 53.2

Tier 2
2nd place   Spanish La Liga – 46.8
3rd place   German Bundesliga – 46.2
4th place   Italian Serie A – 44.1
Drop of 11.6

Tier 3
5th place   French Ligue 1 – 32.5
Drop of 19.9

Tier 4
6th place   Portuguese Primeira Liga – 12.6
7th place   Dutch Eredivisie – 11.1
8th place   Turkish Super Lig – 10.1
9th place   Russian Premier Liga – 9.2
10th place   Belgian Pro League – 8.9

The market value data clearly shows that there are 4 easily distinguishable tiers of soccer in Europe. The EPL stands alone at the very top and is assigned a perfect rating of 100.0 as it has the highest average team value. The drop from first to the next few leagues is substantial. The 2nd tier is composed of: Spanish La Liga: rated at 46.8, German Bundesliga: rated at 46.2, and Italian Serie A: rated at 44.1. After the top 4 leagues, there is another substantial drop. The French Ligue 1 is rated at 32.5 and stands alone in the 3rd tier. The 4th tier leagues and below is where things begin to drop much more linearly. The difference between the 6th ranked Portuguese Primeira Liga (12.6) and the 10th ranked Belgian Pro League (8.9) is a differential of only 3.7 rating points. If league finances as our primary evaluation criterion for quality and talent is an accurate metric, we could logically assume that the league rankings by actual on-field results would closely follow the list above, and should be subject to very similar disparities.

Let's evaluate each league's rating based on the UEFA league co-efficient metric[19], which is based on actual on-field performance in the European inter-league competitions over the past 5 years (2017/18 to 2021/22)

Tier 1
1st place   English Premier League – 100.0
Drop of 9.8

Tier 2
2nd place   Spanish La Liga – 90.2
Drop of 18.0

Tier 3
3rd place   Italian Serie A – 72.1
4th place   German Bundesliga – 70.5
Drop of 14.2

Tier 4
5th place   French Ligue 1 – 56.3
6th place   Portuguese Primeira Liga – 50.1
7th place   Dutch Eredivisie– 46.2
Drop of 9.8

Tier 5
8th place   Austrian Bundesliga – 36.4
9th place   Scottish Premiership – 34.6
10th place   Russian Premier League – 32.3

The data clearly shows that while the ranking order appears to be somewhat similar, the disparity that existed financially drops dramatically when evaluating actual on-field results. The ratings gap in finances between 1st place English Premier League and 9th place Russian Premier League is an enormous 90.8, yet when we compare the actual on-field performance and results of the best teams from those same two leagues, we see the gap has dropped to 67.7. What does this data likely demonstrate? I believe it demonstrates that there are factors that contribute to on-field success other than league size, finances etc. One of these factors, which in my personal opinion is one of the strongest contributors is what I call the "competition factor"; knowing you are the underdog and facing a very formidable opponent normally brings out a different level of play. Athletes rise to the challenge of facing a great opponent.

I cannot talk about this subject without remembering a Europa League game from October 2019. As a matter of fact, I highly recommend looking it up and watching the highlights yourself.[20] The game featured the English Premier League's Arsenal; a team that had a roster then valued at approximately 608 million euros, against humble Vitória de Guimarães from the 6th ranked Portuguese Primeira Liga. At the time, Vitória was valued at approximately 65 million Euros, which for those keeping track is 543 MILLION EUROS LESS! Let's say that another way, the squad value of Vitória de Guimarães was only 12% the value of their opponents'.

On paper it was a huge mismatch, certainly destined to be a massacre of the little Portuguese team. But those of us that actually watched that game were treated to an excellent display of soccer. Vitória took an early 1-0 lead, Arsenal later equalized 1-1. Vitória again took the lead 2-1, and later Arsenal scored a free kick to tie it at 2-2. It wasn't until the dying seconds of the game; 90+1 that Arsenal was awarded another free kick and scored the winner. Despite losing in the last minutes of the game, Vitória looked every bit the equal of the mighty Arsenal. Had their jerseys had a different logo on them, no one would have been able to tell Vitória wasn't a Premier League team. The athletes on that little Portuguese team rose to the occasion of playing an English giant, in London; this is the competition factor in action.

The following pages will graphically depict the decline in average team value of the world's top flight soccer leagues, beginning with the top ranked English Premier League all the way to the 80th ranked Canadian Premier League. The graphs do not include second division leagues.

WORLD'S TOP SOCCER LEAGUES
BY AVERAGE TEAM VALUE (1–5)

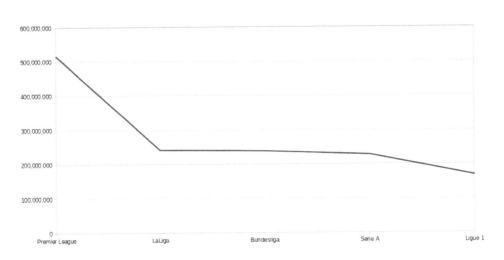

WORLD SOCCER LEAGUES
BY AVERAGE TEAM VALUE (6–13)

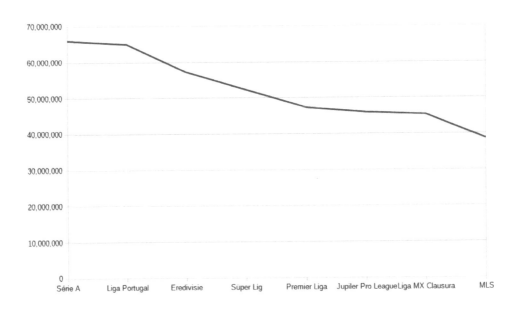

WORLD SOCCER LEAGUES
BY AVERAGE TEAM VALUE (14-80)

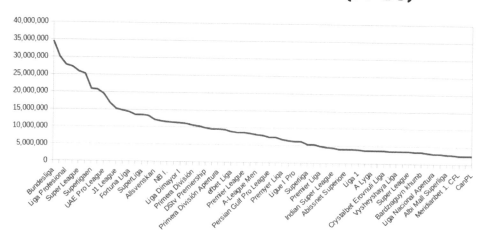

WORLD SOCCER LEAGUES
BY AVERAGE TEAM VALUE (22/23)

1	Premier League	England	516,000,000
2	LaLiga	Spain	241,500,000
3	Bundesliga	Germany	238,333,333
4	Serie A	Italy	227,500,000
5	Ligue 1	France	167,500,000
6	Série A	Brazil	66,000,000
7	Liga Portugal	Portugal	65,000,000
8	Eredivisie	Holland	57,222,222
9	Süper Lig	Turkey	52,275,263
10	Premier Liga	Russia	47,308,125
11	Jupiler Pro League	Belgium	45,921,111
12	Liga MX Clausura	Mexico	45,316,667
13	MLS	USA/Canada	38,620,690
14	Bundesliga	Austria	34,554,167
15	Premiership	Scotland	30,020,833
16	Liga Profesional	Argentina	27,741,071
17	Super League 1	Greece	27,212,857
18	Super League	Switzerland	25,865,000
19	SuperSport HNL	Croatia	25,251,000
20	Superligaen	Denmark	20,840,000
21	Saudi Pro League	Saudi Arabia	20,687,500
22	UAE Pro League	United Arab Emirates	19,427,143

41

23	Premier Liga	Ukraine	16,792,500
24	J1 League	Japan	15,182,778
25	Super liga Srbije	Serbia	14,722,500
26	Fortuna Liga	Czech Republic	14,303,125
27	Ekstraklasa	Poland	13,436,111
28	SuperLiga	Romania	13,428,750
29	K League 1	South Korea	13,281,667
30	Allsvenskan	Sweden	12,118,750
31	Protathlima Cyta	Cyprus	11,732,143
32	NB I.	Hungary	11,508,333
33	Stars League	Qatar	11,355,833
34	Liga Dimayor I	Colombia	11,266,500
35	Eliteserien	Norway	11,051,875
36	Primera División	Chile	10,618,750
37	Ligat ha'Al	Israel	10,364,286
38	DStv Premiership	South Africa	9,890,625
39	Serie A Primera Etapa	Ecuador	9,555,000
40	Primera División Apertura	Paraguay	9,554,167
41	Primera División Apertura	Uruguay	9,462,500
42	efbet Liga	Bulgaria	8,929,375
43	Liga 1 Apertura	Peru	8,670,000
44	Premier League	Egypt	8,598,889
45	Super League	China	8,365,556
46	A-League Men	Australia	8,048,333
47	Botola Pro Inwi	Morocco	7,841,875
48	Persian Gulf Pro League	Iran	7,393,750
49	División Profesional	Bolivia	7,301,765
50	Premyer Liqa	Azerbaijan	6,733,000
51	Fortuna Liga	Slovakia	6,401,667
52	Ligue I Pro	Tunisia	6,220,625
53	Ligue Professionnelle 1	Algeria	6,147,500
54	Superliga	Uzbekistan	5,415,714
55	Prva Liga	Slovenia	5,332,000
56	Premier Liga	Kazakhstan	4,913,571
57	Thai League	Thailand	4,596,875
58	Indian Super League	India	4,475,455
59	Super Liga	Moldova	4,158,750
60	Abissnet Superiore	Albania	4,075,000
61	Virsliga	Latvia	4,068,000
62	Liga 1	Indonesia	4,000,000
63	Premijer Liga	Bosnia- Herzegovina	3,852,500
64	A Lyga	Lithuania	3,850,000

65	Liga FUTVE	Venezuela	3,821,333
66	Crystalbet Erovnuli Liga	Georgia	3,737,000
67	Primera División Apertura	Costa Rica	3,586,667
68	Vysheyshaya Liga	Belarus	3,565,333
69	Prva liga	North Macedonia	3,539,091
70	Super League	Malaysia	3,535,714
71	Leb. Premier League	Lebanon	3,476,667
72	Bardzraguyn khumb	Armenia	3,391,000
73	Veikkausliiga	Finland	3,190,000
74	Liga Nacional Apertura	Honduras	3,044,000
75	Premier League	Malta	2,984,286
76	Albi Mall Superliga	Kosovo	2,745,000
77	V.League 1	Vietnam	2,699,286
78	Meridianbet 1. CFL	Montenegro	2,530,000
79	Hong Kong Premier League	Hong Kong	2,529,000
80	CanPL	Canada	2,460,000

All values from transfermarkt.com

"PEOPLE ASK ME ABOUT THE PLAYERS WHO PLAY THE GAME IN CANADA AND I ALWAYS TELL THEM THEY ARE THE SAME AS THE NFL PLAYERS. MANY CFL PLAYERS HAD THE CHANCE TO PLAY IN THE NFL BRIEFLY, OR WERE LATE CUTS IN NFL CAMPS OVER THE YEARS.

THE MEN IN THE MONTREAL LOCKER ROOM WERE ESSENTIALLY NO DIFFERENT THAN THE MEN IN OUR CHICAGO LOCKER ROOM. THE PLAYERS TRULY LOVE THE GAME, TRAIN EXTREMELY HARD IN THE OFF-SEASON, ARE HIGHLY COMPETITIVE AND "FOOTBALL INTELLIGENT," AND THE GAME IS AS IMPORTANT TO THEM AS THE NFL PLAYERS I HAVE COACHED. THE ONLY DIFFERENCE IS THE CFL PLAYER SALARY IS SIGNIFICANTLY LESS THAN THE NFL PLAYER." [21]

MARC TRESTMAN

NFL HEAD COACH
CHICAGO BEARS

CFL HEAD COACH
MONTREAL ALOUETTES/TORONTO ARGONAUTS

SECTION 5 - SUPPLY AND DEMAND

The preceding section served to illustrate the absolutely vast network of professional soccer leagues in the world. The world's 80 most valuable top division professional soccer leagues have a total of 1,180 teams, which contain a total of 33,764 players. Second division leagues/teams from Europe's top 25 soccer nations will add another 437 teams, with 11,770 more players for a grand total of 1,617 teams with a total of 45,534 professional players at any given time. Keeping these numbers in mind, let's look at the network that supplies the NFL and CFL with talent to see how it compares to the soccer supply chain in terms of numbers.

In North America, colleges and universities are the main suppliers of professional football talent, as there are no de facto second tier professional leagues in either the USA or Canada. Although college football teams can have as many as 125 players on an active roster, to keep things simple and conservative we will assume that each team only has 53 players per active roster in the US, and 46 players per active roster in Canada in keeping with the NFL and CFL active roster limits. The reality is, the number of actual available players are likely double. The amateur football system is divided into the following 7 amateur tiers.

1   NCAA Division 1 – Football Bowl Subdivision (FBS)
    129 teams – 6,837 players

2   NCAA Division 1 – Football Championship Subdivision (FCS)
    125 teams – 6,625 players

3   NCAA Division 2 – Football Championship
    165 teams – 8,745 players

4   USPORTS – Canadian Universities
    27 teams – 1,242 players

5   NCAA Division 3 – Football Championship
    241 teams – 12,773 players

6   NAIA – National Association of Intercollegiate Athletics
    94 teams – 4,982 players

7   NJCAA – National Junior college Athletic Association
    65 teams – 3,445 players

When tallying all the above data, we see that the supply system for professional football talent has a total of 846 teams, with a total of 44,649 players. It is quite remarkable to note that in this example the supply of available football talent appears to be very comparable to the supply of available top professional soccer talent in the world with a very similar number of total players.

	Football	Soccer
Teams	846	1617
Players	44,649	45,534

Each and every season there are approximately 16,380 draft eligible players graduating from NCAA programs[22]. I will repeat that number; 16,380. Every...single...year. If we were to take only the top 2.5%, "the best of the best", the most "pro ready" prospects, we would end up with 410 players. The annual NFL draft could potentially claim 260 players from that number, bringing the number down to 150 players who were a part of the top 2.5% of the most talented players in college football that remain unclaimed and unemployed.

Some of those surplus players may receive an opportunity to sign priority free agent contracts, get camp invites and such, but at that point they have an uphill battle to make a roster that their talent, or lack thereof, will have very little effect on. 150 players who now have to scratch and claw for reps if they manage to even make it to camp. Players that have to attempt to draw their coach's eye away from the incumbents, free agents with previous NFL experience, and draft picks that the organization has spent thousands to scout and evaluate. In short, most of those 150 surplus players will rejoin the other 15,970 who just graduated and will more than likely have to forget their football dreams and get a "real job". It is just the reality of supply and demand. Many of the players that do not get the opportunity to play professional football are in fact talented enough to do so, but are simply casualties of the numbers game. This principle is not unique to professional football, but can be seen in action in virtually any situation in life where the available supply far exceeds the available demand.

With a fresh supply of players regularly being turned over each and every season from the NCAA, Canadian USports, JUCO etc, it would be numerically possible to supply talent to many leagues, with the "performance bell curve" likely looking similar to what it is in world soccer. In a scenario like that, the NFL would top the pyramid as the English Premier League does, with the CFL, XFL, USFL, and other leagues taking on the roles of La Liga, Serie A, Bundesliga etc.

I believe that the enormous supply of football talent available relative to the comparatively scarce demand for professional football players results in the existence of a curious dynamic. Despite NFL teams being able to select any players they want, the surplus of available post-college players, and roster overflow from the NFL itself is still so great that any secondary professional leagues would still be able to create teams that are full of highly talented individuals.

Simple math tells us that for every 260 players drafted into the NFL every year, there are 260 players previously considered good enough to be there that are "drafted" out of the NFL every year as well. It is like an overflowing cup under a running faucet. If fresh water is continually being added to the cup that is already filled to capacity, it overflows. Does that mean that the water that is currently in the cup is "better" than the water that is running down the side of it, or down the drain? Think logically and you tell me!

To further explore the concept of supply and demand as it relates to professional sports, I decided to take 32 clubs with the world's most valuable rosters from the world's top soccer leagues and create an NFL style super league. This super league would be nothing but "the best of the best" and would likely look like the following:

RANK	Team	Players	Team Value	AVG/Player
1	Manchester City	24	1,050,000,000	43,700,000
2	Real Madrid	23	849,000,000	36,910,000
3	Bayern Munich	27	995,700,000	36,880,000
4	Arsenal FC	23	803,000,000	34,910,000
5	FC Barcelona	22	762,000,000	34,640,000
6	Paris Saint-Germain	26	889,050,000	34,190,000
7	Chelsea FC	33	1,040,000,000	31,650,000
8	Liverpool FC	30	931,000,000	31,030,000
9	Tottenham Hotspur	25	711,300,000	28,450,000
10	Manchester United	29	756,100,000	26,070,000
11	Atlético de Madrid	22	489,000,000	22,230,000
12	West Ham United	22	471,500,000	21,430,000
13	Inter Milan	27	555,950,000	20,590,000
14	SSC Napoli	27	543,000,000	20,110,000
15	Aston Villa	23	445,800,000	19,380,000
16	AC Milan	31	571,400,000	18,430,000
17	RB Leipzig	27	493,300,000	18,270,000
18	Leicester City	27	455,100,000	16,860,000
19	Juventus FC	27	442,300,000	16,380,000
20	Newcastle United	29	474,400,000	16,360,000
21	Borussia Dortmund	33	522,700,000	15,840,000
22	Bayer 04 Leverkusen	28	416,350,000	14,870,000
23	Everton FC	25	368,100,000	14,720,000
24	Real Sociedad	26	380,500,000	14,630,000
25	Wolverhampton Wanderers	28	393,700,000	14,060,000
26	Villarreal CF	22	289,700,000	13,170,000
27	Southampton FC	30	387,500,000	12,920,000
28	Crystal Palace	24	309,200,000	12,880,000
29	Brighton & Hove Albion	24	308,600,000	12,860,000
30	Brentford FC	24	305,100,000	12,710,000
31	AS Roma	29	368,000,000	12,690,000
32	Atalanta BC	25	307,450,000	12,300,000
	TOTALS	860	18,085,800,000	
	AVERAGE		565,181,250	21,628,750
	MEDIAN		481,700,000	18,350,000

This super league would be home to 860 players, each with an average value of 21.6 million Euros, with an average team value of 565.2 million Euros.

The combined value of all players in the league was 18.1 billion Euro. The teams above have been colour coded to reflect the 6 rating tiers; elite, above average, high average, low average, below average and poor from a financial value standpoint.

After completing the 32 team super league, I then attempted to create a second professional league with only 9 teams. This mini league could only draw from what the super league had left behind. In other words, players from teams that did not have an average player value high enough to make the cut in the super league. I found I was able to create 9 teams from the "best of the rest" which would all be competitive from a player value standpoint.

The mini league totalled 234 players, each with an average value of 17.5 million Euros, with the league having an average team value of 456.2 million Euros. The combined value of all players in the mini league totalled 4.1 billion Euros.

RANK	Team	Players	Market Value	Average/Player
1	TEAM 1	26	440,000,000	16,923,077
2	TEAM 2	26	451,000,000	17,346,154
3	TEAM 3	26	450,500,000	17,326,923
4	TEAM 4	26	447,500,000	17,211,538
5	TEAM 5	26	460,500,000	17,711,538
6	TEAM 6	26	451,500,000	17,365,385
7	TEAM 7	26	467,500,000	17,980,769
8	TEAM 8	26	462,500,000	17,788,462
9	TEAM 9	26	475,000,000	18,269,231
	TOTALS	234	4,106,000,000	
	AVERAGE		456,222,222	17,547,009
	MEDIAN		451,500,000	17,365,385

If we were to evaluate the results based strictly on the average player values, we find that the mini league sits at roughly four fifths of what the super league is. All 9 teams would transition into the low average category of the super league. It is interesting to note that despite handpicking the most expensive players left available, the mini league did not have any teams which could rival the top 10 super league teams from an average player value standpoint.

I then created a mini league All-Star team by taking the absolute best players available from the mini league and ended up with a roster that had a total value of 815 million Euros, with an average player value of 31.3 million. This team of All-Stars would end up as the 7th most valuable roster in the super league, with an average player value that ranked 8th in the super league. As is evident, the upper echelon of the mini league would not only be competitive against every team in the super league, they could ultimately challenge for championships.

Now, some of you may be reluctant to accept the outcome of this scenario because I had the benefit of being able to blow up existing teams' rosters, rank all available players by value, and choose the most expensive ones to create the mini league's teams. In truth, this would likely not be a realistic way to build a roster, as secondary football leagues would not necessarily have access to, or even be able to sign all the best available players. So what if instead of that I was only able to choose left over teams just as they were, without any modifications to their rosters? In this scenario the mini league was composed of the following teams: Leeds United, Benfica, Ajax, Stade Rennais, Monaco, Marseille, Real Betis, Fulham FC and Sevilla. This league had an average team value of 274.4 million Euros and an average player value of 11.1 million Euros.

This meant the revised mini league was roughly 50% of what the super league was as a whole, however taking a closer look we can observe that even the bottom team in the mini league was only valued at 18.6% lower than the bottom team in the super league from an average player value perspective. This suggests that despite not making the cut from an absolute numbers perspective, I would still expect that even the lowest mini league team would still be reasonably competitive against many of the teams in the super league. This 2023 season in the English Premier League we observed this principle in action as Leeds United (average player value 12.3 million) beat Chelsea (average player value 31.7 million) and Liverpool (average player value 31 million).

I would hypothesize that all factors being equal (rules, field size etc.), all the mini league teams would be able to play respectably against most of their super league counterparts. They most likely would not challenge for the top of the super league, but in fairness, neither would half the super league either! I think this is a point that many CFL haters or NFL elitists are either not aware of or simply refuse to see. Never forget that for every 14-2 Kansas City Chiefs in the NFL, there is an equal and opposite 2-14 New York Jets.

"THE CFL IS THE BEST PROFESSIONAL FOOTBALL OUTSIDE OF THE
NATIONAL FOOTBALL LEAGUE..."

"I BELIEVE EVERY CFL TEAM COULD BEAT THE UNIVERSITY OF ALABAMA.
IF YOU WANNA TALK ABOUT THE QUALITY OF THE FOOTBALL...THAT'S HOW I
EVALUATE THE TALENT LEVEL."

QUESTION:
"SO THIS IS TOUGHER COMPETITION THAN THE TOP LEVEL OF COLLEGE
FOOTBALL IN YOUR OPINION?"

"YES, ABSOLUTELY! THAT'S WHY YOU SEE SO MANY PEOPLE FAIL WITH
THE CFL." [23]

CRIS CARTER

8X PRO BOWL WIDE RECEIVER
INDUCTED TO THE PRO FOOTBALL HALL OF FAME

SECTION 6 – THE RELEGATION VISUALIZATION

One of the most stark differences between sports in Europe and sports in North America is the existence of a relegation system in Europe vs a franchise system in North America. The North American system provides stability, the European system is a sort of meritocracy where teams are either rewarded or punished based on their on-field performance. Both have pros and cons. If we were to simplify things and imagine the NFL as the top division and the CFL as the second division, in a system that included promotion and relegation based on overall performance, what would that league look like? How many CFL teams, if any, would we find plying their trade in the NFL? "Dave; the NFL ONLY fan" says he only watches the NFL because it is the best of the best. Quite reasonably he will say that the Chiefs, Saints, Rams, Patriots, and Ravens are prime examples of that fact. In fairness to Dave; he's absolutely right! Those teams have in fact been elite teams! According to my calculations, over the past 5 years those teams were the most consistent and productive in the entire NFL. But what about the Jets, Giants, Jaguars, Lions and Bengals? Can we just ignore how bad those teams have been over the same period of time? While they all play in the same league, make no mistake, the bottom half of the NFL is **DEFINITELY** not the "best of the best".

Analyzing the past 5 NFL seasons (2017/18-2021/22), I assigned each team a PSC rating based on their actual on-field regular season performance.

1.	Kansas City Chiefs	96.7	17.	San Francisco 49ers	68.3
2.	New Orleans Saints	93.6	18.	Chicago Bears	67.7
3.	Los Angeles Rams	88.7	19.	Atlanta Falcons	63.0
4.	New England Patriots	88.0	20.	Miami Dolphins	62.9
5.	Baltimore Ravens	86.5	21.	Arizona Cardinals	62.6
6.	Green Bay Packers	83.1	22.	Las Vegas Raiders	60.6
7.	Pittsburgh Steelers	82.7	23.	Carolina Panthers	60.4
8.	Tennessee Titans	80.1	24.	Houston Texans	60.3
9.	Buffalo Bills	79.6	25.	Cleveland Browns	59.3
10.	Seattle Seahawks	79.6	26.	Denver Broncos	57.8
11.	Minnesota Vikings	76.5	27.	Washington COMM	57.6
12.	Dallas Cowboys	75.5	28.	Cincinnati Bengals	56.7
13.	Philadelphia Eagles	74.3	29.	Detroit Lions	54.2
14.	Los Angeles Chargers	71.8	30.	Jacksonville Jaguars	52.5
15.	Tampa Bay Buccaneers	71.2	31.	New York Giants	49.2
16.	Indianapolis Colts	70.5	32.	New York Jets	48.1

As we can see in the list above, very unsurprisingly we have the Kansas City Chiefs as the best team over the period, followed closely by the New Orleans Saints, Los Angeles Rams and New England Patriots. The 5th place Baltimore Ravens are already more than 10 full rating points behind the Chiefs in terms of overall production. The disparity in the NFL between the best and worst team over the past 5 years is a differential of 48.6, which indicates the Chiefs and the Jets have been in no way comparable. They have been in "different leagues".

Unlike the super league/mini league example using soccer teams, I am not able to perform the same comparison based on team values for football. The world soccer system is essentially a free market, where there is unrestricted competition for players around the world from multiple teams in multiple leagues. The best, most coveted players see their values rise, while the less desired players values fall. As such, using financial value as an evaluation criterion for quality and talent, although not fully accurate is still more feasible for soccer than it would be for an NFL/CFL comparison. In football, player values are artificially set by the NFL's salary cap system. The disparity we find in values between the NFL and CFL are dictated by the NFL's purchasing power and not actually based on the laws of supply and demand.

In North American gridiron football, I would argue that on-field team performance would be a more accurate method of comparison to evaluate player talent. In a nutshell, the best players perform and obtain results. I analyzed the past 5 CFL seasons and assigned each team a PSC rating based on their actual on-field performance. The disparity observed between the best and worst team in the CFL is 41.0. These ratings indicate that the CFL has slightly more parity than the NFL as the CFL's disparity between the best and worst clubs is 41.0 compared to the NFL's larger 48.6. You'll also notice that beside the PSC rating for each team, there is another number in brackets. This number is the adjusted PSC rating, which will be further explained below.

1. Winnipeg Blue Bombers – 99.1 **(79.3)**
2. Calgary Stampeders – 98.6 **(78.9)**
3. Saskatchewan Roughriders – 83.6 **(66.9)**
4. Hamilton Tiger-Cats – 78.4 **(62.7)**
5. BC Lions – 69.4 **(55.5)**
6. Toronto Argonauts – 66.4 **(53.1)**
7. Edmonton Elks – 65.4 **(52.3)**
8. Montreal Alouettes – 62.1 **(50.5)**
9. Ottawa RedBlacks – 58.1 **(46.5)**

If the dynamic that existed between our fictional soccer super league and mini league were in fact true, we saw that the mini league was roughly 80% of what the super league was from a talent financial value standpoint. Seeing that the supply pipelines for both sports are quite similar in size, I took the same factor and applied it to discount the CFL teams' PSC Ratings to account for the "reduction in level of play". The end results of an "NFL by merit" can be seen below.

NFL BY MERIT

1.	Kansas City Chiefs	96.7	17.	Tampa Bay Buccaneers	71.2
2.	New Orleans Saints	93.6	18.	Indianapolis Colts	70.5
3.	Los Angeles Rams	88.7	19.	San Francisco 49ers	68.3
4.	New England Patriots	88.0	20.	Chicago Bears	67.7
5.	Baltimore Ravens	86.5	**21.**	**Saskatchewan RR**	**66.9**
6.	Green Bay Packers	83.1	22.	Atlanta Falcons	63.0
7.	Pittsburgh Steelers	82.7	23.	Miami Dolphins	62.9
8.	Tennessee Titans	80.1	**24.**	**Hamilton Tiger-Cats**	**62.7**
9.	Buffalo Bills	79.6	25.	Arizona Cardinals	62.6
10.	Seattle Seahawks	79.6	26.	Las Vegas Raiders	60.6
11.	**Winnipeg BB**	**79.3**	27.	Carolina Panthers	60.4
12.	**Calgary Stampeders**	**78.9**	28.	Houston Texans	60.3
13.	Minnesota Vikings	76.5	29.	Cleveland Browns	59.3
14.	Dallas Cowboys	75.5	30.	Denver Broncos	57.8
15.	Philadelphia Eagles	74.3	31.	Washington COMM	57.6
16.	Los Angeles Chargers	71.8	32.	Cincinnati Bengals	56.7

I found it fascinating that in this example 4 of the 9 CFL teams slotted into the 11th, 12th, 21st, and 24th positions in the hierarchy of the NFL based on their adjusted PSC ratings for their on-field performance. This scenario is a bit less optimistic than the original super/mini league scenario we examined in Section 5, as only 4 of 9 teams were able to measure up from a quality of play perspective.

By this point we have considered two different hypothetical comparison scenarios, both based on different criteria. In one case, the above relegation scenario, nearly half the mini league teams would be able to compete in the super league by on-field team performance (44%). In the other scenario, the mini-league team's player values alluded to all of the mini league's teams being able to transition into the super league; albeit at a low average level, and then we observed the modified version of that scenario which saw approximately 50% making the transition. If we average out the results of all three scenarios, we could infer that the mini league is approximately 65% of what the super league is in its totality, considering player values and overall team performance. This is an interesting number that roughly lines up with some of the player and coach quotes we will see a bit later.

The addition of the above mentioned 4 CFL teams would force 4 NFL teams to be "relegated" to the CFL.

1. **BC Lions – 55.5**
2. Detroit Lions – 54.2
3. **Toronto Argonauts – 53.1**
4. Jacksonville Jaguars – 52.5
5. **Edmonton Elks – 52.3**
6. **Montreal Alouettes – 50.5**
7. New York Giants – 49.2
8. New York Jets – 48.1
9. **Ottawa RedBlacks – 46.5**

Even though this is simply a hypothetical scenario, I feel like I can almost see Dave's jugular vein throbbing as he screams ***"The New York Jets would absolutely destroy the Winnipeg Blue Bombers, 65-0! In the first quarter alone!!!"*** Take it easy Dave, watch that blood pressure. Nevertheless, I think this concept is interesting to consider.

The majority of the "second division teams" would more than likely not be able to compete for championships in the super league, however from a talent standpoint would still be comparable to the majority of the super league's teams. Some of you might say that seeing a bunch of CFL teams slot into the high average and low average categories of the NFL isn't impressive at all. As a matter of fact you might be thinking this hypothetical scenario only confirms what you already believed; that the CFL is bad football. The only problem with this is: **you cannot have it both ways**!

You cannot say it is unimpressive that Saskatchewan and Hamilton would slot into the low average category in the NFL by performance, yet in the same breath sing the praises of teams like the Jaguars, Giants, Jets and Lions who have been perennial below average teams in the NFL. In the above fictional "relegation" scenario none of those teams are even participants in the NFL anymore due to their terrible play!

A quick look at the final standings from the 2022 NFL season really helps us visualize the concept: Chicago Bears; 3-14. Houston Texans; 3-13-1. Arizona Cardinals; 4-13. Indianapolis Colts; 4-12-1. Do these look like the records of elite football teams?

The San Francisco 49ers scored 450 points with only 277 against for a net point differential of +173. Meanwhile, the Indianapolis Colts scored 289 points and allowed 427 against for a net point differential of -138. That is "only" a difference of 311 points from first to worst. No big deal right? They are both elite teams? They are both the "best of the best"? Sure, they are both in the NFL, but if you can read numbers the answer to those questions quickly becomes very clear. The hypocrisy of some "football fans" and the sheer blind faith they have in the NFL shield boggles my mind at times.

This is one thing I find great about the promotion/relegation that exists in the European leagues. The teams that are in the top divisions are there and stay there by merit. They are there because they proved themselves to be better than the other teams in the lower leagues and earned the right to be in the top division, competing against the best of the best. Notwithstanding the fact that some teams in the European leagues have virtually unlimited funds compared to their fellow league compatriots, and as such some would argue can "buy" their way to remaining in the top flight leagues. Nevertheless, despite all the money, they are still not above being relegated based on play. The North American sports leagues are completely closed circuits. There are a relatively small amount of spots in the league, and those spots are not for teams that deserve it necessarily, but for teams that have essentially bought their place in the league via purchase or expansion fees. As such, they are always in the league and always considered "top tier", which I personally think is a highly debatable title for some of them.

"CONTRARY TO POPULAR OPINION, I BELIEVE THAT THE TALENT IN THE CFL IS A LOT CLOSER TO THE TALENT IN THE NFL THAN PEOPLE MIGHT WANT TO BELIEVE." [24]

MARKUS HOWELL
CFL RECEIVERS COACH

SECTION 7 – REASONS FOR REJECTION

While those that hate the CFL will state that "lack of talent" is unequivocally the one and only reason players get cut from the NFL, any logical person can understand that as with anything in life, there are many reasons why things turn out the way they do. The following are a few of the many reasons players cannot "stick" on an NFL roster.

Nerves

Society seems to think of professional athletes as superhuman. While it is true that professional athletes are far stronger and faster than the average human, they continue to be human! As such, they are not immune to the same issues regular people deal with such as fear, nervousness, anxiety etc. Some players who ultimately have the potential to play pro are just not quite ready yet when they get their first and many times their only NFL opportunity. Performance anxiety, lack of confidence, failure to rise to the occasion on the big stage are some of the reasons players can fail to impress.

7 time Pro Bowler Steve Tasker explained it this way *"What happens as an athlete, you're out there and you're playing, and you finally got to this point where you've always wanted to be or you've gone further than you ever thought you could, you start to think about the consequences if it goes wrong. It dominates your train of thought...'if I make a mistake now, it's all gone'. That's the mindset you slip into as a young player instead of just the opposite."*[25]

Like everything else in life there are a wide range of people in the world who all deal with stress in different ways, athletes are no exception to this human characteristic. When confronted with a high stress situation the human being is led to either "fight, flight or freeze". Many times players finding themselves on the big stage allow the moment to grow too big for them and simply "freeze" when their number is called. Does it mean they are not talented enough to play? Definitely not. It means they let their nerves or anxiety get the better of them and did not perform up to their potential. For players that find themselves in this position, seldom will they get a second chance unless the team has already invested significant capital in them, be it draft capital or actual financial capital.

Sunk Cost Fallacy

People and businesses often take previous expenditures or previously invested capital into account when considering future decisions; this principle is called the sunk cost fallacy. A team will often put up with inconsistent play or mistakes from a first or second round draft pick, or even a player that signs a free agent contract with a significant signing bonus. That team will normally be highly reluctant to cut them, simply because of the time and money they have already invested into them. If that player under performs, the team will most likely continue to provide that player opportunities to clean up their game. Whereas if another player had signed as a free agent with no bonus and had performed comparably, the second player likely would have been cut while the first player continued on, being given opportunities to play and improve. This mentality is that of "we have already invested all this money. If we cut them now we lose it all with little to no return on our investment."

As regular people, think of it this way. You have just purchased a used car. You spent $10,000 on the vehicle and shortly after purchase you realize you are going to need some repairs. Upon taking the vehicle to the mechanic, you are advised the vehicle has a transmission issue that will cost $2000 to fix. Despite the cost being steep, you will more than likely pay for the repair. After all, you have just spent $10,000 of your hard earned money on it. A short time later, the vehicle again begins giving you problems. Another trip to the mechanic reveals it requires a new suspension, which again costs you another $2000. At this point the vehicle has already cost you $4000 in repairs in a short period of time, but even still you would not easily be inclined to just cut your losses and sell the vehicle. There is always that feeling that things are going to improve and you'll eventually start reaping the benefits of your investment. Assuming the vehicle continues breaking down at the current rate, you will eventually reach the point where you say "losses be damned, I have to get rid of this car." You gave the vehicle as many opportunities as you believed yourself to be financially able to bear. In theory, if you hold onto the vehicle long enough without considering how much money you have already sunk into it, at some point it will likely stop giving you problems and function as it should. You would have replaced pretty much everything there was to replace by that point but once the vehicle began chugging along with no issues, you would have received "confirmation" that you made the right decision in keeping and investing in the vehicle as it eventually became a dependable car.

Now assume you receive that same vehicle for free as a gift from a friend. At the very first sign of issues would you be inclined to spend the $2000 to fix the transmission, or would you be more inclined to scrap the car and simply move on? If we are honest with ourselves, we all know the answer. There is no way we would invest that kind of money into a defective vehicle that we did not purchase. This is the principle of the sunk cost fallacy in action.

When a team invests heavily in a player, they will be highly reluctant to cut that player. Another player may come along, perhaps even with a higher potential than the first, but the team will believe that the player they have financially invested in has to get them a return on their investment. They will not be inclined to cut the former to keep the latter.

Injuries

Over the years there have been countless individuals who have been highly promising college players. Some have gone on to be highly sought after pro prospects after great bowl game and combine performances toward the end of their college careers. Unfortunately, upon hitting the professional ranks they are faced with a set back that they may not have had to deal with previously; serious injury.

Many times, players that are unbelievably talented get injured early into their professional careers. Imagine a draft pick with a high potential suffering a torn ACL in his first training camp which will keep him off the field the entire season. The team will certainly not cut the player right away, after all, they have already invested a draft pick in them. The most likely scenario is the team will assist the player in rehabbing and getting healthy, hoping to get them back up to speed and on the field the following season.

But what would happen if during that second season, the player made it through training camp and made the opening day roster, however early into the season they ended up sustaining another serious injury which kept them sidelined for a majority of that season? By the end of year two, the player would have been on the team for 2 seasons with very little to show for it. The team may begin to lose confidence in the player's ability to ever get on the field in any regular capacity. Perhaps they decide to draft another player the following season or they sign a free agent who ends up taking that role on the team. Even something as simple as a change in the coaching staff could be enough to prompt a release of the injured player as the incoming coach(s) may not believe that particular player is a fit for the system they wish to run.

In the end, the highly talented draft pick who ran into injury troubles early in his career may end up completely out of the league within 2-3 years. With the sheer amount of talent available, teams would be reluctant to hang onto a player who at that point would surely have been labelled "injury prone". In most cases like this, the player quickly runs out of options to continue playing. With very little NFL film available from the player's first two seasons, and his excellent college tape now a distant (and irrelevant) memory, his chances of continuing on a roster in the NFL would at that point be slim to nil.

Trouble with the Law

There are numerous examples of players that were highly talented, but for one reason or another ran into trouble with the law; take Willie Jefferson for example. He was a promising young wide receiver/tight end who was recruited by Baylor University. In October 2010, he was arrested with his Baylor teammate; wide receiver Josh Gordon, after they fell asleep in a drive-through at a Taco Bell. Police were called and ultimately allegedly found marijuana in Jefferson's car. A week later Jefferson was again arrested for minor drug possession, and as a result was kicked off the Baylor team for violating unspecified team rules.[26]

Jefferson transferred to Stephen F. Austin State University where he switched to defensive end and put up 19 sacks in two seasons. Those numbers, coupled with his NFL size were enough to get him an undrafted free agent contract with the Houston Texans after graduating. Unfortunately once again, Willie ran into some issues and in October of 2013 he was released by the NFL club along with two other players for allegedly "violating team rules". With an ejection from the Baylor Bears football program and then another from the Houston Texans, it was highly unlikely that Willie would ever get another true opportunity in the NFL, as at that point he already had two strikes going against him. It was only after getting an opportunity in the CFL and getting some playing time that Jefferson began his ascent to being an All-Star calibre player. A modest 4 sacks in 17 games (0.24 sacks per game) with the Edmonton Elks in his first season led to eventually recording a career best 12 sacks in 18 games (0.67 sacks per game) with Winnipeg during the 2019 season.

Trouble with the law while in college will normally scare NFL teams away from drafting players who would otherwise have been drafted from a talent standpoint. Teams not only look for quality, talented players, but they are also looking for "good character guys". Having criminal charges, multiple team rule violations, or even a bad reputation in the locker room would more than likely be enough to have most teams pass on highly talented players in the draft because they deem them to be more trouble than they are worth.

This mentality obviously does not give young, immature players the ability to make up for their past mistakes, all too often for very minor rule violations. This phenomenon unfortunately ensures that some potential All-Pro players never get to see the field.

Casualties of the Numbers Game

Many players sign contracts and are released well before they have even had a single opportunity to get on the field in any capacity; a fact that is hardly their own faults and certainly not an accurate indication of their talent or ability. There is a reason that some say that NFL stands for "Not For Long". Let's be honest, very few players ever get the opportunity to see the inside of an NFL facility. If a player is on a team, whether on the active roster, the practice roster, or even the off season roster, that player is among the best of the best. Even the so-called "training camp bodies" are excellent players, most of whom enjoyed good to great college careers or even stints with other professional clubs. When you have large numbers of players who all have potential to play pro, but only have a limited number of roster spots available, it is inevitable that many players will simply become casualties of the numbers game.

NFL off season rosters can have a maximum of 90 players and must be reduced to 53 by the time the season starts. The fact is, each team will cut 37 players before the season even begins. Make no mistake, players are not invited to NFL camps because they are terrible, much to the contrary, every single player present has the potential to play professional football. Taking into account the returning players already under contract, the newest draft picks the team has invested in, and other free agents that have significant NFL experience already under their belt, it is simply impossible to keep every good player.

Inability to Adjust to/Learn the Playbook

Depending on where a player played their amateur football, their exposure to the complicated "pro style" offences used in the NFL can be slim. There are likely many players that have the size, strength and speed to play professional, however their inability to learn the complicated playbooks in the NFL in a short amount of time gets them released. These are players that perhaps with more time, coaching, and film study could play and become stars, however the rigours of professional football and the pressure to "win right now" does not afford many players enough time to get acclimated to the particular offensive or defensive scheme a team runs. Coaches in the NFL do not get paid to develop talent, rather they are paid to win football games. Most players that hit training camps and have difficulty learning their respective playbooks will get cut simply because pro football coaches are under such immense pressure to win immediately. Frankly, they do not have the time to wait for those who are a little slower to catch up, as their jobs quite literally depend on winning as much as possible as quickly as possible.

Lack of Avenues for Development/Not Quite Ready Yet

The fact is, there are no other well established, fully professional football leagues outside of the NFL and CFL. As such, there are no other high level options available to allow players to play and develop after college. Some players, although highly talented, are just not "pro ready" right out of college and require some additional playing time at a high level to develop into true professionals. Bucky Brooks, well respected NFL scout and analyst explained it this way: *"The general rule in the National Football League it takes about three years to figure out if a guy can play or not...when we talk about quarterbacks the number that's been frequently thrown out has been 30-32 starts."*[27] It is unbelievable to think that despite the knowledge that one can not truly know what a player is capable of until they hit that 3 year mark, there are hundreds of players each and every year that are cut well before they get anywhere near that mark, and well before their true potential is ever reached or even seen.

This sentiment was echoed by former NFL guard turned author Geoff Schwartz on the PFF NFL Podcast: *"There's this pressure now to have these guys play so quickly and be good so fast, otherwise (as a coach) you lose your job, and it used to be, a first round draft pick you might not even start the first year...year two you get better, and year three you're ready to go. Now if you're a first round draft pick and you don't play right away 'what's wrong with this kid...he's a bust'...There's so much pressure now to 'win now' this idea of the developmental part of the game it's hard to grasp for all the coaches because they have to get these guys ready so quickly."* Podcast host Sam Monson then made this very correct observation *"It also makes it almost impossible for guys that aren't high draft picks to play. Those guys may be capable of doing it, but they are going to take the same developmental time as anybody else, and if you have just a 4th round pick ends up starting for you, getting his ass kicked for the first year, like that dude's not playing, alright, he's not 'good enough'. Bye, next guy. And we're on to the next one. Even if he just needed that year of development, maybe year two he would actually become a good starter for you."²⁸*

Andrew Hawkins; one of my chosen profiled players said the following about his time in the CFL which illustrates the very same principle: *"I learned the game. I learned to play against grown men. In an environment where I wasn't like 'hey, you have to be the MAN right now' or you can't stay, which is the NFL. You gotta bring it NOW, if you're coming from where I was coming from. The only people who get time are the guys who get in the first round, second round, those kind of guys."²⁹* Note that he is essentially referring to the sunk cost fallacy principle when he describes that only 1ˢᵗ and 2ⁿᵈ round players are actually afforded additional developmental time to 'get it right'.

In that same podcast he describes a story of an interaction he had in the Cincinnati Bengal's locker room as an NFL rookie that illustrates how the CFL permitted him to develop into a true professional, and how his pro experience from the CFL was noticeable to other NFL veterans.

"Being in the NFL, when I came back down after 2 and 3 years, playing for the Bengals I was a rookie, when AJ Green and Andy Dalton came in and I remember being in the weight room and Reggie Nelson who was a free safety was like:

RN - How many years you been in the league?
and I'm like
AH - 'Oh, I'm a rookie'.
He was like
RN - 'You're not no rookie.'
AH - I'm like 'Yeah, it's my first year in the NFL'
RN - 'Where did you play at?'
AH - I'm like 'Canada'
RN - He said 'Yeah I can tell you played against grown men.

That's a thing. Once you learn to play against grown men it's a different mindset. That's the thing CFL can do for a lot of players who may have a chance to stick but there's nowhere for them to develop those skills and hone that mentality."

I found this conversation between Hawkins and Nelson absolutely fascinating. A similar comment was made by Indianapolis Colts veteran linebacker Pat Angerer about Jerrell Freeman when he first broke into the NFL.

When discussing Freeman's play Angerer said *"He's been around. He made a ton of tackles in Canada. He's a great player. It might be his first year in the (NFL), but he's a veteran. He knows what to do."*[30]

These examples illustrate that there is in fact a difference between playing college, even high level college, and playing professionally against grown men. For both Hawkins and Freeman (and virtually all other players that transition to the NFL after a stint in the CFL) the experience gained from playing professionally in the CFL was instrumental in preparing them for the rigours of the NFL. Without their CFL experience, they would not have been able to make it in the NFL because they were players that for one reason or another were just not quite ready yet coming out of college. They required a little additional time to hone their skills and become true pros; both of which were later able to go on to the NFL and play at a high level.

It is one thing to rely on your natural ability in college where the level of play is lower than the professional ranks. In fact, some players are likely able to make it through their entire college career on sheer raw talent alone, depending on where they play. Unfortunately for them, talent alone is not enough to enjoy a successful professional career as the amount of time invested in film study, practice, and exercise is significantly higher than any college player is used to investing. Some players take some time to adjust to life as a professional athlete. They may be afforded an opportunity in the NFL right out of college, however their lack of maturity or inability to deal with the requirements of the job end up getting them released. With no other football options in the United States, most players end up moving away from football altogether. Those that refuse to give up on their football dreams and are afforded an opportunity in Canada away from the glitz, glamour and money of the NFL, can often times develop into high level professionals when all the other distractions have been removed and only football is left.

"I THINK ANYBODY THAT DISMISSES THE CFL IS DOING THEMSELVES AN INJUSTICE BECAUSE THEY'RE SHOWING THEIR IGNORANCE." [31]

"IF ANYBODY DOESN'T THINK THAT (CFL) IS PROFESSIONAL FOOTBALL, THEY'RE INSULTING THE LEAGUE AND INSULTING ALL OF US THAT HAVE PLAYED THIS GAME. THIS IS BIG TIME PROFESSIONAL FOOTBALL, AND I'M VERY PROUD TO HAVE PLAYED UP HERE, AND PROUD TO HAVE PUT ON THE DOUBLE BLUE." [32]

I DON'T THINK THERE'S DOUBT IN ANYBODY'S MIND THAT THE CFL IS BIG-TIME FOOTBALL. IT'S JUST THEY DON'T HAVE THE MARKETING OR PUBLIC RELATIONS BEHIND IT IN THE UNITED STATES. YOU DON'T HAVE THAT VEHICLE OUT THERE PUSHING THE PLAYER NAMES. THE PEOPLE IN THE KNOW, KNOW WHAT'S GOING ON, BUT THE CASUAL FANS ARE NOT AS FAMILIAR. [33]

JOE THEISMANN

2X PRO BOWL QUARTERBACK
SUPERBOWL CHAMPION
2X CFL ALL STAR

SECTION 8 – FITTING THE MOLD

According to the traditional football philosophy, each position in football requires a precise combination of size, power, and speed. If one of the characteristics is not what has been determined to be ideal for the position, many players will not even get a look simply because they are too short, too light, too heavy, or do not have the other desired measurables the league has over the years determined to be the right combination for a particular position. All one has to do is pay attention to the annual NFL Combine to see how much of a role the measurables play in getting a player drafted. Everything down to hand size is measured. In recent years, the NFL has begun to change its tune with regard to players fitting the mold and has in fact begun to provide more opportunities to players that are smaller, more agile types, although the old mentality still permeates the league and will likely never disappear completely.

When Doug Flutie played in the NFL he was an outlier, as the smaller, mobile quarterback was something the NFL just did not believe in. The prototypical quarterback was 6'4", 230lbs and a traditional pocket passer that took the vast majority of snaps from under centre. In today's NFL, as more and more elements of college offences are implemented, we see more and more smaller more agile quarterbacks being given starting opportunities. Players like Russell Wilson (5'11", 215lbs), Bryce Young (5'10", 204lbs) and Kylar Murray (5'10" 207lbs) would never have been afforded an opportunity to start in the NFL years ago, simply because they represented such a dramatic departure from the traditional school of thought on required NFL body types.

Earlier in this book I quoted Doug Flutie as having said: *"Most of the guys (in the CFL) were NFL calibre talent, but were undersized or just didn't fit the mold in one way or another"*.

Flutie also famously made this statement:

"...In the NFL, they just want big guys who just throw the ball," Flutie said. "They want to program everything." "I was winning but I wasn't flashy enough for them, or big enough. In the NFL, it's, you know, 'Let's put in a guy who's 6-4. We'll lose but we'll look good losing.' It amazes me the guys who hang around, sitting on the bench in that league. There are guys in the NFL that I've never lost to."[34]

I decided to actually compile an average height and weight for every position in the NFL and CFL to see if there was in fact any detectable difference in player sizes per position. I compiled data from the 2016 and 2019 CFL and NFL seasons, and came up with an average height/weight for each position in each league. Prior to compiling the complete list from each league, I hypothesized that if there were detectable differences between positions in each league, the positions that had the greatest discrepancies would likely be the positions where we observed the least successful transitions from one league to another. By contrast, the positions where we observed the smallest discrepancies would likely be the positions where we observed the most successful transitions.

The results of the player size analysis comparison between leagues can be seen in the tables below.

Year	Position	CFL	NFL	DIF	% DIF	CFL	NFL	DIF	% DIF
		Centimetres				Pounds			
		Height	Height			Weight	Weight		
2016	Receivers	185	184	-1	-0.5	201	201	0	0.0
2016	Defensive Backs	182	182	0	0.0	193	195	2	1.0
2016	Offensive Line	195	195	0	0.0	309	314	5	1.6
2016	Running Back	179	180	1	0.6	206	215	9	4.3
2016	Safety	181	183	2	1.1	198	207	9	4.4
2016	Quarterback	187	192	5	2.6	213	225	12	5.5
2016	Defensive Ends	190	193	3	1.6	256	279	23	8.6
2016	Linebackers	184	188	4	2.2	224	245	21	9.0
2016	Interior D-Line	189	191	2	1.1	270	309	39	13.5

Year	Position	CFL	NFL	DIF	% DIF	CFL	NFL	DIF	% DIF
		Centimetres				Pounds			
		Height	Height			Weight	Weight		
2019	Receivers	185	184	-1	-0.5	199	200	1	0.5
2019	Defensive Backs	181	182	1	0.6	193	194	1	0.5
2019	Offensive Line	195	194	-1	-0.5	306	310	4	1.3
2019	Safety	187	183	-4	-2.2	200	205	5	2.5
2019	Quarterback	188	191	3	1.6	215	222	7	3.2
2019	Running Back	178	180	2	1.1	207	218	11	5.2
2019	Linebackers	185	188	3	1.6	223	242	19	8.2
2019	Interior D-Line	189	190	1	0.5	282	310	28	9.5
2019	Defensive Ends	190	193	3	1.6	247	274	27	10.4

Amalgamating the data of both tables above, a few things become evident. The positions which were most compatible between leagues from a size perspective were: receivers, defensive backs, and offensive linemen; as their height and weight discrepancies between leagues were marginal at best. The largest discrepancies observed in either table were significant, and mainly associated to the weight of front seven defenders; defensive interior, edge defenders and linebackers. These positions in the NFL outweighed their CFL counterparts by an average of 33.5, 25, and 20 pounds respectively.

Based on size differences alone I would logically hypothesize that receivers, defensive backs, and offensive linemen could most easily transition between leagues. In contrast, linebackers and defensive linemen represented the most drastic size differences and as such would likely present the biggest challenge to transitioning between leagues based solely on height and weight metrics. It was interesting to note that exactly half of the 20 players profiled in this book are defensive backs and receivers. 3 are running backs, 3 are linebackers, 2 are quarterbacks, 2 are defensive ends and none were defensive interior players. This represents a composition similar to what we could have reasonably expected to see from the data above.

Another issue we run into when analyzing this data is understanding that from a size perspective, not all positions are actually equivalent. For example, while receiver, defensive back, and offensive lineman are close enough to be considered equivalent positions, we observe a very different story with some of the other positions on defence.

On average a CFL linebacker is too big, and likely not quick enough to be an NFL safety, but too small to be an NFL linebacker. A CFL defensive end is roughly equivalent in size to an NFL linebacker, but likely not quick enough to play linebacker in the NFL. A CFL interior defensive lineman is roughly equivalent in size to an NFL defensive end, but likely does not possess the required explosiveness to get to the quarterback off the edge. While there are in fact players in the CFL who are NFL interior defensive lineman size, we do not often see defensive tackles that size being very successful in the CFL.

Let's see if this theory applies to the best/most productive players in these three position groups as it pertains to real-world, on-field production.

Interior Defensive Linemen

According to PFF, the top 5 best interior defensive linemen entering the 2021 NFL season were:

1. Aaron Donald – 6'1", 285lbs
2. Chris Jones – 6'6", 310lbs
3. Cameron Heyward – 6'5", 295lbs
4. Grady Jarrett – 6'1", 305lbs
5. DeForest Buckner – 6'7", 295lbs

The average height and weight of the top 5 interior defensive linemen in the NFL was **6'4", 298lbs.**

In comparison, PSC's top 5 most productive interior defensive linemen in the CFL for the 2021 season were:

1. Shawn Oakman – 6'9", 287lbs
2. Mike Rose – 6'2", 270lbs
3. Tim Bonner – 6'5", 250lbs
4. Jake Ceresna – 6'5", 295lbs
5. Woody Baron – 6'1", 270lbs

The average height and weight of the top 5 most productive interior defensive linemen in the CFL was **6'4", 274lbs.** As is evident, there is a noticeable difference in interior defensive lineman bulk. In the above "top 5" comparison, the NFL defensive interior players are on average 24 pounds heavier than their CFL counterparts. This is less than the average difference for the entire league as shown in the tables above (33.5lbs), but is still a statistically significant difference.

Defensive Ends

According to PFF, the top 5 best defensive ends entering the 2021 NFL season were:

1. Khalil Mack – 6'3", 252lbs
2. TJ Watt – 6'4", 252lbs
3. Joey Bosa – 6'5", 280lbs
4. Myles Garrett – 6'4", 272lbs
5. Nick Bosa – 6'4", 266lbs

The average height and weight of the top 5 defensive ends in the NFL was **6'4", 264lbs.**

In comparison, PSC's top 5 most productive defensive ends in the CFL for the 2021 season were:

1. AC Leonard – 6'2", 250lbs
2. Jackson Jeffcoat – 6'3", 245lbs
3. Willie Jefferson – 6'7", 252lbs
4. Ja'Gared Davis – 6'1", 238lbs
5. Shawn Lemon – 6'1", 249lbs

The average height and weight of the top 5 most productive defensive ends in the CFL was **6'3", 247lbs.** The weight disparity between NFL and CFL defensive ends is an average of 17lbs in this comparison. This number is smaller than the average discrepancy we observed in the tables above (25lbs), however once again, still represents a significant difference on average.

Linebackers

Entering the 2021 NFL season, according to PFF, the top 5 NFL linebackers were:

1. Bobby Wagner – 6'0", 242lbs
2. Fred Warner – 6'3", 230lbs
3. Eric Kendricks – 6'0", 232lbs
4. Lavonte David – 6'1", 233lbs
5. Demario Davis – 6'4", 256lbs

The average height and weight of the top 5 linebackers in the NFL was **6'1", 239lbs.**

In comparison, PSC's top 5 most productive linebackers for the 2021 CFL season were:

1. Simoni Lawrence – 6'1", 231lbs
2. Bo Lokombo – 6'2", 225lbs
3. Dexter McCoil Sr – 6'2", 220lbs
4. Darnell Sankey – 6'1", 245lbs
5. Avery Williams – 5'10", 223lbs

The average height and weight of the top 5 most productive linebackers in the CFL was **6'1", 229lbs.**

The average weight disparity between NFL and CFL linebackers in this comparison is 10lbs. This number is also smaller than the average we observed in the tables above (20lbs). Although a 10lbs difference is not a large difference, it is still a clearly noticeable one.

We have just finished looking at two different comparisons, one which encompassed all players in each league per position, and the other which compared only the best/most productive players at their position. In both cases, we can in fact observe a noticeable difference in weight between players in the NFL and CFL. Former CFL defensive end Philip Hunt ended the 2010 season with 16 sacks for the Winnipeg Blue Bombers. The following season he signed in the NFL with the Philadelphia Eagles as an outside linebacker/defensive end. He had this to say when asked about putting on weight from a CFL playing weight of 245 lbs to an NFL weight of 257 lbs. *"Coming into the season, coming from the CFL where it's just a pass happy league, I was built more for just pass rushing on every down, but I realized here there's a lot more girth and a lot more size when it comes to offensive linemen, and the weight is needed."*[35]

Imagine the following: a player has played his entire life at a certain weight. All throughout college and during their time in the CFL they played at that same weight, eventually becoming elite at their position. Once they gain notoriety and eventually get themselves an NFL opportunity, they all of a sudden have to put on 10-20 pounds because the coaching staff there believes they will require the additional weight. At that point, the player is expected to continue to produce at that same high level, all while having to carry additional weight they never had to before. Former Toronto Argonaut cornerback and Philadelphia Eagle strong safety Byron Parker had this to say: *"The Eagles had me on a weight program and I bulked up to 227 pounds," Parker said. "It wasn't meant for my body. I'm now down to 210 pounds. I'm feeling good because I'm now lighter on my feet."*[36]

Sometimes players are able to gain weight and continue being as productive as they were previously, however most are just not able to adapt in the relatively short amount of time the adaptation is usually required. In a practical sense, think of it this way. How many push-ups can you regularly do? 30? 50? 10? Whatever the number is does not matter much. Now grab a weighted vest and try to do the very same number that just a moment ago was regularly within your reach. Despite the vest only adding 10-20 pounds, the difference is VERY noticeable.

Unfortunately, many players end up returning to the CFL after a brief stint in the NFL. For some, their inability to adapt to playing the same at a higher weight is what ultimately gets them cut. Expecting talented players to gain weight, simply to fit the mold has no doubt resulted in hundreds if not thousands of players being cut over the years. A situation that armchair quarterbacks immediately attribute to a "lack of talent", is in fact just a simple inability to adapt to being a player they were really never meant to be.

While doing research for this section, I came across a draft prospect page on NFL.com.[37] Based on his play in college, NFL draft analysts had assigned this player a grade of 5.90. For context, this grade meant that this NFL scout believed the player had the potential to be an "average backup or special-teamer". Under his player bio he is described as follows:

*"**Short**, **scrappy**, instinctive, highly productive defensive lineman who **does not look the part**, but inspires confidence he **can be an exception to the rule**. Is the type you root for and has the quickness, athleticism and motor to earn a spot as a **rotational three-technique** in a fast-flowing 4-3 scheme."*

Under the heading "Weaknesses" they had this to say:

*"**Marginal height** and frame is nearly maxed out. **Hands are more active than strong** -- could play with more pop and power. Overpowered in the run game and ground up by double teams. **Gets snared and controlled by bigger, longer blockers**. Not a two-gap player. **Has some tweener traits -- lacks ideal length** and bend to play outside."*

The scouting report above is obviously not a glowing review of this player. Despite this player being a "highly productive" player at the college level, he clearly did not fit the mold that was necessary for success. To this NFL talent evaluator this player was short, scrappy, did not look the part, had marginal height, did not have strong hands, and was a "tweener" who lacked "ideal length". Would it surprise you to learn that this player was Aaron Donald?

If we average the data from the tables and from the top 5 size comparisons, the prototypical defensive tackle in the NFL is 6'3", 305lbs. As you have seen above, Aaron Donald is 6'1", 285lbs. This means that according to traditional football philosophy on player sizes, he was 2 inches too short and 20lbs too light. Although today, after he proved himself to be a dominant player despite his "size shortcomings", it would be ridiculous to claim that Aaron Donald was not NFL starting material, however this is EXACTLY what some experts thought of him prior to the NFL combine believe it or not!

Aaron Donald has been the best defensive tackle pretty much since he entered the NFL, however even he was looked down on for not fitting the mold coming out of college. If it were not for a dominant performance after being **<u>INVITED</u>** to participate in the senior bowl, and another dominant performance after being **INVITED** to attend the NFL combine, it is highly possible that he could have been drafted much lower. A situation which could have prompted a very different career trajectory despite clearly being a productive player in college. Among defensive line players for the 2013 NCAA season Aaron Donald was the top rated defensive tackle in the nation, and 5th most productive defensive line player that year earning a PSC rating of 85.0. An interesting side note, who was the number 1 most productive defensive line player in the entire NCAA that season? Texas Longhorn defensive end, turned Winnipeg Blue Bomber: Jackson Jeffcoat who earned a PSC Rating of 91.5.

Although things have changed somewhat over the years, and will likely continue to change, fitting the mold will always be a factor that NFL talent evaluators find it hard to look beyond. Unfortunately, often times it takes more than talent and production to get an NFL opportunity...

It takes fitting the mold.

SECTION 9 – THE "TALENT GAP"

As with pretty much anything we can evaluate in life, I believe football talent exists on a normal distribution bell curve. Practically everything in life exists on a spectrum; with a small percentage at the very top, a small percentage at the very bottom, and the overwhelming majority somewhere in between the two extremes. As previously mentioned, with 44,649 amateur football players in the United States and Canada at any given time, if we were to apply a normal bell curve to the talent available in college football programs we would find a curve as depicted in the following graphic.

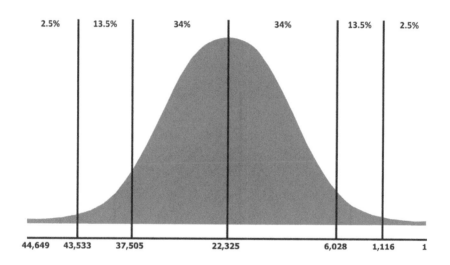

| 2.5% | 13.5% | 34% | 34% | 13.5% | 2.5% |

| 44,649 | 43,533 | 37,505 | 22,325 | 6,028 | 1,116 | 1 |

LESS TALENTED   50th PERCENTILE   MORE TALENTED

Assuming the talent spectrum in the college football system fell like a normal distribution bell curve, the graphic would indicate that the talent distribution can be broken down as follows:

Number of Players

ELITE – 1,116

ABOVE AVERAGE – 4,912

HIGH AVERAGE -16,297

LOW AVERAGE – 16,297

BELOW AVERAGE – 4,912

POOR – 1,116

To those that hate the CFL, the talent bell curve between the NFL (Red) and CFL (Yellow) would likely look something like the following graphic.

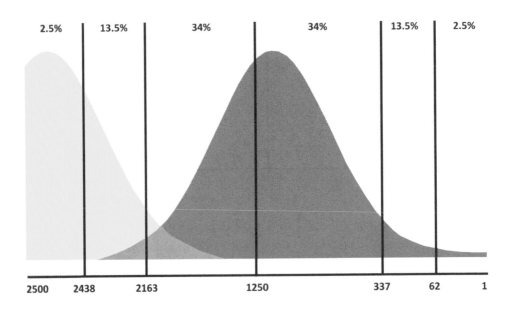

| 2.5% | 13.5% | 34% | 34% | 13.5% | 2.5% |

| 2500 | 2438 | 2163 | 1250 | 337 | 62 | 1 |

LESS TALENTED   50th PERCENTILE   MORE TALENTED

In this fictional scenario, there is very little overlap between both leagues. As we can see even the very best CFL players cannot even begin to compare to the 50th percentile of the NFL. The overwhelming majority of CFL players fall within the lowest 2.5% of all 2,500 professional football players, with basically only the best 15% even being able to hang around on the bottom of an NFL roster. The haters would absolutely agree that this graphic is an exact representation of reality. It is a fact that most CFL players return to the CFL after a brief stint in the NFL, as such being "unable to stick" on an NFL roster would be considered by many to be conclusive evidence of the CFL player's inferiority. As I detailed in section 7, the reasons for a player not making an NFL roster very often have little to do with their talent, therefore I do not believe the inability to stick is any true indication of a players level of talent and ability.

Thankfully, as we have already seen in the college football bell curve above, there are 6,028 players in the top 15 percent of the talent curve at any given moment. This means that there are more than enough players available to supply talent to 2-3 NFL sized leagues. This scenario assumes that not a single one of the remaining 84% could be trained and coached to become dependable starters or rotation players at the professional level, which is virtually a statistical impossibility given the sheer number of players left available outside the top 15%; which is an absurd 38,621 players!

Based on my extensive analysis, and statements made by numerous players and coaches over the years, I believe the actual talent curves between both the NFL (RED) and CFL (YELLOW) likely look something like the following graphic.

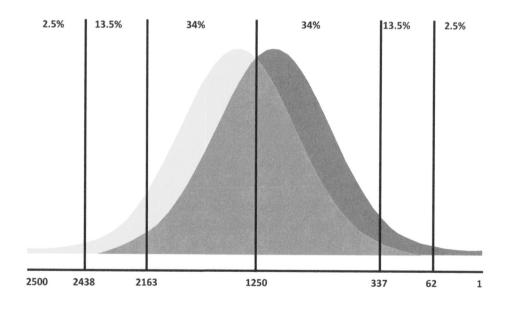

| 2.5% | 13.5% | 34% | 34% | 13.5% | 2.5% |

| 2500 | 2438 | 2163 | 1250 | 337 | 62 | 1 |

LESS TALENTED   50th PERCENTILE   MORE TALENTED

As we can see in the above example, the top 5-10% of NFL talent has no CFL equivalent. This would indicate that of the 1,696 active roster players in the NFL, the top 85-170 players simply have no CFL equals. These would be the players often labelled "physical freaks". These players are those that possess an extremely rare combination of speed, strength, size, explosiveness and football intelligence, which for want of a better term I will call the "football pentagon". While there are CFL players that are just as fast, just as strong, just as big, or just as intelligent, it can be a challenge to find similarly freakish athletes that possess all of the above plus that elite explosive power and speed north of the border. Most, if not all of these so-called freaks are drafted into the NFL because of that elite athleticism.

As with anything in life there are exceptions, and a bit later I will profile players that are examples of this, but I would hypothesize that the main difference between CFL players and their NFL counterparts is the relatively small number of NFL players that possess that rare combination previously described as the "football pentagon".

If we look closely at the graph above, note that as a whole, the bulk of players in the NFL are slightly over the 50th talent percentile, while the bulk of CFL players are slightly under the 50th percentile, however there is a significant amount of overlap between the two leagues as illustrated by the area shaded in ORANGE.

As an example, let's compare the combine/pro day numbers for one of the NFL's premier defensive tackles; Aaron Donald, with one of the CFL's premier defensive tackles; Almondo Sewell. Both players have enjoyed highly successful careers, and have produced at a high level consistently since entering their respective leagues.

Almondo Sewell	Aaron Donald
Height: 6'1"	Height: 6'1
Weight: 280lbs	Weight: 285lbs
40 time: 4.88	40 time: 4.62
10 yd: 1.62	10 yd: 1.63
20 yd: 2.83	20 yd: 2.69
20 yd shuttle: 4.68	20 yd shuttle: 4.39
3 cone: 7.50	3 cone: 7.11
Vert: 28.5"	Vert: 32"
Broad jump: 8'5"	Broad jump: 9'8"
Bench Press: 44	Bench Press: 35
PSC Rating: 95.3	**PSC Rating: 97.9**

Above we can see their metrics side by side. Aaron Donald's numbers are from the 2014 NFL Combine, and Almondo Sewell's are from his 2011 Pro Day. Both players are virtually the same size and weight, with Donald being only 5 pounds heavier. We begin to observe discrepancies in metrics that reflect the player's explosive athleticism. Despite being a very similar height and weight, Aaron Donald was 2 tenths of a second faster in the 40 yard dash. Donald's vertical jump of 32" was a full 3.5" higher than Sewell's 28.5". Donald's broad jump of 9'8" was a full 15 inches farther than Sewell's 8'5". The only metrics where Sewell gets the nod is 10 yard split time (by only a hundredth of a second), and bench press where he was able to put up a full 9 more reps of 225lbs. Speaking of the bench press, had he been invited to the NFL combine, Almondo Sewell's 44 bench press reps would have ranked him tied for sixth best ALL-TIME! As such, no one can deny Sewell's absolutely elite strength. I applied my PSC rating system to the 10 metrics referred to above and the results were impressive. Almondo Sewell was rated at 95.3, which compared very favourably to Aaron Donald's 97.9; The difference between them athletically coming out of college was quite small.

In summary, both Donald and Sewell have the size, strength, speed and football intelligence to be professional football players. The main difference between them is the explosiveness that Donald demonstrated to be superior to Sewell. Do not get me wrong, athleticism is an unquestionably important aspect of being a professional football player. While elite athleticism in and of itself does not necessarily guarantee a player success at the professional level, it will normally mean the difference between being provided an NFL opportunity or not. Do I believe Almondo Sewell could have played in the NFL? Without a doubt! His slower 40 time, despite still being quick for a man that size, his "unimpressive" explosion metrics, and his lack of prototypical size are most likely the reasons he was never afforded an opportunity in the NFL.

Some will be confronted with my previous statement, will look at the combine PSC Ratings and will still think 'Sewell would never be able to stick in the NFL'. To that I would say, think reasonably; is every defensive tackle in the NFL like Aaron Donald? If you answer honestly you'll come to the conclusion that Aaron Donald is an absolute beast who really does not have any equals in the NFL at his position; he has been in a league of his own. Although as we saw in the previous section, even Aaron Donald had "experts" who doubted his ability to make it in the NFL! Backup/special-teamer indeed.

Sewell might not have the "Aaron Donald factor", but in fairness, neither does anyone else in the NFL! At the end of the day, aside from the most elite players, one would be hard pressed to find major differences in the quality, talent, and level of play from the NFL to the CFL.

FIRST HAND TESTIMONIALS

There is no better testimony than first hand testimony. When someone has actually "been there and done that" they can talk about a matter with a certain authority that most others just do not have. As such, when attempting to evaluate the talent gap between the NFL and CFL, I believe the most important things we can consider are the opinions of people who have actually experienced the level of play in both leagues. The following are quotes from players and coaches who have been involved in and/or have played in both the NFL and CFL when they were asked to compare the talent or level of play of both leagues.

Hall of Fame GM/CFL head coach Wally Buono:

"No one appreciates the talent (in the CFL) until you get into it. The guy who comes from the NFL doesn't appreciate it until he plays against it. The guy from the major college doesn't appreciate how strong the players are. The guy from the CIS comes and has his eyes wide open. The players in the league are the ones who appreciate it most. Most of the guys come from the NFL and feel they should dominate right off the bat. They don't realize how tough (the CFL) really is."[38]

Linebacker Adam Bighill:

"I would say like in the NFL every team will have about three or four guys that I would call physical freaks. Guys that you would never see in the CFL. Guys that are in their own class of the NFL...every team has a few of those guys and those would be the main difference."[39]

Wide Receiver Duron Carter:

"I wouldn't say that there's a huge difference between the talent (of the NFL and CFL); maybe in the top players or top one player at a position."[40]

Offensive Lineman Brett Jones:

"The one thing about the CFL is it always seems to get a hard time — people don't always think it's as good a league as some believe," Jones said. "But there's a lot of great players that I think, given the right opportunity and the right circumstances, they can be players in the NFL and be stars."[41]

NFL Quarterback Coach/CFL Head Coach Scott Milanovich:

"Two-thirds or three-quarters of a CFL roster are guys that can play in the NFL, for whatever reason they didn't. It's hard for some guys, they think NFL their whole life and anything else isn't good enough," Milanovich said. "This is what I tell guys that come to the CFL all the time because I went through it as a player as well... they think that they are just going to come up and dominate and they do not realize how good the players are."[42]

Running Back James Wilder Jr:

"I was thinking, when I come here there wasn't going to be a lot of talent. From the NFL, it's a lot of guys here that played in the NFL...I thought the talent level was going to be dropped off more than what it is, and it's not that, I mean I was definitely wrong, it's a lot of talent here, and you know it's a lot of guys that's been from the league (NFL), it's a lot of great guys who haven't been to the league (NFL) that COULD be in the league easily. And I definitely found out the hard way. I thought it was going to be a big drop off, and it's not. It's not as much as people would think."[43]

Defensive End Victor Butler:

"I came up to the CFL with the misconception that these were second-tier players in a third-tier league. I was completely wrong about the PLAYERS! There are a number of guys that could not only start on an NFL team but play at a Pro Bowl level. The football in the CFL is top-notch, but the same cannot be said about the league or its organizations, particularly Toronto."[44]

Linebacker Donnie Baggs:

"It's real competition up here." Baggs said. "It's no joke. The athletes and the players out here are just as good as NFL athletes. That's the biggest thing I've taken away from it. Even though it's a smaller league and the players don't get paid as much, the athletes still play the same. It's really good competition and a lot of fun."[45]

Running Back Chris Jennings:

"There is a lot of talent here. It's just the same as the NFL...The only difference is three downs instead of four and the field is wider and longer."[46]

NFL Head Coach Mike McCoy:

"I'm a firm believer that that's a great league up there. Having played up there for the short amount of time I was up there, there's a lot of talented players..."[47]

Former NFL/CFL Defensive Back/TSN Analyst Davis Sanchez:

"A lot of the times, people don't realize that it's a huge jump (from college to the CFL), even when you're coming from a powerhouse."[48]

Defensive Tackle Drake Nevis:

"If you don't come ready to play, you will get exposed. A lot of people have been in the (NFL), so the talent is up there."[49]

Linebacker Derrick Moncrief:

"The CFL game is way faster. The biggest difference is some of the trenches as far as offensive line and defensive line...You can tell these are some of the best guys in the world at what they do (in the NFL)...but the CFL game is way faster. I'll tell anybody that."[50]

Wide Receiver Reggie Begelton:

"There are a lot of guys up there (that should be playing in the NFL)...I know for a fact there are a lot of ballers up there that can ball down here."[51]

Wide Receiver Chad Owens

"People who don't know, believe the CFL is not a legit league, a semi-pro league, not too much talent up there...When you finally get to play, and you get in the game, you see the speed of the game, you watch film you see the talent, you sit back and realize, damn, this is real, this is real football."[52]

Defensive Back Jonathan Dowling:

"I was telling T.J. Heath that I see no drop off from the NFL to the CFL. There are guys working hard every day and competing. I feel the DBs I've been working out with are just as talented as the DBs I worked with in the NFL, good hands, good feet."[53]

Linebacker Samuel Eguavoen:

"A lot of people may look down on the CFL, but it is still professional football. A bunch of other players out there just like me trying to make the next jump. They attack the game the same way I do. So being there three years I learned a lot, I matured a lot."[54]

Defensive Back Will Blackmon:

"I honestly came out there with no ego. I loved the CFL, it's incredible football, there's amazing players there."[55]

Defensive Tackle Rakim Cox:

"When you've been (in the NFL) and you've seen the attention you get in America and the cheques you get there, it's great, it's wonderful and you can't knock it. When you come here (CFL) and it's not like that, but on the field the play is just as intense, then you've got to respect it."[56]

Over the years, I have accumulated a great number of quotes from players, coaches, analysts and others who have ties to both leagues. The above quotes represent only a fraction of the total gathered. Yet as of the writing of this book, I have yet to find one single individual who has gone on record stating that the CFL is in fact bad football that represents a large gap in talent from the NFL. I have certainly never heard anyone who has real knowledge of both leagues refer to the CFL as a "bush league" as the CFL haters love to refer to it as. While I will concede that there are a great number of people who hold this opinion, **none** of them are players, coaches, or have in any way, shape or form experienced either league, besides watching on TV. Many of these naysayers would state that an NCAA team, or even more ridiculously a US high school team could beat a CFL team! Sometimes one just has to shake their head and wonder what planet we are living on where someone actually believes high school children could beat a team of grown men, the vast majority of whom were stars at the college level.

In the quotes mentioned above, we have Drake Nevis who was first team All-SEC, and a BCS National Champion with LSU stating that players who do not come prepared *"will get exposed"* because *"the talent is up there"* in the CFL.

Donnie Baggs who played collegiately in the SEC with Texas A&M said *"The athletes and the players out here are just as good as NFL athletes."*

Coach Milanovich who spent significant time coaching in both leagues stated that approximately 66% to 75% of CFL players would be able to play in the NFL, inferring that the bottom 25-33% of the CFL would not.

Brett Jones advised that he believed there were *"a lot of great players"* in the CFL that could play and be stars in the NFL.

Duron Carter stated that although there might be a difference between the top players at each position, there isn't a huge difference in the talent of the majority.

Adam Bighill advised each team has 3-4 players dubbed the *"physical freaks"* that are the main difference. In other words, the absolute top 96 to 132 players in the NFL are the main difference between both leagues, approximately 2 teams worth of players.

Victor Butler, an NFL veteran with 91 tackles and 11 sacks to his name stated *"There are a number of guys (in the CFL) that...play at a Pro Bowl level. The football in the CFL is top-notch, but the same cannot be said about the league or its organizations"*. This quote is of particular note because he did not hold back the negative statement regarding the league as an organization, or the team he played for in the Toronto Argonauts.

Will Blackmon; a Superbowl Champion and a veteran of 10 NFL seasons stated the CFL was *"incredible football"* with *"amazing players"*.

I could go on, and on. The more we look into the opinions and perceptions of people with first hand experience in both leagues, the more we come to the conclusion that while there is a distinct and enormous difference in the finances of both leagues, the level of play is actually much closer than that financial disparity would imply.

Some players even go so far as to say there is no difference at all in the talent of CFL players compared to their NFL counterparts; Chris Jennings and

Jonathan Dowling above, and as you will see a bit later, Delvin Breaux as well. Most others acknowledge there is some discrepancy between the absolute most elite players in the NFL and basically everyone else in football, CFL or NFL for that matter.

I am reminded of a comical exchange I observed on Twitter some time ago. The exchange was in relation to a Tweet TSN Analyst Jason Gregor (@JasonGregor) had made regarding Coach Scott Milanovich's statement referenced above where he indicates that the majority of the CFL (67-75%) could play in the NFL. Immediately people on both sides of the argument jumped on and gave their viewpoints. One individual had taken a particularly hard stance against the CFL and posted *"The only thing is that 100% of an #NFL roster can play in the NFL"*. Thanks Captain Obvious...OK. What else? He then went on to a back and forth with numerous others until he dropped these beauties: *"CFL can't even compete with the SEC"* and *"#CrimsonTide or #LSU will stomp a mudhole in the Toronto astronauts maybe even a TX HS team or 2 as well."* Now then. If you thought he was a savvy football mind before, you must be even more impressed with his logic now. My sarcasm notwithstanding, that was the comical part of the exchange. It got to the point where the original poster, Mr. Gregor, intervened and wrote back: *"you are mistaken. Please fine [SIC] me one SEC player who played in CFL who agrees with you. Find them and let me know. Because every former NCAA player in the CFL who I spoke with says CFL would school any NCAA team for fun."*

But therein lies the problem with the CFL hate. Oftentimes more credibility is given to the statements and opinions of "armchair quarterbacks", than is given to people that have **LITERALLY** been involved in both leagues and can actually speak from first hand knowledge and experience. It would be akin to getting parenting advice from a 12 year old who does not have any children but has watched half an episode of Dr. Phil, and an episode of Modern Family; it just would not make sense.

I believe the testimony of hundreds over the years confirms that while there is in fact a relatively small gap in the overall level of play in favour of the NFL, the talent level between both leagues is far closer than casual observers would want to believe. Just as I detailed in section 5 of this book, with the amount of available talent there is still enough surplus talent to create another handful of high quality leagues. While the lesser leagues may be a notch or two below the juggernaut, they would still have a very high level of play, and be filled with hundreds of world-class players, which in any event would be leagues well worth watching.

I believe that one of the biggest reasons CFL players return to the CFL after a brief stint in the NFL is simply the fact that they are not given an opportunity to play! Sounds simple, but it is true! It is a major difference I noticed when studying the dynamic between CFL/NFL and Premier League/other Euro leagues in soccer. When a Premier League team purchases a player from a lower league, they often get significant opportunities to play and as a result, they "prove themselves worthy" of being considered a big league player.

Take the example of Bruno Fernandes of Manchester United. He was an excellent player in the 6th ranked Portuguese Primeira Liga. While playing for Sporting CP in Portugal, he was Europe's top scoring midfielder. During his final two seasons in Portugal, over the course of 50 league games he scored an average of **0.56 goals per game**, and made **0.40 assists per game**.

Upon signing in Manchester, numerous experts advised caution with Fernandes, stating that in the Premier League he would just not be able to do some of the amazing things he did in the Portuguese League as the difference in quality between the leagues is just too great. *"He will first have to adjust to a significant jump in quality. While there is plenty of conjecture over the standard of this year's Premier League, it is evidently a more physical, quicker and technically demanding competition than the Primeira Liga."*[57]

When he made the jump to the Premier League he was immediately thrust into a starting role, and lo and behold, continued playing soccer at a high level, actually playing just as he had in the "lowly" Portuguese league. He was immediately considered one of the best players in England, and AGAIN proved himself to be one of the most productive offensive midfielders in all of Europe.

During his first two seasons in the Premier League, over the course of 51 league games he scored an average of **0.51 goals per game**, and made **0.37 assists per game**. As is evident from these numbers, his decline in production was negligible. Do I believe this means the Portuguese league is equal to the Premier League? No. However, are there many Premier League quality players playing in the Portuguese league? Without a doubt! This is the point I am trying to make with this comparison.

What do you think would have happened however, if he was purchased and trained with the team but was relegated to riding the bench in a manner similar to how many CFL players are only afforded opportunities on an NFL practice squad? He would have lost his form, probably lost his confidence, and if/when he was actually given a starting opportunity would just not have made an impact. A situation that would then "confirm" the players in the Portuguese league are just not Premier League material. In the same way, to many fans when a CFL player only makes an NFL practice squad, that is a situation that "confirms" that those players are just not up to the task of being regular contributors. They are just not "talented enough" to play in the big league.

Unfortunately, overly simplistic conclusions are often drawn from situations like these, and that is exactly the type of thinking I wanted to dispel with this project. Remember the expression I used in the very beginning of this book? "Success occurs when **OPPORTUNITY** meets preparation." A player might be highly talented, and very well prepared. But if that opportunity never materializes, then they never get to show the world how good they really are, and are labelled as "rejects", "not good enough" and a million other terms that in reality are completely unfair and not at all justified.

Think about the example of Tom Brady. I do not think there are many people out there who would disagree that he was the best quarterback of all time, but let's go back about 20 years. He was drafted in the 6th round of the NFL draft; 199th overall. This was almost a miracle in and of itself as it is widely known that he was not the most athletic quarterback coming out of college. I am sure we have all seen the image of a very unimpressive looking young Tom Brady in his boxers at the combine. His 5.28 second 40 yard dash was a number that would be slow even for an offensive lineman who weighed 300+ pounds. While everyone is quick to jump on the bandwagon today and agree that Tom Brady is the greatest of all time, the reality is that if Coach Belichick had not made the bold decision to keep Brady as the starter over New England's then franchise quarterback Drew Bledsoe, Brady would have remained a backup. Imagine Bledsoe ends up leading the Patriots to a Superbowl victory, where would Brady have gone then?

An unathletic, 6th round backup quarterback? I cannot imagine that would have sounded very appealing to any NFL GM's at the time. After all, they had all passed on drafting him numerous times before New England finally picked him up. I highly doubt there would have been much interest in any team bringing in Brady as a backup, let alone starter. But just stop and think for a moment, if it were not for that <u>ONE SINGLE DECISION</u> made by his head coach. One single decision that was completely out of Brady's control could have led us to have never heard of Tom Brady at all. He could have very easily faded away into oblivion, maybe even coming north of the border to continue his football career if Coach Bill Belichick had not made a highly controversial decision; one that many experts believed was the wrong decision at the time. Whether it was foresight or just plain good luck, even a player who ended up being as monumental as Tom Brady needed someone in his corner who believed in him enough to take a chance. Many highly talented players never encounter that coach or GM that is willing to take such a risk on them.

There is also another factor which I believe also contributes to the perceived talent gap that exists between the CFL and NFL, and it is one that is not often talked about; practice time! Let's consider for a second how a typical NFL season develops. The Superbowl ends in February and players have a couple of months of legitimate time off. However, as early as April voluntary workouts are already being started. Rookie mini camps are followed by OTA's in May, and by June mandatory mini camp is in full swing. There are a few weeks off in between, but training camp begins in earnest toward the end of July, followed by four weeks of preseason games in August.

Contrast this with how the CFL season develops. The Grey Cup is typically concluded in November, and players then have 5 long months completely off before short mini camps begin at the end of April. CFL mini camps are normally less than a week long, and they are followed by another 3 weeks of inactivity before training camp begins in mid to late May. There is then a two week preseason in early to mid June, and the season officially begins mid to late June. If we look at the schedule for the two leagues side by side, we can see a clear difference in the amount of time players are allowed to dedicate to working and training as a team.

In simple terms, CFL players have roughly 5 weeks of preparation before the season begins, where NFL players have roughly 15 weeks of preparation before their season begins.

CFL	**NFL**
Season concludes end of November	Season concludes mid February
5 months off	2 months off
1 week mini camp	2 weeks of strength and
3 weeks off	conditioning/physical rehabilitation
10-15 day training camp	3 weeks of on-field workouts; player
2 week pre-season	instruction and drills
Regular season begins	4 weeks of OTA's (10 drill practice days
	allowed total)
	2 weeks of training camp
	4 weeks of pre-season
	Regular season begins

88

It does not take a rocket scientist to see there is a staggering difference between the amount of practice players in the NFL get vs their CFL counterparts. Player A and player B might be equally strong, fast, talented and intelligent, however if player A practices triple the amount of time that player B practices, who do you think will likely make less mistakes? Who do you think will know their playbook better? Who do you think watched more film? We have all heard the expression that "practice makes perfect". It should therefore not be surprising that at times early season CFL games seem a bit more sloppy than early season NFL games. That difference most likely has much more to do with the longer off-season and less practice time in the CFL than it does with NFL players being more talented. Unfortunately these are factors that the average Joe does not understand, but which lead to the perception that CFL players are vastly inferior to their NFL counterparts.

Ricky Williams was quoted as saying "consistency" was one of the main differences between the NFL and CFL. Consistency can be defined as "unchanging in nature, standard, or effect over time". The fact that Ricky Williams observed more inconsistency in the CFL than in the NFL could possibly be attributed, at least in part, to the dramatic differences in the amount of time each league's players dedicate to improving their craft.

Further evidence of this point comes from former Saskatchewan Roughrider and current Miami Dolphin linebacker Samuel Eguavoen. He echoed those same sentiments when he stated the following: *'Besides the rules, Eguavoen has found another major difference (between the CFL and NFL). "I'd say film," he said. "There's so much film study out here...I'd say the CFL is more, I don't want to use the term laid-back, but it just wasn't as redundant as the NFL, as severe as the NFL."*[58]

Contrary to the opinions of uninformed football fans, the talent gap between the CFL and NFL is much much smaller than they could ever imagine. Throughout the preceding sections we have explored numerous concepts and situations which helped us to gain a broader understanding of just how many factors impact professional football in North America.

The differences in practice time, available supply of players, and required body types for each league, are only a few of the many different factors that affect how players are perceived and whether or not a player makes a professional roster. Armed with this knowledge as our base, we will now get into studying the playing lives of our featured players, and gain an even more detailed understanding of the differences between reality and perception when it comes to talent or lack thereof.

SECTION 10 – PLAYER PROFILES

Now that I have laid the ground work of explaining the previous 9 sections of this book, keeping the principles we learned in mind I can begin the work of actually profiling and comparing the performances of the 20 players I selected for this exercise. As previously mentioned, some of these players will be obvious and easily remembered, others not so much. The ultimate goal of this entire book was to answer a simple question:

How does the level of competition in the CFL compare to the NFL?

The truth is, there is no single factor that can give us a truly objective and conclusive answer to the question, as such this book takes a multifaceted approach. Evaluating each player's performance in either league, comparing that performance to other players playing the same position, during the same season, comparing a player's performance in one league relative to his performance in the other, and probably most important of all, understanding the opinion of the player that has actually experienced the play in both leagues. Let's not forget that there is nothing quite as weighty as first hand testimony.

With regards to player quotes, I have been compiling quotes from numerous sources such as web articles, podcasts, and interviews over the past decade plus. While I reference each and every quote with the source I obtained it from, some of the web links are unfortunately no longer active as the content has either been moved, or has been deleted altogether. Nevertheless, the links are all listed in the end notes starting on page 290. Wherever possible I attempted to provide direct quotes from the players I profiled to understand their personal perspective on the matter.

The most important conclusion I arrived at after exhaustively comparing the production of these 20 exceptional players was "**A player is who he is**". This statement needed to be highlighted, in bold, and underlined. After all the analysis, comparison, and evaluation, this statement became the bedrock of the hypothesis of this book, and time and again proved itself to be true with few exceptions.

We will be examining the following CFL to NFL player transitions, all of whom were overlooked and undrafted by the NFL:

Diontae Spencer – NCAA division I FCS – McNeese State

Brandon Browner – NCAA division I FBS - Oregon State
Andrew Hawkins – NCAA division I FBS – Toledo
Jerrell Freeman – NCAA division III – Mary Hardin Baylor
Dontrelle Inman – NCAA division I FBS – Virginia
Delvin Breaux – NCAA division I FBS – LSU[59]
Marcus Thigpen – NCAA division I - Indiana
Alex Singleton – NCAA division I FCS – Montana State
Erik Harris – NCAA division II – California University of Pennsylvania
Cameron Wake – NCAA division I FBS - Penn State

These players will be followed up by the following NFL to CFL player transitions:

Cassius Vaughn – Undrafted – NCAA division I FBS – Ole Miss
Jumal Rolle – Undrafted – NCAA division II - Catawba College
Jonathan Newsome - 5th round – NCAA division I FBS – Ball State
Troy Smith - 5th round – NCAA division I FBS – Ohio State
Tre Mason - 3rd round – NCAA division I FBS – Auburn
Jalen Collins - 2nd round – NCAA division I FBS – LSU
Trent Richardson - 1st round – NCAA division I FBS – Alabama
Johnny Manziel - 1st round – NCAA division I FBS – Texas A&M
Shane Ray - 1st round – NCAA division I FBS – Missouri

These 19 players will be followed by a special section titled "Big-time players make big-time plays in big-time games" which will feature CFL to NFL wide receiver:

Chris Matthews – NCAA division I FBS – Kentucky.

In addition to comparing each player's most productive season in either league, some players will get an additional level of profiling as I will be comparing their college career and combine or pro day numbers to other very well known NFL players from the same draft year. The reasoning behind this is simple: People tend to think and act like NFL 1st round picks are leaps and bounds above those lower round players, and entire galaxies apart from players who go undrafted. However, when we actually analyze their college production and combine or pro day performances, we can start to see that the gap is definitely not as large as all that, and in many cases is in fact razor thin.

Please keep in mind that nothing we will be discussing is intended to be viewed or interpreted as an absolute rule! The only thing I know for sure is that life is a wide spectrum with a multitude of variables at play at any given moment. As such, we should not draw overly simplistic conclusions from a single factor when there are in fact so many variables which impact performance, especially in a team sport like football.

For example, taking a player like Cassius Vaughn whose most productive NFL season at 24 years of age saw him produce at a high average level, and comparing that to a 29 year old Cassius Vaughn who performed at an above average level in the CFL as one of the most productive defensive backs in the league. This situation can not be interpreted as conclusive evidence that the NFL is a higher level of play than the CFL in isolation. It would not be reasonable to infer that an average NFL player would instantly be one of the best CFL players simply from that information alone. There are always other factors involved. One of which could be as former NFL/CFL cornerback Anthony Orange stated when he said *"I love the game of football but up here (CFL) it's more tailored to a defensive back. It's like, a passing league. Big field and long throws, so there's more opportunities to get interceptions."*[60] In Vaughn's case, perhaps the bigger field provided more opportunities and space to get those interceptions, but even this idea is still subject to defensive schemes among a myriad of other factors! Keep an open mind and try to focus on the big picture instead of one or two factors only.

There was an interesting principle I came across as I studied the playing lives of my chosen profiled players. The vast majority of them had multiple points in their careers that could be considered cross roads; one wrong move and they would have found themselves unemployed, literally. Despite being highly talented, they could all have found themselves on the outside looking in had they not made the conscious choice to continue pressing toward their ultimate goal, and had the good fortune of running into some coaching staffs along the way that believed in them, plus just a hint of luck.

At the end of the day, the whole point of this book was to try to get people to think beyond the basic train of thought that is normally associated with a CFL/NFL comparison. There is a large number of ignorant football fans who believe *"NFL players are all elite talents, and CFL players couldn't beat high school kids."* This project aims to combat such garbage opinions by providing knowledge! I encourage all of you to consider all the information in its totality, and think for yourselves to come to your own conclusions!

Without further ado, let's get into the actual numerical analysis and see what I believe the data demonstrates.

DIONTAE
SPENCER

UNDRAFTED FREE AGENT

DENVER BRONCOS

"The level of play in the CFL is VERY CLOSE TO THE NFL"

DIONTAE SPENCER[61]

Diontae Spencer played his collegiate football at McNeese State, a program that competes in the NCAA FCS's Southland Conference. He was a highly productive player at that level setting a program record with 365 all purpose yards in a single game against Stephen F. Austin. In that game he returned two kick offs and a punt return for touchdowns, and added seven receptions for 152 yards at an average of 21.7 yards per reception with two receiving touchdowns! Despite showing an elite ability to play on multiple phases of the game, he was not invited to the 2014 NFL combine.

I will be comparing his production during his final college season as well as his pro day/combine metrics with another well known wide receiver from the same draft year; Odell Beckham Jr.

SENIOR COLLEGE SEASON

Diontae Spencer	Odell Beckham Jr.
Receptions: 50	Receptions: 59
Yards: 835	Yards: 1,152
Average: 16.7	Average: 19.5
Touchdowns: 9	Touchdowns: 8
Kick Returns: 29	Kick Returns: 32
KR Yards: 853	KR Yards: 845
Average: 29.4	Average: 26.4
TD: 2	TD: 0
Punt Returns: 20	Punt Returns: 19
PR Yards: 152	PR Yards: 160
Average: 7.6	Average: 8.4
TD: 1	TD: 0
PSC Rating: 93.2	PSC Rating: 81.1
PSC Rating Omitting Return TDs: 91.9	PSC Rating Omitting Return TDs: 97.3

When looking at their production side by side, it is clear that Odell Beckham Jr. had a more productive season on offence, making more receptions and gaining more yards with a higher average per reception. Their return stats are remarkably comparable however, with the main difference between them being the 3 return touchdowns Spencer scored compared to Beckham Jr.'s 0. Spencer's higher PSC rating reflects the difference in return touchdowns scored. Some might see it as a fluke that Spencer managed to score all 3 return touchdowns in the same game, so for argument's sake I will be nullifying the return touchdowns scored, but keep all the other metrics in play.

As such, the modified college production ratings would be 97.3 for OBJ, and 91.9 for Diontae Spencer. I will use the modified numbers going forward for further calculation.

PRO DAY/COMBINE

Diontae Spencer	Odell Beckham Jr.
Height: 5'8"	Height: 5'11-1/4"
Weight: 173lbs	Weight: 198lbs
40 yard dash: 4.34	40 yard dash: 4.43
10 yard split: 1.53	10 yard split: 1.57
20 yard split: 2.59	20 yard split: 2.58
20 yard shuttle: 4.30	20 yard shuttle: 3.94
3 cone drill: 7.22	3 cone drill: 6.69
Vertical jump: 40.0"	Vertical jump: 38.5"
Broad jump:10'3"	Broad jump:10'2"
Bench press: 13 reps	Bench press: 7 reps
PSC Rating: 98.0	**PSC Rating: 93.1**

When comparing their pro day/combine metrics, we observe that they are fairly comparable overall. Beckham Jr. was taller and heavier, slightly slower in the 40 yard dash, and faster in the agility drills. The main difference was Spencer's 13 reps of 225lbs on the bench press, compared to only 7 for Beckham Jr. This all adds up to a PSC Rating of 98.0 for Diontae Spencer and 93.1 for Odell Beckham Jr.

All things considered, Spencer's performance objectively proved he was not an inferior athlete to Odell Beckham Jr. Even omitting the effect on the PSC Ratings of the return touchdowns that Spencer scored, and using the modified PSC ratings we discussed above, we still arrive at the following final PSC Ratings:

Odell Beckham Jr: 95.2
Diontae Spencer: 95.0

In this scenario, the statistically insignificant difference of 0.2 rating points proves Diontae Spencer was an elite athlete. Yet, in the infinite wisdom of every NFL scout Spencer was still 3" too short, 25 pounds too light, and played against *vastly inferior* competition in the FCS. Compared to Odell Beckham Jr. who had played for LSU in the SEC, Spencer was obviously *just not big enough, or talented enough to play in the NFL*.

Although their college production and combine metrics were fairly comparable, Odell Beckham Jr. went on to be drafted in the 1st round of the 2014 NFL draft (12th overall), and Diontae Spencer went undrafted. Spencer was invited to the Chicago Bears' mini camp but was released. He subsequently signed with the St. Louis Rams, but was again cut before the beginning of training camp.

It was at that point with no further opportunities in the NFL available to him that Spencer turned his focus north and signed with the Toronto Argonauts. Spencer spent the next 4 seasons in the CFL, playing two seasons in Toronto and another two in Ottawa maturing into a true professional.

He saw action both on offence as well as special teams and displayed his skills in both phases of the game. Interestingly, just as he had in college he famously also set a single game all-purpose yards record when he recorded 496 all purpose yards against the Hamilton Tiger-Cats; 133 yards receiving, 165 kick return yards, and 169 punt return yards.

While conducting research for this book I had the privilege of briefly chatting with Diontae over Twitter. During that conversation he provided me a personal quote he had created:

"In order to be 'him',
you must do something 'him' has never done before."

I will admit it took me a moment to fully understand it, but the quote became more and more clear when I considered everything he had been able to accomplish in his career, both in college as well as the CFL. In his case, setting the single game all-purpose record both in college as well as the CFL was in fact doing something that no one had ever done before. It seemed "HE" had arrived.

When I asked him about comparing the level of talent between the CFL and NFL, he advised me the following: *"Same game, just faster besides the rules. But in the CFL you can get away with not being 100 percent every rep. In the NFL there is no room for error. Players are faster and smarter. Everyday is a job interview."* He then proceeded to tell me that all things considered, the level of play in the CFL is *"very close"* to the NFL.[62] If he had to put a number to it, he would estimate the CFL is approximately "75 percent" of what the NFL is; a factor that I found very interesting as it roughly went in line with other factors we have already examined in previous sections.

Diontae's play in the CFL was good enough to earn him a league All-Star selection in 2018, when he recorded his most productive season for kick returns as well as receiving. His most productive season for punt returns in the CFL was 2017. All his production in the CFL was enough to land him an opportunity with the Pittsburgh Steelers for the 2019 season, however he was waived at the end of training camp. He was subsequently claimed off waivers by the Denver Broncos where he was finally provided a legitimate opportunity as a return specialist. His most productive seasons in the NFL were the 2019 season for kick returns, and the 2020 season for punt returns. The graphics on the following pages depict his statistical performance for those seasons.

MOST PRODUCTIVE SEASON
DIONTAE SPENCER

★★★★★★★☆☆☆

YEAR	2018
GP	17
KR	38
KR YDS	815
AVG	21.4
RET TD	0
LONG	47
RANK	5TH

55.9
PRODUCTION RATING

HIGH AVERAGE

MOST PRODUCTIVE SEASON

DIONTAE SPENCER

YEAR	2019
GP	16
KR	15
KR YDS	436
AVG	29.1
RET TD	0
LONG	60
RANK	17TH

SPENCER

11

56.6
PRODUCTION RATING

HIGH AVERAGE

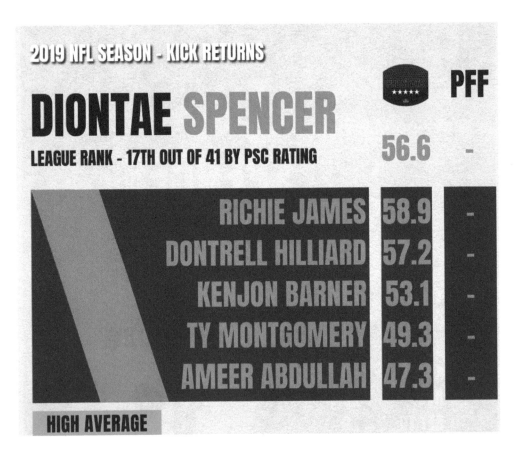

DIONTAE SPENCER

LEAGUE RANK - 17TH OUT OF 41 BY PSC RATING

PFF

56.6 -

RICHIE JAMES	58.9	-
DONTRELL HILLIARD	57.2	-
KENJON BARNER	53.1	-
TY MONTGOMERY	49.3	-
AMEER ABDULLAH	47.3	-

HIGH AVERAGE

Diontae Spencer's performance in kick returns during the 2019 season was comparable to the above mentioned players. His 436 kick return yards were 13th highest, while his 29.1 average yards per return was 4th best in the NFL. As a result of this production, he landed in the high average rating category as the 17th most productive kick returner in the NFL.

In the CFL, during his most productive season for kick returns he ranked 5th on the list of most productive kick returners earning a high average rating. He was comparable to Christion Jones (6th, PSC Rating 53.3), Stefan Logan (7th, PSC Rating 52.8), and Loucheiz Purifoy (8th, PSC Rating 51.8). His 815 kick return yards were 3rd best in the league, but his 21.4 average yards per return were only good for 14th highest in the CFL, rated low average. His CFL PSC Rating for kick returns of 55.9 was actually slightly lower than his best PSC Rating in the NFL of 56.6, although as evidenced, his performance in either league was very comparable.

MOST PRODUCTIVE SEASON
DIONTAE SPENCER

★★★★★★ ★★★★

YEAR	2017
GP	18
PR	70
PR YDS	929
AVG	13.3
RET TD	1
LONG	96
RANK	3RD

SPENCER
85

73.5
PRODUCTION RATING

ABOVE AVERAGE

MOST PRODUCTIVE SEASON

DIONTAE SPENCER

YEAR	2020
GP	11
PR	16
PR YDS	253
AVG	15.8
RET TD	1
LONG	83
RANK	3RD

SPENCER

11

79.6
PRODUCTION RATING

ABOVE AVERAGE

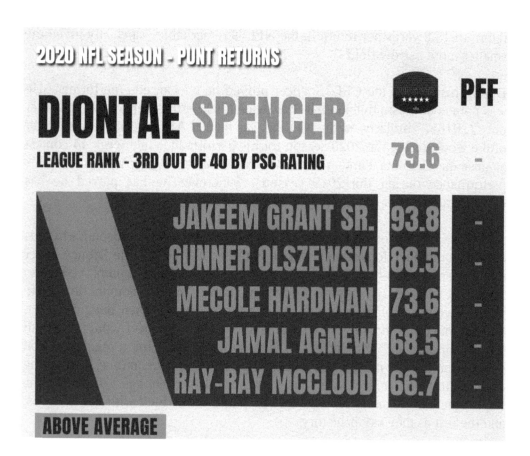

DIONTAE SPENCER

PFF

LEAGUE RANK - 3RD OUT OF 40 BY PSC RATING

79.6 -

JAKEEM GRANT SR.	93.8	-
GUNNER OLSZEWSKI	88.5	-
MECOLE HARDMAN	73.6	-
JAMAL AGNEW	68.5	-
RAY-RAY MCCLOUD	66.7	-

ABOVE AVERAGE

Spencer's most productive season on punt returns saw him put up comparable production to the above listed players. His performance was good enough for 3rd most productive punt returner in the entire NFL, rating him above average. His 253 punt return yards were 7th highest in the league, while his 15.8 average yards per punt return was second best in the NFL[63].

During his most productive season in the CFL for punt returns he was the 3rd most productive punt returner in the league. He put up comparable production to Martese Jackson (2nd, PSC Rating 74.5), Christion Jones (4th, PSC Rating 69.1) and Kevin Fogg (5th, PSC Rating 68.2). His 929 punt return yards were 2nd best in the CFL, and his 13.3 average yards per punt return was good for 4th highest in the league.

It is interesting to note some characteristics of Spencer's game that were similar in either league. He was a more prolific punt returner than kick returner in either league, and in his best seasons ended up as the 3rd most productive punt returner in either league. The fact that he was able to improve his already impressive CFL punt return average of 13.3 yards per return to 15.8 yards per return in the NFL is remarkable, especially given the smaller more narrow field.

During his time in the CFL, Spencer proved he was an elite performer. He was named an East Division All-Star twice (2017, 2018), and a CFL All-Star once (2018). Similarly, in the NFL he was named AFC special teams player of the week during the 2020 season for his performance in a week 14 contest against the Carolina Panthers, and was voted a Pro Bowl Alternate for his performance during the 2019 season. Wherever he has played he has demonstrated the same elite play making ability.

Just like so many other players before him, imagine for a second what his career would have looked like had he not been claimed by the Broncos after the Steelers waived him at the end of training camp? At that point, he had no NFL film to speak of, only his CFL film against "inferior competition". He might have been able to continue on with the Steelers on their practice roster, but at some point most likely would have been cut. Spencer would have run out of options, and without ever seeing an NFL field for a regular season game, would have most likely returned to the CFL to continue his playing career. An *"NFL reject"* who was *"just not talented enough"* to play in the big league. Fortunately for him, he ran into a bit of luck with the Broncos, and the rest as they say is history.

An All-Star calibre returner in the CFL proved himself to be a Pro Bowl calibre returner in the NFL. He was an above average punt returner in either league, and a high average kick returner in either league. 3rd best in the CFL became 3rd best in the NFL? Could it be that...

"A player is who he is"

BRANDON BROWNER

UNDRAFTED FREE AGENT

SEATTLE SEAHAWKS

"Guys that played with us...feel they can be here...and I personally feel there's a lot of guys up there that CAN PLAY HERE"

BRANDON BROWNER[64]

Brandon Browner played collegiate football at Oregon State University and was named Freshman All-American and second team All PAC-10 conference. He ended his two year college career with 87 tackles (74 solo), 1 sack, 5 tackles for a loss, two forced fumbles, 15 pass deflections, 6 interceptions and an interception return touchdown. I will be comparing his college pro day/combine metrics to another well known defensive back from the same draft year: Antrel Rolle.

Brandon Browner	Antrel Rolle
Height: 6'4"	Height: 6'1"
Weight: 221lbs	Weight: 201lbs
40 yard dash: 4.68	40 yard dash: 4.48
20 yard shuttle: 4.24	20 yard shuttle: 3.94
3 cone drill: 7.20	3 cone drill: 6.68
Vertical jump: 36.5"	Vertical jump: 37.0"
Broad jump:10'3"	Broad jump:10'3"
Bench press: 13 reps	Bench press: 15 reps
PSC Rating: 94.5	**PSC Rating: 100.0**

While the PSC rating makes it clear that Rolle was the more athletic of the two players, earning himself a perfect rating of 100.0, Browner's production rating of 94.5 is still quite close. In fact, seeing that Browner is three inches taller and 20 pounds heavier makes Browner's pro day performance that much more impressive. Below I compare their production during their final college season.

Brandon Browner	Antrel Rolle
Total Tackles: 44	Total Tackles: 58
Solo Tackles: 37	Solo Tackles: 37
Assisted Tackles: 7	Assisted Tackles: 21
Passes Defended: 9	Passes Defended: 6
Sacks: 1	Sacks: 1
Forced Fumbles: 0	Forced Fumbles: 0
Interceptions: 0	Interceptions: 1
Interception return yards: 0	Interception return yards: 6
PSC Rating: 51.1	**PSC Rating: 83.3**

Despite there being a large disparity in their ratings, if we look closely we can see that the difference between them is essentially the 1 interception for 6 yards that Rolle managed.

For example, if we were to nullify the interception and return yards, Rolle's final college season would have earned him a production rating of 58.3, which is fairly close to Browner's 51.1. As it stands however, Rolle's final college season production rating of 83.3 was significantly better than Browner's 51.1.

Combining their ratings for college and athleticism, their final PSC ratings are:

Brandon Browner – 72.8
Antrel Rolle – 91.7

The 18.9 point gap in favour of Rolle from an athletic and college production standpoint saw Antrel go on to be drafted in the 1st round of the 2005 NFL draft (8th overall), while Browner did not get drafted at all. Despite this, Browner was signed as an undrafted free agent by the Denver Broncos, however after a preseason injury he was placed on injured reserve and eventually released.

It was at that point that Browner came north to play in the CFL. His CFL career spanned 4 seasons with Calgary from 2007 to 2010. He was able to translate his CFL success into another opportunity in the NFL where he then played from 2011 to 2015. During those seasons, he posted the following career statistics:

	CFL		**NFL**
Games Played	68		61
Solo Tackles	196		187
Tackles/Game	2.87		3.87
Interceptions	12		12
Interceptions/Game	0.18		0.20
Interception Return Yards	78		340
Interception TD	1		2
Forced Fumbles	8		3

After signing with the Calgary Stampeders in the CFL, Browner became known as a highly physical player who possessed dominant size and speed. At 6'4" 221lbs he was an imposing figure who's physicality often ended up in him being one of the most penalized players in the league. Nevertheless, he was voted a CFL All-Star in 3 of the 4 seasons he played in the CFL.

Some of the highlights of Browner's most productive CFL season (2010) were 48 solo tackles at a rate of 2.67 per game, 5 interceptions at a rate of 0.28 per game, with no touchdowns. Browner's CFL production was rated high average. His production rating of 53.7 ranked him as the 11th most productive DB in the league by PSC rating. In the CFL, his most productive season saw him putting up comparable production to Brandon Smith (PSC Rating 55.6 – 9th), Lin-J Shell (PSC Rating 55.5 – 10th), and Dante Marsh (PSC Rating 53.5 – 12th). High level production no doubt, as players like Marsh and Smith were perennial All-Stars, although still quite short of league leaders James Patrick (PSC Rating 94.8 – 1st), Dwight Anderson (PSC Rating 90.5 – 2nd), and Chris Thompson (PSC Rating 72.2 – 3rd).

After signing in the NFL the very next season, he took a remarkable step up from his already impressive performance in the CFL. His very first NFL season he earned the distinction of being the number one most productive DB in the NFL by PSC Rating, rated elite. His numbers in the NFL were virtually all improvements over what he produced in Canada. 51 solo tackles at a rate of 3.19 per game, 6 interceptions at a rate of 0.38 per game, tied for second most in the league, 2 interceptions returned for touchdowns, tied for most in the league and 23 passes defended, most in the league at a rate of 1.44 passes defended per game. This rate was second highest in the league and higher than Darrelle Revis (1.31), Charles Woodson (1.13) and Richard Sherman (1.06).

At no point during his 4 year CFL career was Browner ever able to crack into the top 10 highest producing DB's in the league. His career high tackles per game ratio in the CFL was 3.22 during the 2008 season, which was actually lower than his career high NFL tackles per game ratio of 3.94 recorded during the 2015 season. His most productive interception per game ratio in the CFL was 0.28 which put him into a 4-way tie for 4th highest in the CFL, rated above average. Very similarly, his best NFL interception per game ratio was his most productive season at 0.38 per game, higher than his best CFL production and a season that saw him similarly placed into a 3-way tie for 5th highest in the NFL, rated above average as well.

As a matter of fact, when examining Browner's career stats side by side as we saw on the previous page, Browner actually demonstrated himself to be a better and more productive NFL player than CFL player! He is an impressive example of a player that went from a CFL top 15 player to the most productive player at his position in the NFL, and all in the span of a single year! One wonders what would happen if more CFL players were allowed to transition straight into the NFL as Browner did? I would hypothesize they would continue their run of form and would continue to play at a high level just as they did previously in the CFL.

I found an interesting parallel between a couple of key stats from both leagues. As I previously detailed, his most productive interception per game ratio was good enough to tie him for 4th best in the CFL during his most productive season, rated above average. That same metric in the NFL saw him rank tied for 5th best in the NFL, also rated above average. His tackles per game ratio of 2.67 in the CFL ranked him 23rd most productive DB in the league, rated high average. Comparing that to his NFL tackles per game ratio of 3.19, and we see it ranked him 69th most productive DB in the league, rated high average as well.

The graphics on the following pages depict his most productive CFL and NFL seasons.

MOST PRODUCTIVE SEASON
BRANDON BROWNER

YEAR	2010
GP	18
TACKLES	48
TCK/GM	2.67
INT	5
INT/GM	0.28
INT TD	0
RANK	11TH

BROWNER

27

53.7
PRODUCTION RATING

HIGH AVERAGE

MOST PRODUCTIVE SEASON
BRANDON BROWNER

★★★★★★★★★★★

YEAR	2011
GP	16
TACKLES	51
TCK/GM	3.19
INT	6
INT/GM	0.38
INT TD	2
RANK	1ST

BROWNER
39

95.7
PRODUCTION RATING

ELITE

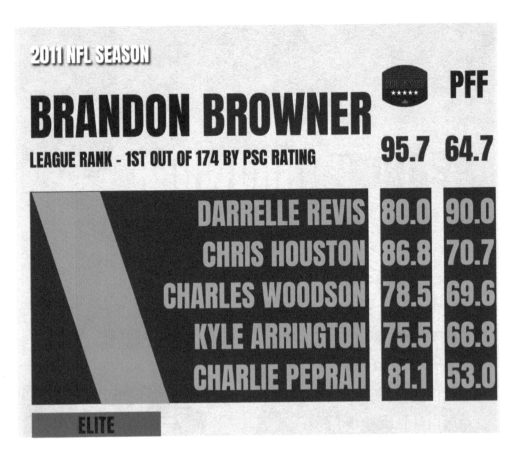

BRANDON BROWNER

LEAGUE RANK - 1ST OUT OF 174 BY PSC RATING

PFF

95.7 64.7

	PSC	PFF
DARRELLE REVIS	80.0	90.0
CHRIS HOUSTON	86.8	70.7
CHARLES WOODSON	78.5	69.6
KYLE ARRINGTON	75.5	66.8
CHARLIE PEPRAH	81.1	53.0

ELITE

Browner's performance during the 2011 NFL season put him on the same level of production as players like Chris Houston, Charlie Peprah, Darrelle Revis, Charles Woodson and Kyle Arrington. The chart above compares his PSC and PFF Overall Grade to theirs.

Browner is an example of a player that obviously had talent and above average size and speed, but did not "light the CFL on fire". While he had high average production, as previously detailed he did not make the top 10 most productive DB's from a statistical standpoint in any of his CFL seasons. Upon signing and immediately being afforded an opportunity to play in the NFL he continued his run of form and even improved to become the top producing DB in the NFL, a Pro Bowler, and a founding member of the "Legion of Boom" in Seattle; one of the most feared secondaries in NFL history. Browner later went on to win a Superbowl with Seattle in 2013, and another the very next year with the New England Patriots becoming one of the few players in NFL history to win back to back championships with two different teams. He was also one of only a small handful of players to have won a Superbowl and a Grey Cup.

Even though he managed to improve his performance in the NFL from his CFL numbers, his performance down south was not a dramatic departure from what he produced in Canada. He was an All-Star calibre player in the CFL, and subsequently proved himself to be a Pro Bowl calibre player in the NFL.

Despite improving on his CFL numbers in virtually all relevant metrics upon becoming an NFL starter, a closer look at his career best metrics in either league makes one thing exceedingly clear:

<table>
<tr><td align="center"><u>CFL</u></td><td align="center"><u>NFL</u></td></tr>
<tr><td align="center">Solo Tackles: 58 (2008)</td><td align="center">Solo Tackles: 63 (2015)</td></tr>
<tr><td align="center">Solo Tackles/Game: 3.22 (2008)</td><td align="center">Solo Tackles/Game: 3.94 (2015)</td></tr>
<tr><td align="center">Interceptions: 5 (2010)</td><td align="center">Interceptions: 6 (2011)</td></tr>
<tr><td align="center">Interceptions/Game: 0.28 (2010)</td><td align="center">Interceptions/Game: 0.38 (2011)</td></tr>
<tr><td align="center">Forced Fumbles: 4 (2007)</td><td align="center">Forced Fumbles: 3 (2012)</td></tr>
<tr><td align="center">Forced Fumbles/Game: 0.24 (2007)</td><td align="center">Forced Fumbles/Game: 0.25 (2012)</td></tr>
</table>

"<u>A player is who he is</u>"

ANDREW
HAWKINS

UNDRAFTED FREE AGENT

CLEVELAND BROWNS

"There's a thin line between starting in the NFL and working in a factory. ONE BAD DECISION and I'm on the wrong end of it."

ANDREW HAWKINS⁶⁵

Andrew Hawkins played collegiately at the University of Toledo, which competes in the NCAA FBS's Mid-American Conference. His college career was not very productive as by its end he had only made 65 receptions for 633 yards and 4 touchdowns in 36 games, having been WR3 virtually his whole college career. This unimpressive production was likely one of the main reasons he was not invited to the 2008 NFL scouting combine. As a point of comparison, I will be comparing Hawkins' Pro Day performance and athleticism to another wide receiver from the same draft class: DeSean Jackson.

Andrew Hawkins	DeSean Jackson
Height: 5'7"	Height: 5'10"
Weight: 182	Weight: 175
40 yard dash: 4.34	40 yard dash: 4.35
10 yard split: 1.53	10 yard split: 1.55
20 yard split: 2.52	20 yard split: 2.53
20 yard shuttle: 4.03	20 yard shuttle: 4.19
Three-cone drill: 6.81	Three-cone drill: 6.82
Vertical jump: 38"	Vertical jump: 34-1/2"
Broad jump: 9'6"	Broad jump: 10'2"
PSC Rating: 99.3	**PSC Rating: 97.8**

As evidenced above, Andrew Hawkins' numbers are either virtually identical, or better in almost every single metric except broad jump and height. His PSC Rating of 99.3 beats DeSean Jackson's 97.8 from an athleticism standpoint. He demonstrated himself to be physically just as gifted as Jackson in virtually every metric. Although his lacklustre college production was likely the main reason he wasn't considered "draftable", his height: listed at 5'7" was likely a very scary number to NFL teams. Remember that the NFL highly values all the measurables, as such a 5'7" wide receiver who had only made 65 receptions in college was just not going to turn the heads of any NFL scouts.

Hawkins' and Jackson's college careers could not have been more different. Hawkins was used very sparingly during his 3 year career at Toledo while Jackson made 162 receptions for 2,423 yards and 22 touchdowns during his. In terms of college production, there was no comparing these two players as DeSean Jackson wins that comparison hands down.

DeSean Jackson was drafted into the NFL in the 2nd round 49th overall, while Hawkins wasn't drafted at all. Although Hawkins' athleticism was enough to afford him a brief opportunity with the Cleveland Browns in early 2008, he was not signed to a contract and was left unemployed.

Hawkins then famously appeared on Michael Irvin's football reality show "4th and Long", and was a runner-up at the conclusion of the season. He was out of football for the entirety of the 2008 season, however he signed with the Montreal Alouettes for the 2009 season. Upon making the team, he played 2 seasons in the CFL, both with Montreal, and was a part of winning two Grey Cups in the process. He was later able to translate that experience into an NFL career that ended up spanning 6 seasons; 2011-2016.

Below you will find his career stats for both leagues.

CFL	NFL
Games played: 13	Games played: 74
Receptions: 41	Receptions: 209
Receptions/Game: 3.2	Receptions/Game: 2.8
Targets: 58	Targets: 343
Targets/Game: 4.5	Targets/Game: 4.6
Reception %: 70.7	Reception %: 60.9
Yards: 457	Yards: 2,419
Yards/Game: 35.2	Yards/Game: 32.7
Average/Reception: 11.1	Average/Reception: 11.6
Touchdowns: 5	Touchdowns: 9
Touchdown/Game: 0.38	Touchdown/Game: 0.12

Hawkins' most productive seasons in the CFL and NFL were the 2010 and 2014 seasons respectively. Highlights of his 2010 CFL season production include 28 receptions for 326 yards with an average of 11.6 yards per reception, 68.3% receiving percentage, and two touchdowns at a rate of 0.12 per game. This production rated him as low average, and landed him as the 38th most productive receiver in the league. His play in the CFL was comparable to Cary Koch (PSC Rating: 51.6, 32nd), Prechae Rodriguez (PSC Rating: 48.0, 34th), and James Robinson (PSC Rating: 44.1, 39th).

Hawkins is an example of a player who was never relied on to be a top receiver in the CFL, as can be demonstrated by his relatively low production. He ended his most productive CFL season 7th in receiving yards on the Alouettes behind Jamel Richardson (1,271 yards), Kerry Watkins (970 yards), S.J. Green (875 yards), Ben Cahoon (702 yards), Avon Cobourne (556 yards), and Brian Bratton (530 yards).

Despite the low production, he was still afforded an NFL opportunity which he was subsequently able to translate into a 6 year career. His NFL numbers for his most productive season (2014) were 63 receptions for 824 yards with an average of 13.1 yards per reception, all improvements over his CFL production. His reception percentage dipped to 55.8% and similarly he also had two receiving touchdowns at a similar rate of 0.13 per game. This production rated him as high average, and ranked him the 49th most productive receiver in the NFL. Despite the smaller field size in the NFL his average yards per reception climbed to 13.1 vs 11.6 yards per reception in the CFL. He was counted on for 54.9 yards per game in the NFL vs. only 40.8 yards per game in the CFL.

The graphics on the following pages depict his statistics and league rankings for his most productive seasons.

MOST PRODUCTIVE SEASON

ANDREW HAWKINS

YEAR	2010
GP	8
REC	28
TARGETS	41
YARDS	326
AVERAGE	11.6
TD	2
RANK	38TH

HAWKINS

0

45.8
PRODUCTION RATING

PRO STATS
★★★★★

LOW AVERAGE

MOST PRODUCTIVE SEASON
ANDREW HAWKINS

PRO STATS
★★★★★

YEAR	2014
GP	15
REC	63
TARGETS	113
YARDS	824
AVERAGE	13.1
TD	2
RANK	49TH

HAWKINS
16

60.2
PRODUCTION RATING

HIGH AVERAGE

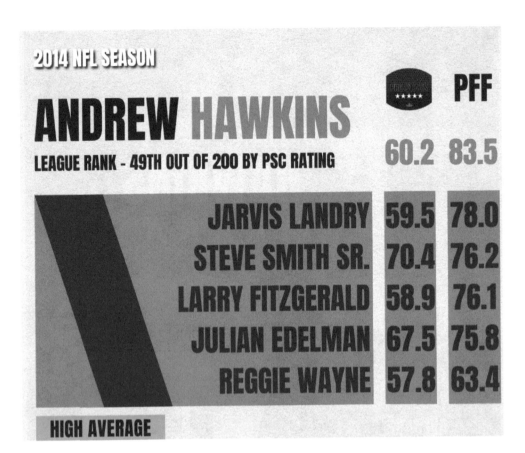

ANDREW HAWKINS

LEAGUE RANK - 49TH OUT OF 200 BY PSC RATING

PFF

60.2 83.5

JARVIS LANDRY	59.5	78.0
STEVE SMITH SR.	70.4	76.2
LARRY FITZGERALD	58.9	76.1
JULIAN EDELMAN	67.5	75.8
REGGIE WAYNE	57.8	63.4

HIGH AVERAGE

Hawkins' performance during the 2014 season was comparable to some all-time great players. His production that season was comparable to Steve Smith Sr, Julian Edelman, Jarvis Landry, Larry Fitzgerald, and Reggie Wayne. As a matter of fact, Hawkins' PFF overall grade was actually higher than all the players mentioned, with his PSC rating being comfortably average in that group.

Despite his lack of production in the CFL, when he eventually signed with the Browns his most productive season saw him become the legitimate number one receiver on that team and the above noted production is the end result. His lack of opportunity in the CFL could have resulted in him being deemed "not talented enough" to play professional football. Instead, he was able to capitalize on the opportunities afforded him and translated modest production in the CFL into team leading production in the NFL. Hawkins was a low average production CFL receiver, who turned into a high average production NFL receiver. Strangely enough, he was an example of a player who was a WR3/4 at best on his stacked Alouettes team, who ended up turning in production comparable to the NFL Pro Bowl calibre players listed above when his number was called.

This is certainly a curious dynamic, yet one that much like the other examples we have studied speaks more to the quality of players in the CFL than to anything else. Hawkins not being targeted much in Montreal was not because he wasn't talented enough, but because he was behind some hall of fame receivers on the depth chart. Had he been required as a WR1 in Montreal I have no doubt he would have been as productive as his WR1 gig in the NFL, perhaps even more so.

Because his work load was so much higher in the NFL overall, let's take a quick look at his career best metrics side by side from seasons where he had over 20 receptions and analyze his highest P.R.O.P. on a per game basis.

CFL

Receptions/Game: 3.5 (2010)
Targets/Game: 5.1 (2010)
Receiving %: 68.3 (2010)
Yards/Game: 40.8 (2010)
Average/Reception: 11.6 (2010)
Touchdowns/Game: 0.25 (2010)

NFL

Receptions/Game: 4.2 (2014)
Targets/Game: 7.5(2014)
Receiving %: 67.6 (2011)
Yards/Game: 54.9 (2014)
Average/Reception: 13.1 (2014)
Touchdowns/Game: 0.29 (2012)

While we can see slight improvements in certain metrics and a slight decline in others, most of his career best metrics are within reasonable proximity of each other. Considering that most of the above NFL metrics were gleaned from seasons where he played at least 13 games, compared to his CFL best of 8 games played (2010), let's quickly compare his 2010 CFL season to his 2015 NFL season head to head as these two seasons were the most comparable from a total work load standpoint.

CFL

GP: 8
Receptions: 28 (7th on team)
Receptions/Game: 3.5
Targets: 41 (7th on team)
Targets/Game: 5.1
Receiving %: 68.3
Yards: 326 (7th on team)
Yards/Game: 40.8
Average/Reception: 11.6
Touchdowns: 2
Touchdowns/Game: 0.25

NFL

GP: 8
Receptions: 27 (6th on team)
Receptions/Game: 3.4
Targets: 44 (6th on team)
Targets/Game: 5.5
Receiving %: 61.4
Yards: 276 (5th on team)
Yards/Game: 34.5
Average/Reception: 10.2
Touchdowns: 0
Touchdowns/Game: 0.00

The above head to head comparison makes it clear that when given similar work loads in either league, and occupying a similar position on the team from a targets standpoint, Hawkins performed very comparably aside from his touchdown numbers. As a matter of fact, even if we expand the comparison to include his metrics from his entire career in either league, we still find his numbers are very comparable. Remember that...

"A player is who he is"

JERRELL
FREEMAN

UNDRAFTED FREE AGENT

INDIANAPOLIS COLTS

"NFL guys come up here and they think, 'I've been in the NFL, this is gonna be a cakewalk';
THEY GET HUMBLED REALLY FAST"

JERRELL FREEMAN[66]

The University of Mary Hardin-Baylor. I would be surprised if you had even heard of it. It is a small division III school in Belton, Texas, and is the alma mater of Jerrell Freeman. It is the place where during his illustrious college career he became the first UMHB player to make over 300 tackles. He ended his college career with 15 sacks, 16 pass break ups, 6 interceptions, 5 forced fumbles, and had 48.5 career tackles for a loss to his credit.[67] During his time at UMHB he won a D3football.com defensive player of the year award, and multiple All-American selections, proving he was a heck of a player in college. However, due to having plied his trade in division III against "vastly inferior" competition, as expected, the NFL would not take the risk of drafting him after he completed his time as a student athlete.

Despite not being drafted, his college resume and athleticism was good enough to get him a brief look with the Tennessee Titans. Professional football being what it is, he was not actually afforded a true opportunity to prove what he was capable of. He was cut from the team after OTA's in 2008, was brought back a week later as a result of some injuries sustained by other Titans players, however was again cut a mere week after that, thus ending his career as a professional. Freeman stated the Titans staff had told him *"you are an NFL linebacker, but not here, and not now.'* Freeman further advised that having played college football in division III had always been a strike against him. *"You had to prove you could compete beyond the level of competition you faced in college. It was hard for me personally, I needed to add weight, and I needed to erase the stereotype."*[68]

Freeman was eventually approached by the Saskatchewan Roughriders of the CFL and ultimately ended up signing with the team. However, even in the CFL his division III pedigree still hampered his opportunities to play. He was used mainly on special teams during his first 2 seasons, although even there he excelled recording a team high 25 special teams tackles during the 2009 season. 2010 saw him get some additional playing time as a regular contributor on defence, where he ended that season having made 23 solo tackles, and a team leading 7 sacks, at a rate of 0.41 sacks per game. After completing his first two seasons, he was finally promoted to full-time defensive starter where he was at long last given a legitimate opportunity to prove what he was capable of. His most productive season in the CFL saw him make 103 solo tackles, at a rate of 6.06 tackles per game, with 6 sacks, 4 forced fumbles and 3 interceptions. That production was good enough to rate him elite as the most productive linebacker in the league. He translated that production into an opportunity with the Indianapolis Colts in the NFL and never looked back playing 6 total seasons in the NFL from 2012-2017. Below you will find his career statistics in both leagues.

<table>
<tr><td>CFL</td><td>NFL</td></tr>
<tr><td>Games Played - 51</td><td>Games Played - 70</td></tr>
<tr><td>Solo Tackles - 140</td><td>Solo Tackles - 389</td></tr>
<tr><td>Tackles/Game - 2.75</td><td>Tackles/Game - 5.55</td></tr>
<tr><td>Sacks - 13</td><td>Sacks - 12</td></tr>
<tr><td>Sacks/Game - 0.25</td><td>Sacks/Game - 0.17</td></tr>
<tr><td>Forced Fumbles - 7</td><td>Forced Fumbles - 8</td></tr>
</table>

Freeman's most productive seasons in the CFL and NFL were the 2011 and 2013 seasons respectively. His CFL tackles per game ratio of 6.06 was good enough for second best in the league behind only Solomon Elimimian. His sacks per game ratio of 0.35 was good enough for third best for a linebacker, behind Jamall Johnson (0.40, 1st), and Rod Davis (0.36, 2nd). His 3 interceptions at a rate of 0.18 per game was good for best in the CFL for linebackers. Freeman's PSC Rating of 98.4 rated him elite, and ranked him as the most productive linebacker in the CFL ahead of such notable players as Chip Cox (PSC Rating 84.2, 2nd) and Solomon Elimimian (PSC Rating 75.9, 3rd).

When Freeman transitioned to the NFL, his most statistically productive season overall came two seasons later in 2013 where he ended up with 83 solo tackles at a rate of 5.19 tackles per game. If we include his "assisted tackles" which the NFL tracks, his number jumps up to 126 total defensive tackles at a rate of 7.88 tackles per game. The 2013 season also saw him rack up 5.5 sacks, 2 interceptions and 6 forced fumbles; a very similar output to his most productive CFL season.

His NFL production was good enough to rate him above average in 2013 as the 6th most productive player in the NFL at his position by PSC rating. While his tackles per game ratio of 5.19 was only good enough for 24th best that season, it was comparable to players such as Chad Greenway (5.19), Bobby Wagner (5.14) and D'Qwell Jackson (4.69).

The graphics on the following pages depict his statistics and league rankings for his most productive professional seasons.

MOST PRODUCTIVE SEASON
JERRELL FREEMAN

★★★★★★ ★★★

YEAR	2011
GP	17
TACKLES	103
TCK/GM	6.06
SACKS	6.0
SCK/GM	0.35
FF	4
RANK	1ST

FREEMAN

50

98.4
PRODUCTION RATING

ELITE

PROSTATS
★★★★★

MOST PRODUCTIVE SEASON
JERRELL FREEMAN

YEAR	2013
GP	16
TACKLES	83
TCK/GM	5.19
SACKS	5.5
SCK/GM	0.34
FF	6
RANK	6TH

FREEMAN

50

79.5
PRODUCTION RATING

ABOVE AVERAGE

JERRELL FREEMAN

LEAGUE RANK - 6TH OUT OF 117 BY PSC RATING

PFF

79.5 70.6

NAVORRO BOWMAN	95.6	88.6
LAVONTE DAVID	88.4	86.0
KARLOS DANSBY	91.4	81.1
PAUL POSLUSZNY	86.4	63.4
ALEC OGLETREE	85.2	63.0

ABOVE AVERAGE

Freeman's overall performance during the 2013 season was comparable to players such as: Navorro Bowman, Karlos Dansby, Lavonte David, Paul Posluszny, and Alec Ogletree. In Freeman we see a player that sat atop the CFL as the league's most productive player in his best season, who when provided comparable playing time in the NFL resulted in him landing squarely in the top 10 most productive players at his position.

Even more interesting is that Freeman's evolution as a player continued. Although he never put up another season as statistically productive overall as his 2013 season, he continued to improve as an already elite NFL player. Three seasons later during the 2016 season, Freeman's tackling efficiency exploded as he made 86 solo tackles in only 12 games at a rate of 7.17 solo tackles per game. This number was not only better than his previous career best in the CFL, this performance was good for best in the NFL, ahead of Luke Kuechly (7.10), Kwon Alexander (6.75), and Vontaze Burfict (6.64). If we included his assisted tackles as well, we end up with 110 total tackles at an absurd rate of 9.17 tackles per game. This proved that despite being an NCAA division III player, he was able to dominate at the professional level, both in the CFL and later with even better production in the NFL.

During the 2016 season PFF assigned him an overall grade of 90.9 which rated him elite and ranked him as the 3rd best front seven defender in the entire NFL, behind only Khalil Mack (92.3), and Luke Kuechly (91.0). This was an absolutely amazing accomplishment given his humble beginnings.

Freeman was living proof that elite talent can come from anywhere, and that sometimes all a player needs is a genuine opportunity to prove what they can do. He was a tackling machine in division III college, he became a tackling machine in the CFL, and finally a tackling machine in the NFL as well. Who would have thought? No matter which level Freeman played at, he conclusively proved

"A player is who he is"

DONTRELLE
INMAN

UNDRAFTED FREE AGENT

SAN DIEGO CHARGERS

"It's a very good league, and a professional league, so they have a lot of talent...
IT'S VERY CLOSE TO THE NFL"

DONTRELLE INMAN [69]

Dontrelle Inman played collegiately at the University of Virginia which competes in the NCAA division I FBS's Atlantic Coast Conference. He was used sparingly during his 4 year career only really coming into his own during his final season in 2010 where he made 51 receptions for 815 yards at an average of 16.0 yards per reception with 3 touchdowns. He was eligible for the 2011 NFL Draft, however was not selected by any team. As a baseline, I will be comparing Inman's final college season and combine/pro day numbers with another well known wide receiver from the same draft class; A.J. Green.

FINAL COLLEGE SEASON

Dontrelle Inman	**A.J. Green**
Receptions: 51	Receptions: 57
Yards: 815	Yards: 848
Average: 16.0	Average: 14.9
Touchdowns: 3	Touchdowns: 9
Long: 52	Long: 50
PSC Rating: 83.8	**PSC Rating: 97.9**

As we can see from the above cited numbers, the main difference between each player's final college season production was the touchdowns scored. Inman only had 3 compared to Green's 9. That difference alone was enough to have the disparity we can see in their PSC ratings. Both had reasonably comparable final seasons, although most experts would argue that Inman played against "inferior competition" in the ACC, whereas Green played for Georgia in the SEC.

Let's take a look at how they compared from an athleticism standpoint coming out of college.

131

Dontrelle Inman

Height: 6'3"
Weight: 198lbs
40 yard dash: 4.47
10 yard split: 1.60
20 yard split: 2.63
20 yard shuttle: 4.13
3 cone drill: 6.53
Vertical jump: 34.0"
Broad jump: 9'10"
Bench press: 11 reps
PSC Rating: 93.9

A.J. Green

Height: 6'3-5/8"
Weight: 211lbs
40 yard dash: 4.50
10 yard split: 1.56
20 yard split: 2.63
20 yard shuttle: 4.21
3 cone drill: 6.91
Vertical jump: 34.5"
Broad jump: 10'6"
Bench press: 18 reps
PSC Rating: 99.0

When examining their combine/pro day numbers, things become a lot closer than the college production. They were both 6'3" tall, although Inman was 198lbs vs Green's 211lbs. As we can see from the actual numbers, they were virtual mirrors of each other. Inman was 3 hundredths of a second faster in the 40 yard dash, Green was 4 hundredths of a second faster in the 10 yard split, and they were exactly equal in the 20 yard split.

When all was said and done, Inman's PSC rating of 93.9 was very comparable to A.J. Green's 99.0. As we previously saw in the Almondo Sewell/Aaron Donald comparison, the explosive strength metrics are usually the main difference. In this case, evidenced by Green's broad jump being 8" farther, and him having put up 7 more reps of 225lbs on the bench. As the NFL highly values all the physical metrics, the fact that A.J. Green runs a 4.50 at 211 lbs, is regarded much more favourably than Inman running 4.47 at 198. It may seem like that is splitting hairs, but it can be the difference between being drafted in the 1st round of the NFL (Green) and not being drafted at all (Inman).

Combining their ratings for their final season of college production, and their pro day/combine metrics, we arrive at the following final PSC Ratings:

A.J. Green: 98.5
Dontrelle Inman: 88.9

As we see time and again, the difference between players drafted high in the NFL and those that end up undrafted and unemployed is often times quite small. Inman's final college season was comparable to A.J. Green's. His pro day metrics also compared very favourably to Green's in almost every way possible, yet as previously mentioned, Inman went undrafted in the 2011

NFL draft, while A.J. Green was selected in the 1ˢᵗ round, 4ᵗʰ overall to the Cincinnati Bengals.

Inman was signed by the Jacksonville Jaguars as an undrafted free agent in 2011, but he was later released at the end of training camp. Like so many before him, when faced with no other professional opportunities south of the border, Inman looked north and signed with the Toronto Argonauts of the CFL. He played two seasons in double blue before being afforded another opportunity in the NFL. He initially signed with the San Diego Chargers, and ultimately played in the NFL for a total of 7 years. The following are his career statistics from both leagues.

CFL	NFL
Games played: 28	Games played: 75
Receptions: 100	Receptions: 188
Receptions/Game: 3.6	Receptions/Game: 2.5
Targets: 161	Targets: 308
Targets/Game: 5.8	Targets/Game: 4.1
Reception %: 62.1	Reception %: 61.0
Yards: 1,542	Yards: 2,445
Yards/Game: 55.1	Yards/Game: 32.6
Average/Reception: 15.4	Average/Reception: 13.0
Touchdowns: 11	Touchdowns: 13
Touchdown/Game: 0.39	Touchdown/Game: 0.17

The graphics on the following page depict Inman's most productive seasons in the CFL and NFL; the 2013 and 2016 seasons respectively.

MOST PRODUCTIVE SEASON
DONTRELLE INMAN

★★★★★★★★★★★

YEAR	2013
GP	13
REC	50
TARGETS	76
YARDS	739
AVERAGE	14.8
TD	6
RANK	18TH

INMAN

11

68.7
PRODUCTION RATING

HIGH AVERAGE

MOST PRODUCTIVE SEASON
DONTRELLE INMAN

YEAR	2016
GP	16
REC	58
TARGETS	94
YARDS	810
AVERAGE	14.0
TD	4
RANK	55TH

INMAN

15

61.0
PRODUCTION RATING

HIGH AVERAGE

DONTRELLE INMAN

LEAGUE RANK - 55TH OUT OF 178 BY PSC RATING

PFF

61.0 72.3

DESEAN JACKSON	69.4	73.0
GOLDEN TATE	74.5	71.6
ROBERT WOODS	50.4	71.4
BRANDON MARSHALL	60.8	69.2
TED GINN JR.	59.0	69.2

HIGH AVERAGE

Inman's most productive NFL season saw him put up production comparable to DeSean Jackson, Golden Tate, Robert Woods, Brandon Marshall and Ted Ginn Jr. His PFF overall grade was second best in this group, only 0.7 rating points behind DeSean Jackson. While in the CFL, Inman established himself as a solid WR3/4. His 6 touchdowns were good for 3rd on the Toronto Argonauts behind John Chiles (1st) and Jason Barnes (2nd), and his 739 receiving yards were good for 3rd on the team behind Andre Durie (1st) and Chad Owens (2nd).

During his most productive CFL season, Inman's play was comparable to players like: Adarius Bowman (PSC Rating 71.1, 16th), Clarence Denmark (PSC Rating 69.5, 17th), Greg Ellingson (PSC Rating 68.5, 19th), and Bakari Grant (PSC Rating 68.0, 20th). Once he transitioned to the NFL, his most productive season saw him occupy a similar role as a WR2/3 on the San Diego Chargers. His 810 yards were good for 2nd on the team behind only Tyrell Williams (1st), while his 4 touchdowns ranked him tied for 4th behind Hunter Henry (1st), Tyrell Williams (2nd), and Antonio Gates (3rd).

He was a dependable, high average WR3 in the CFL, and transitioned to a dependable, high average WR2/3 in the NFL with very similar production. He was never selected as an All-Star in the CFL, and was similarly not ever voted to the Pro Bowl in the NFL.

What about our old friend A.J. Green? How did his 2016 season compare to Inman's? Let's examine a couple of basic metrics:

A.J. Green	**Dontrelle Inman**
Receptions: 66	Receptions: 58
Targets: 100	Targets: 94
Receiving %: 66.0	Receiving %: 61.7
Yards: 964	Yards: 810
Average/Reception: 14.6	Average/Reception: 14.0
Touchdowns: 4	Touchdowns: 4
PSC Rating: 71.8	**PSC Rating: 61.0**
Ranked 23rd	**Ranked 55th**

A.J. Green was the bona fide WR1 on the Bengals. As such, he was targeted far more than Inman on a per game basis. His production was accomplished in only 10 games, compared to Inman's full slate of 16 games played. Nevertheless, when looking at them side by side as we are, I can only say 'Not bad for an undrafted former CFL'er!'

If one were to ask the "experts" how close of a season these two would have, 6 years into Green's career, all with the same team as WR1, and 5 years into Inman's career after playing for two different teams in two different leagues and never being counted on to be the top receiver? Most would have stated there would be no comparison at all! However, ending the 2016 season only 8 receptions and 6 targets behind, falling only 4.3% short on receiving percentage, being 0.6 yards per reception behind, and scoring the same amount of touchdowns is closer than anyone could have reasonably expected to see!

As with the majority of the profiled players in this book, Inman is a perfect example of the statement:

"A player is who he is"

DELVIN
BREAUX

UNDRAFTED FREE AGENT

NEW ORLEANS SAINTS

"The talent level is the SAME"

DELVIN BREAUX [70]

Delvin Breaux has a heck of a story. He suffered a severe neck injury during a game at the end of his high school career that doctors believed should have ended his life. His medical team believed that at the very least, the injury would forever rob him of his ability to walk or run. At the time, he had already committed to play college football at LSU. Against all odds, he rehabbed from that devastating injury and in fact attended LSU as a student, however he was never allowed on the field as a player and he completed his entire college program without ever having played a single down of football. After college, he worked his way through various different teams at various levels of semi-professional football until the Hamilton Tiger-Cats came calling. Breaux played in the CFL from 2013 to 2014, and then again from 2018-2022. In between those two stints, he played in the NFL for 2 seasons from 2015-2016. During that time he posted the following career statistics:

CFL	NFL
Games Played - 58	Games Played - 22
Solo Tackles - 133	Solo Tackles - 53
Tackles/Game - 2.29	Tackles/Game - 2.41
Interceptions - 2	Interceptions - 3
Interceptions/Game - 0.03	Interceptions/Game - 0.14
Interception Return Yards - 27	Interception Return Yards - 22
Interception TD - 2	Interception TD - 0
Forced Fumbles - 7	Forced Fumbles - 0

Breaux was a player that did not put up overwhelming stats regardless of where he played. One of the reasons for that was, he was an excellent DB that quarterbacks would rather not throw to. He was normally tasked with covering the opposing team's best receiver man to man. His performance during the 2014 CFL season earned him not only an East Division All-Star nod, but also saw him become a CFL All-Star for the first time in his career.

Upon his transition to the NFL the very next season, not only did he make his hometown New Orleans Saints' 53 man roster, he became one of their starting cornerbacks, and even more impressively, graded at a Pro Bowl level. In fact, if it were not for an improperly diagnosed leg injury leading to a subsequent falling out of favour with the Saints' management, we would likely have never seen him back in the CFL ever again. Proving just how short lived NFL careers can be, despite his stellar play for the Saints, no other NFL team was willing to take a chance on him after he fully recovered from his leg injury. Teams may have been reluctant to sign him due to believing him to be injury prone, his previous neck injury, or perhaps even his undeserved "bad reputation", which arose as a result of Head Coach Sean Payton not believing he was truly injured. Whatever the reason, a Pro Bowl calibre player was left unemployed at the end of the 2017 season and returned north to continue his professional career with the Tiger-Cats, where he went on to another league All-Star nomination for the 2018 season and ultimately made the CFL All-Decade team 2010-2019.

The graphics on the following pages depict Breaux's performance for his most productive CFL and NFL seasons.

MOST PRODUCTIVE SEASON
DELVIN BREAUX

★★★★★★★★★★★

YEAR	2014
GP	16
TACKLES	33
TCK/GM	2.06
INT	1
INT/GM	0.06
INT TD	1
RANK	14TH

BREAUX

27

54.2
PRODUCTION RATING

HIGH AVERAGE

MOST PRODUCTIVE SEASON
DELVIN BREAUX

★★★★★

YEAR	2015
GP	16
TACKLES	37
TCK/GM	2.31
INT	3
INT/GM	0.19
INT TD	0
RANK	41ST

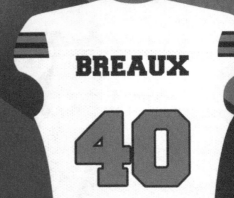

43.8
PRODUCTION RATING

HIGH AVERAGE

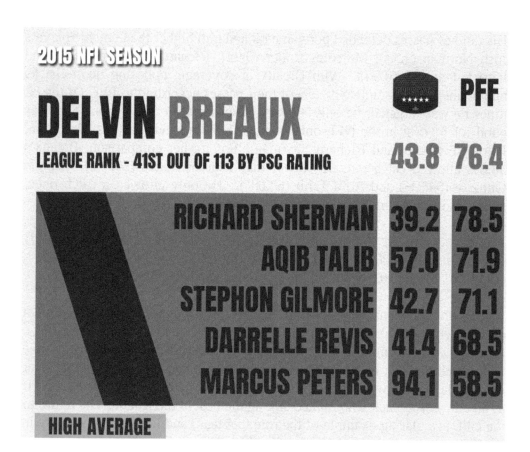

Delvin Breaux's performance in the NFL during the 2015 season was comparable to Richard Sherman, Aqib Talib, Stephon Gilmore, Darrelle Revis, and Marcus Peters. He ranked among the top DB's in the league and although he was not voted to the Pro Bowl, was playing at a Pro Bowl level; the metrics prove this fact. His performance was so good in fact that he was voted the Saints' defensive MVP by fans on the Saints' website.[71]

Like Browner before him, Breaux is another example of a player who within a single year transitioned from the CFL to the NFL and improved on his already impressive performance. His 2014 CFL season saw him make 33 solo tackles at a rate of 2.06 per game, rated below average, and 1 interception at a rate of 0.06 per game, rated low average. The very next season in the NFL he improved to 37 solo tackles at a rate of 2.31 per game, rated low average, and 3 interceptions at a rate of 0.19 per game, rated high average. Even more impressive were his 19 passes defended at a rate of 1.19 per game, rated above average, which ranked him 6th and 9th in the NFL respectively.

His ratio of passes defended per game ranked him higher than notable players Josh Norman (1.13), Malcolm Butler (0.94), Richard Sherman (0.88) and Patrick Peterson (0.50). With Breaux in coverage, opposing quarterbacks only managed to complete 48.8% of their passes according to PFF. Of the 82 times he was targeted, he only allowed 40 catches for 565 yards. This was good for 5th best in the NFL only behind Darrelle Revis, Leodis McKelvin, Patrick Peterson, and Richard Sherman. For further comparison, Breaux's 48.8% allowed catch rate was better than Marcus Peters (50.4%), Stephon Gilmore (54.3%) and Aqib Talib (63.0%). He only allowed a catch once, every 13.5 snaps which was ninth best in the NFL.[72]

A Bleacher Report article titled *"B/R NFL 1000: Ranking the Top 101 Cornerbacks from 2015"* listed Breaux as the 13th best cornerback in the NFL out of 101 for his 2015 NFL rookie season, rating him 87/99.[73]

As previously mentioned, Delvin Breaux was one of those exceptional players who's numbers did not necessarily translate into scorching ratings, however when examining his performance in its totality we can truly see what an elite player he really was. Breaux dominated the CFL as an All-Star calibre player, and when given a starting opportunity also dominated the NFL as an elite cornerback who ranked among the best in the league. His return to the CFL is a glaring example of the role that team and league politics play in many personnel decisions in professional football.

The NFL's loss was the CFL's gain. Once again, Breaux proved the statement true:

"A player is who he is"

MARCUS
THIGPEN

UNDRAFTED FREE AGENT

MIAMI DOLPHINS

"I got out there and I said (the NFL) is not what everyone is making it out to be...
I CAN COMPETE WITH THESE GUYS"

MARCUS THIGPEN⁷⁴

Marcus Thigpen played his college football for the Indiana University Hoosiers. During his 4 seasons with the team he was used in a variety of ways; receiving, rushing and kick returning. He proved himself equally able to exercise any of the roles thrown his way and was a highly versatile player, having ended his college career with 1,600+ rushing yards, 1,000+ receiving yards, and 2,000+ kick return yards.

As a baseline, I will be comparing Thigpen's college career and combine/pro day numbers with another well known wide receiver/kick returner from the same draft class; Percy Harvin. As Harvin did not return kicks in college I will only be comparing their receiving and rushing numbers. We will just have to keep in mind that Thigpen had that additional element to his game in college that Harvin did not.

COLLEGE SEASONS

Marcus Thigpen – Receiving

Receptions: 84
Yards: 1,028
Average: 12.2
Touchdowns: 9
Rec/TD: 9.3
Long: 79
PSC Rating: 78.3

Percy Harvin - Receiving

Receptions: 133
Yards: 1,929
Average: 14.5
Touchdowns: 13
Rec/TD: 10.2
Long: 70
PSC Rating: 96.6

Marcus Thigpen - Rushing

Rushes: 337
Yards: 1,621
Average: 4.8
Touchdowns: 9
Carries/TD: 37.4
Long: 78
PSC Rating: 68.4

Percy Harvin - Rushing

Rushes: 194
Yards: 1,851
Average: 9.5
Touchdowns: 19
Carries/TD: 10.2
Long: 80
PSC Rating: 92.9

COMBINE/PRO DAY

Marcus Thigpen	**Percy Harvin**
Height: 5'9"	Height: 5'11-1/8"
Weight: 184lbs	Weight: 192lbs
40 yard dash: 4.45	40 yard dash: 4.41
10 yard split: 1.53	10 yard split: 1.47
20 yard split: 2.58	20 yard split: 2.51
Vertical jump: 35.0"	Vertical jump: 37.5"
Broad jump: 10'6"	Broad jump: 10'1"
Bench press: 21 reps	Bench press: 17
PSC Rating: 97.6	**PSC Rating: 96.1**

Looking at all the above in its entirety, Harvin obviously had the more productive college career from an offensive perspective. His overall college PSC Rating for offensive production (combination of receiving and rushing) was 94.8. In comparison to Thigpen's 73.3 it represents a 21.5 point differential. The production gap would likely be smaller if we factored in Thigpen's return metrics, as again, it added an additional element to his production that Harvin did not possess in college.

When examining their combine/pro day metrics, it becomes interesting as Thigpen's PSC Rating of 97.6 is actually higher than Harvin's 96.1. While Thigpen was 2 inches shorter and 8 pounds lighter, their quickness was virtually identical. The only significant difference was their strength metrics, where Thigpen demonstrated that despite being smaller, he was actually stronger, putting up a full 4 additional reps of 225lbs on the bench press.

On an interesting side note, both athletes were also involved in track and field throughout high school and college. Thigpen's personal best 100 metre dash time of 10.34 bested Harvin's personal best time of 10.43. The tables turned when comparing their 200 metre dash times with Harvin's personal best of 21.19 beating Thigpen's personal best of 21.27.

Combining their combine metrics with their college production metrics, we arrive at the following pre-draft final overall PSC Ratings:

Percy Harvin: 95.2
Marcus Thigpen: 81.4

While 13.8 rating points is certainly a difference, it is hardly a galaxy apart. In any event, once again as we have seen before, Percy Harvin got drafted in the 1ˢᵗ round of the 2009 NFL draft 22ⁿᵈ overall, while Marcus Thigpen went undrafted.

Thigpen was brought in by the Philadelphia Eagles for the 2009 off-season, however was cut prior to the start of the season. He subsequently spent 10 days with the Denver Broncos, however was also cut and at that point saw his professional opportunities in the NFL completely extinguished without ever having played a single down. He looked north after that, signing with the Saskatchewan Roughriders as a practice squad player and spending the remainder of the season with the team. The Roughriders cut him early in the 2010 season and he later signed with the Hamilton Tiger-Cats where he was finally provided a real opportunity. The 2010 season was the most productive of his CFL career, where he became the first player in CFL history to score a touchdown five different ways in a single season: Kickoff return, punt return, missed field goal return, rushing and receiving.

In total, Thigpen played in the CFL from 2010 to 2011 and then 2017-2019. Between those stints, he played in the NFL from 2012 to 2015.

During that time he posted the following career **KICK RETURN** statistics:

CFL	NFL
Games Played - 68	Games Played - 50
Kickoffs Returned - 115	Kickoffs Returned - 107
KR/Game - 1.7	KR/Game - 2.1
KR Yards – 2,459	KR Yards – 2,525
KR Yards/Game - 36.2	KR Yards/Game - 50.5
KR Average - 21.4	KR Average - 23.6
TD - 3	TD - 1
LONG - 100 Yards	LONG - 96 Yards

Thigpen's most productive seasons in the CFL and NFL were the 2010 and 2012 seasons respectively. The graphics on the following pages depict his statistics and league rankings for those seasons.

One of the most noteworthy discoveries I made when analyzing his inter-league performance was how remarkably similar his metrics were in both leagues. Despite transitioning between two different leagues where the field size and rules have a much more profound impact on special teams than necessarily on any other phase of the game, his numbers were ultra-consistent.

During the 2010 CFL season his performance was rated above average and he was ranked 2nd in the CFL by PSC rating for kick returns. He put up 784 kick return yards at an average of 20.1 yards per return, with 1 KR touchdown. Upon transitioning south during the 2012 season he was very similarly rated above average and ranked as the 5th most productive kick returner in the NFL. Despite playing on the smaller field, he was actually able to improve on his CFL numbers putting up 1,040 kick return yards at an average of 27.4 yards per return, with 1 KR touchdown.

MOST PRODUCTIVE SEASON
MARCUS THIGPEN

★ ★ ★ ★ ★ ★ ★ ★ ★ ★

YEAR	2010
GP	18
KR	39
KR YDS	784
AVG	20.1
RET TD	1
LONG	93
RANK	2ND

94.4
PRODUCTION RATING

ABOVE AVERAGE

MOST PRODUCTIVE SEASON
MARCUS THIGPEN

YEAR	2012
GP	16
KR	38
KR YDS	1040
AVG	27.4
RET TD	1
LONG	96
RANK	5TH

THIGPEN

34

80.1
PRODUCTION RATING

ABOVE AVERAGE

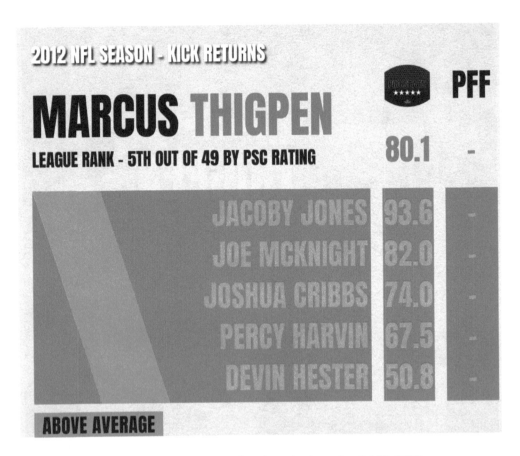

MARCUS THIGPEN

LEAGUE RANK - 5TH OUT OF 49 BY PSC RATING

PFF

80.1 -

JACOBY JONES 93.6 -
JOE MCKNIGHT 82.0 -
JOSHUA CRIBBS 74.0 -
PERCY HARVIN 67.5 -
DEVIN HESTER 50.8 -

ABOVE AVERAGE

Marcus Thigpen's kick return production during the 2012 NFL season was comparable to Jacoby Jones (2nd), Joe McKnight (4th), Josh Cribbs (6th), Percy Harvin (10th), and Devin Hester (21st). He was one of only 8 players in the NFL to accumulate more than 1000 kick return yards.

On an unrelated but nevertheless interesting note, while analyzing the 2012 NFL season's kick return statistics, I discovered that among the 49 players to be included in my analysis, a total of 7 of them had either come from the CFL, or would later transition to the CFL. The list includes:

Joe McKnight (4th); rated above average
Chris Rainey (8th); rated above average
Stefan Logan (22nd), rated high average
William Powell (24th), rated high average
Brandon Banks (26th), rated low average
Armanti Edwards (38th), rated low average
Cassius Vaughn (41st), rated low average

Thigpen's career **PUNT RETURN** statistics are as follows:

CFL	NFL
Games Played - 68	Games Played - 50
Punts Returned - 178	Punts Returned - 95
PR/Game - 2.6	PR/Game - 1.9
PR Yards – 1,617	PR Yards - 919
PR Yards/Game - 23.8	PR Yards/Game - 18.4
PR Average - 9.1	PR Average - 9.7
TD - 1	TD - 2
LONG - 93	LONG - 75

Thigpen's most productive punt return seasons in the CFL and NFL were the 2010 and 2012 seasons respectively. The graphics on the following pages depict his statistics and league rankings for those seasons.

Thigpen's statistics for punt returns between leagues were not as consistent as his kick return metrics. During his most productive CFL season he returned 63 punts for a total of 554 yards at an average of 8.8 yards per return, with one punt return touchdown. This production was good for 4th most productive punt returner in the league, earning him a high average rating.

During his most productive NFL season he returned 26 punts for 316 yards at an average of 12.2 yards per return, with one punt return touchdown. This production was rated high average and ranked him as the 9th most productive punt returner in the NFL. While most of his metrics were fairly similar to his CFL numbers, his average yards per punt return was significantly improved from 8.8 yards per return in the CFL to 12.2 yards per return in the NFL. Although as could reasonably be expected, he fielded significantly less punts in the NFL only returning 26 compared to the 63 that he returned in the CFL.

A factor that possibly contributed to his average yards per punt return metric being higher in the NFL is the "no yards/touchback" differences between the games. Where in the CFL he had to return every single punt, in the NFL he could signal a fair catch and only actually attempt to return a punt where the conditions were more favourable, and therefore more conducive to gaining bigger average yardage.

MOST PRODUCTIVE SEASON
MARCUS THIGPEN

★ ★ ★ ★ ★ ★ ★ ★ ★ ★ ★

YEAR	2010
GP	18
PR	63
PR YDS	554
AVG	8.8
RET TD	1
LONG	93
RANK	4TH

68.7
PRODUCTION RATING

HIGH AVERAGE

MOST PRODUCTIVE SEASON
MARCUS THIGPEN

★★★★★★★★★★★★

YEAR	2012
GP	16
PR	26
PR YDS	316
AVG	12.2
RET TD	1
LONG	72
RANK	9TH

THIGPEN

34

73.3
PRODUCTION RATING

HIGH AVERAGE

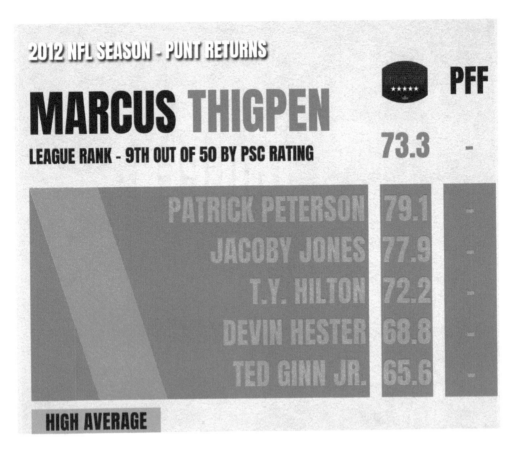

MARCUS THIGPEN

LEAGUE RANK - 9TH OUT OF 50 BY PSC RATING

PFF

73.3   -

PATRICK PETERSON	79.1	-
JACOBY JONES	77.9	-
T.Y. HILTON	72.2	-
DEVIN HESTER	68.8	-
TED GINN JR.	65.6	-

HIGH AVERAGE

Marcus Thigpen's punt return production during the 2012 NFL season was comparable to Patrick Peterson (5th), Jacoby Jones (6th), T.Y. Hilton (13th), Devin Hester (16th), and Ted Ginn Jr. (18th). His 12.2 yards per punt return was rated above average and was good enough for 6th highest in the NFL.[75]

As previously mentioned, the higher average yards per return in the NFL is possibly attributable to fielding less punts, and signalling "fair catch" on those that did not present favourable conditions for return. Despite this, the consistency in his production was still quite notable. The smaller field and much tighter running lanes that the smaller more narrow NFL field affords returners did not hamper him much as he still landed firmly in the top 10 at his position in the NFL.

"A player is who he is"

ALEX
SINGLETON

UNDRAFTED FREE AGENT

PHILADELPHIA EAGLES

"The speed of the game is MUCH FASTER IN THE CFL compared to the NFL and it's not even close"

ALEX SINGLETON[76]

Alex Singleton played his collegiate football at Montana State which competes in the NCAA division I FCS's Big Sky Conference. I will be comparing his college production and pro day metrics to another notable linebacker from the same draft class; Denzel Perryman from the University of Miami.

Alex Singleton	Denzel Perryman
GP: 35	GP: 43
Solo Tackles: 164	Solo Tackles: 228
Solo Tackles/Game: 4.69	Solo Tackles/Game: 5.30
Total Tackles: 260	Total Tackles: 337
Tackles/Game: 7.43	Tackles/Game: 7.84
Tackles for Loss: 35.5	Tackles for Loss: 27.0
Sacks: 3.5	Sacks: 4.5
Forced Fumbles: 3	Forced Fumbles: 7
Interceptions: 5	Interceptions: 2
PSC Rating: 83.4	**PSC Rating: 87.8**

As we can see from their college production PSC ratings, Singleton's college career was very comparable to Perryman's as he ended up only 3.7 rating points below him. Overall, Singleton had less tackles and played in less games, however he demonstrated great versatility as he had more tackles for loss, and more interceptions despite significantly less playing time. He seemed to be as comfortable getting through the line of scrimmage into the backfield, as he was at dropping into pass coverage situations. If we examine their total tackles broken down on a per game basis, we observe their production is virtually identical. Denzel Perryman was invited to participate in the 2015 NFL Combine, while Alex Singleton was not.

Below we can observe their PSC ratings for some of their combine/pro day metrics.

Alex Singleton	Denzel Perryman
Height: 6'2"	Height: 5'11"
Weight: 240lbs	Weight: 236lbs
40 yard dash: 4.62	40 yard dash: 4.68
Broad jump: 10'0"	Broad jump: 9'5"
Vertical Jump: 31"	Vertical Jump: 32"
Bench press: 15	Bench press: 27
PSC Rating: 92.1	**PSC Rating: 97.8**

Just as we saw with their college careers, we also find their athleticism was very comparable. Singleton was taller, roughly the same weight, a little faster, and similarly explosive. The main difference was Perryman clearly demonstrated himself to be the stronger athlete by benching 12 more reps of 225lbs. Their combine/pro day PSC ratings had Perryman besting Singleton by a mere 5.7 rating points. If we combine their PSC ratings for their college careers and combine/pro day performances we end up with a final pre-draft PSC rating of 92.8 for Denzel Perryman and 87.8 for Alex Singleton. Even though their college production and athleticism was demonstrably similar, with only 4.7 rating points separating them, Singleton having played against "inferior competition" in the FCS was likely enough to ward off any thoughts of an NFL team drafting him. All 32 NFL teams decided he just wasn't good enough to spend a draft pick on. Denzel Perryman however went on to be drafted in the 2nd round of the 2015 NFL draft (48th overall).

Singleton managed to sign with the Seattle Seahawks as an undrafted free agent following the draft, however he was released prior to the start of the season. He was then signed to the practice squad of the New England Patriots for all of 7 days and then released once again. Following the season he was signed to the Minnesota Vikings' practice squad however he never made it to camp and once again was released prior to ever taking a single snap. It was at that point with all his NFL opportunities exhausted that Singleton acquired his Canadian citizenship and declared for the 2016 CFL draft. He was selected in the 1st round (6th overall) by the Calgary Stampeders and played 3 seasons in the CFL from 2016 to 2018. He later transitioned back to the NFL where he played from 2019 to the present (2023). During that time he posted the following career statistics:

CFL	NFL
Games Played: 54	Games Played - 59
Solo Tackles: 311	Solo Tackles - 258
Solo Tackles/Game: 5.76	Solo Tackles/Game – 4.37
Sacks: 4	Sacks – 2
Interceptions: 1	Interceptions: 2
Sacks/Game: 0.07	Sacks/Game – 0.03
Forced Fumbles: 6	Forced Fumbles - 2

During his most productive season in the CFL Singleton was the most productive linebacker in the league, ending the season with an elite PSC Rating of 93.2. This was comparable to other notable players such as: Kyries Hebert (PSC Rating 92.2, 2nd), Larry Dean (PSC Rating 86.7, 3rd), Kenny Ladler (PSC Rating 84.3, 4th) and Henoc Muamba (PSC Rating 83.2, 5th).

His tackles per game ratio of 6.83 was second best in the league, only behind Solomon Elimimian's 8.00 tackles per game. Singleton's 4 sacks at a rate of 0.22 sacks per game was also second best in the league for a linebacker, only behind Simoni Lawrence's 6 sacks at a rate of 0.35 sacks per game.

It is remarkable to note that Singleton's 123 solo tackles in the CFL ended up being very comparable to his total tackle output during his first season actually getting meaningful reps on defence in the NFL. During the 2020 NFL season he recorded double digit tackles in 6 of 14 games, although Singleton only became a starting linebacker in week 6 of that season. Prior to then he had only made 5 tackles in 5 weeks as a rotational player who's main role had been on special teams. It therefore becomes even more impressive that with 5 weeks of essentially missed time, he was still able to rack up 120 total tackles, at a rate of 7.50 total tackles per game. A ratio that was actually higher than his career best 6.83 tackles per game in the CFL. Despite the disadvantage of starting less games, Singleton's PSC rating of 69.4 still landed him firmly in the top 20 most productive linebackers in the NFL (18th) for the 2020 season.

The graphics on the following pages depict his statistics and league rankings for his most productive CFL and NFL seasons, 2017 and 2021 respectively.

MOST PRODUCTIVE SEASON
ALEX SINGLETON

YEAR	2017
GP	18
TACKLES	123
TCK/GM	6.83
SACKS	4.0
INT	1
FF	1
RANK	1ST

SINGLETON

49

93.2
PRODUCTION RATING

ELITE

MOST PRODUCTIVE SEASON
ALEX SINGLETON

★★★★★★

YEAR	2021
GP	16
TACKLES	81
TCK/GM	5.06
SACKS	0.0
INT	1
FF	1
RANK	12TH

77.5
PRODUCTION RATING

ABOVE AVERAGE

SINGLETON
49

PRO STATS
★★★★★

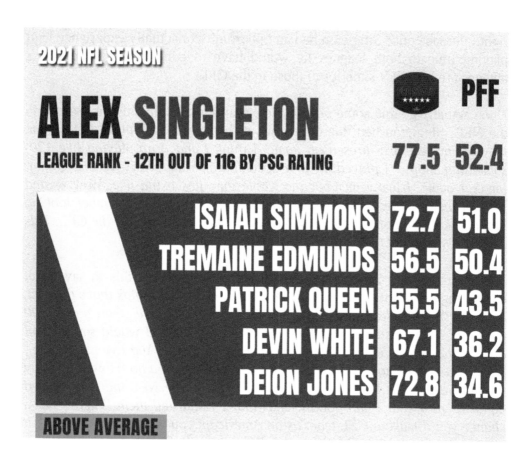

ALEX SINGLETON

LEAGUE RANK - 12TH OUT OF 116 BY PSC RATING

PFF

77.5 52.4

ISAIAH SIMMONS	72.7	51.0
TREMAINE EDMUNDS	56.5	50.4
PATRICK QUEEN	55.5	43.5
DEVIN WHITE	67.1	36.2
DEION JONES	72.8	34.6

ABOVE AVERAGE

During his most productive NFL season in 2021, Singleton's play was comparable to the above noted players. He made a total of 137 tackles at a rate of 8.56 tackles per game which was good for 11th best among linebackers. In addition to yet again proving he was a tackling machine with the highest tackle output of his professional career up until then, NFL or CFL, he also demonstrated coverage skills. He had 4 passes defended and 1 interception which he returned 29 yards for a touchdown. He was one of only 6 linebackers in the NFL to score an interception return touchdown, the second of his NFL career. Just as we saw with Jerrell Freeman, here again we find another player who was the CFL's most productive at his position who transitioned to the NFL and ultimately ended up a top 15 player. Note that all the players compared to Singleton above were 1st and 2nd round picks in their respective draft years, yet Singleton had the highest PSC rating, and highest PFF grade among them.

Prior to joining the CFL, Singleton reached out to some of his peers who had played in the NFL that then played in the CFL to find out what the level of competition was like. What he learned from them was revealing: *"They say game-wise the players are just as good as in the NFL."*[77] But that cannot be right. Perhaps once Singleton had an opportunity to actually experience legit playing time in both leagues he would have to admit that all the NFL's athletes are VASTLY superior to those in the CFL.

Upon actually getting some playing time with Philadelphia his first season in the NFL, Singleton had this to say about the intensity of play: *"This year, playing in the fourth preseason game, I think I ended up playing like 120-something snaps. I played all four special teams and every defensive snap for that game. I just remember the whole time just being like, Wow — and most of the other guys were dead and dying — and I just remember looking around like 'Man, this is not as bad as even playing defence in the CFL. This is nice. I'm not that tired.'"*[78]

In an interview on "The Waggle" podcast, Singleton had this to say about comparing the talent of players in the NFL and CFL: *"I think that's the best, or funniest or saddest thing about the CFL is you're there...there's only 600 guys and I would say, especially out of the Americans, I would say 90% of them had a chance or had a cup of coffee in the NFL. And I would say that just about every single one of them at a point on film you go 'How is this guy still not in the NFL'...There are plenty of guys in the NFL that I've played against, know, that I call good friends that I would tell them 'There's not a chance you'd make a CFL team as an American, you wouldn't be able to', it goes both ways I think. I tell people all the time...there's that 1% in the NFL that everybody knows...they're the guys that people go to the games for, to watch anyways. I would say the other 99% of the guys in the league are no different than your last American dude getting cut at the end of a CFL camp. That 99% from that last guy getting cut in the CFL camp to your starting offensive guard for the Patriots is one or two circumstances going right your way, and one or two circumstances going wrong your way, and you don't know when that's ever going to happen."*[79]

After experiencing first-hand what each league's level of play was like, Singleton echoes the sentiments of numerous other players who believe that aside from the absolute best of the best in the NFL, a number Singleton advised was the top 1%, basically everyone else is interchangeable between both leagues. At the very least, Singleton's comments add weight to the idea that the talent discrepancy between the CFL and NFL is in fact much smaller than many CFL haters seem to believe it is.

During the 2022-23 NFL season, Singleton nearly re-wrote the NFL record books with the Broncos for single game production. On Monday Night Football against the Los Angeles Chargers, he made 19 solo tackles, (21 total), 2 tackles for loss, 1 pass defended, and a QB hit. For context, this performance ranked as the second highest single game tackle output in NFL history. It destroyed the Broncos' single game record of 15, and completely obliterated his best ever single game CFL production of 13 solo tackles and 1 sack recorded during the 2017 season.

Although the 2022-23 season was not his most productive overall, he ended that season having made a total of 163 tackles in 17 games played which ranked him 5th in the NFL rating him elite. He was one of only 6 players in the league to make 100 or more solo tackles, and his P.R.O.P. of 5.88 solo tackles per game ranked as the 6th highest of any linebacker in the NFL, again rating him elite.

If we take his 2019 season out of the equation we find his NFL career production as a starter to be staggering. 49 games played, 420 total tackles at a rate of 8.57 per game, 256 solo tackles at a rate of 5.22 per game, 2 sacks, 2 forced fumbles, 2 interceptions, 2 interception return touchdowns, 8 passes defended and 18 tackles for loss.

Singleton was an elite tackler in the CFL and upon being provided a legitimate opportunity in the NFL once again proved he was a dominant tackling machine there as well.

"A player is who he is"

ERIK HARRIS

LAS VEGAS RAIDERS

"If the CFL paid NFL money, I'd think about playing CFL STYLE FOOTBALL"

ERIK HARRIS[80]

Erik Harris played collegiate football as a safety at California University of Pennsylvania which competes in the NCAA's division II. As a baseline comparison of his athleticism, I will be comparing his pre-draft combine metrics to another notable safety from the same draft class: Harrison Smith.

COMBINE PERFORMANCES

Erik Harris	Harrison Smith
Height:6'2"	Height: 6'1-7/8"
Weight: 226lbs	Weight: 213lbs
40 yard dash: 4.57	40 yard dash: 4.57
10 yard split: 1.65	10 yard split: 1.56
20 yard split: 2.70	20 yard split: 2.66
20 yard shuttle: 4.48	20 yard shuttle: 4.12
Three cone drill: 6.96	Three cone drill: 6.63
Broad jump: 9'2"	Broad jump: 10'2"
Bench press: 23	Bench press: 19
PSC Rating: 95.8	**PSC Rating: 97.5**

As we can see, Harris and Smith were in fact very comparable from an athleticism standpoint. They were virtually the same height, while Harris was 13 lbs heavier. Their 40 yard dash time was identical, and Smith demonstrated himself to be a little quicker in the other agility metrics, although not by much. Harris was the stronger of the two putting up 4 more reps of 225lbs, and Smith demonstrated greater explosive power recording a broad jump which was a full 12 inches farther than Harris'.

Smith played his college ball at Notre Dame and was ultimately a 1st round draft pick, 29th overall in the 2012 draft. Despite Harris demonstrating he was athletically virtually equal to Smith, the fact he played against "inferior competition" in division II resulted in him not being drafted and not being invited to any NFL camps. According to every team in the NFL, Harris' division II pedigree was just not up to standards for the NFL; his athleticism notwithstanding.

Harris' first taste of professional football came with the Hamilton Tiger-Cats during the 2013 CFL season where he played from 2013 to 2015. He later transitioned to the NFL where he played from 2016 to the present (2023).

During that time he posted the following career statistics:

CFL	NFL
Games Played - 45	Games Played - 91
Solo Tackles - 71	Solo Tackles - 202
Tackles/Game - 1.58	Tackles/Game – 2.22
Interceptions - 3	Interceptions - 5
Interceptions/Game - 0.07	Interceptions/Game - 0.05
Interception Return Yards - 46	Interception Return Yards - 167
Interception TD - 1	Interception TD - 2
Forced Fumbles - 0	Forced Fumbles - 1

During Harris' most productive season in the CFL, his PSC Rating of 46.5 was good enough for 25th most productive DB in the league, rating him low average. His production was comparable to Demond Washington (PSC Rating 49.5, 23rd), Ronnie Yell (PSC Rating 46.2, 26th), Sam Hurl (PSC Rating 43.3, 27th), and Antoine Pruneau (PSC Rating 42.1, 30th).

Harris was ultimately afforded his opportunity in the NFL in 2016 in large part because friend and former Ticats teammate Delvin Breaux, at that time a starting cornerback for the New Orleans Saints, convinced his team's management to bring Harris in for a workout. Harris's role with the Saints was limited in his first season in the NFL only making one solo tackle in 4 appearances. He suffered a torn ACL at the end of his first season with the Saints, and was later released.

After his release from New Orleans, he signed a deal with the Raiders and was forced to bide his time as a special teamer and backup safety for a couple of seasons until finally in 2019 he was promoted to starter after teammate Jonathan Abram sustained an injury. When finally provided a legitimate opportunity to participate in meaningful starting reps, he excelled and put up the most productive season of his professional career.

Harris' most productive seasons in the CFL and NFL were the 2015 and 2019 seasons respectively. The graphics on the following pages depict his statistics and league rankings for those seasons.

MOST PRODUCTIVE SEASON
ERIK HARRIS

★★★★★★★★★★★

YEAR	2015
GP	18
TACKLES	41
TCK/GM	2.28
INT	2
INT/GM	0.11
INT TD	1
RANK	25TH

HARRIS

41

46.5
PRODUCTION RATING

LOW AVERAGE

MOST PRODUCTIVE SEASON
ERIK HARRIS

★★★★★★★★★★★★

YEAR	2019
GP	16
TACKLES	64
TCK/GM	4.00
INT	3
INT/GM	0.19
INT TD	2
RANK	6TH

HARRIS

25

73.1
PRODUCTION RATING

ABOVE AVERAGE

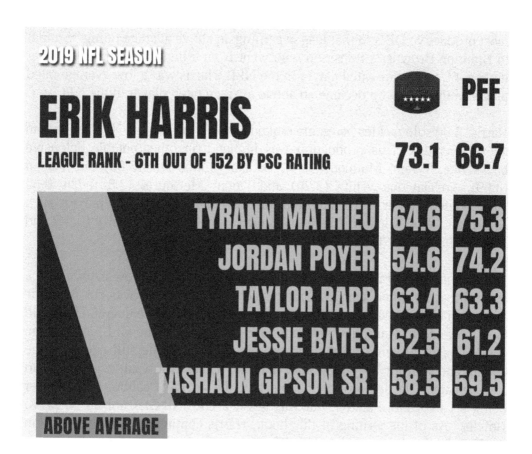

Harris' performance on the field during the 2019 season was comparable to Jordan Poyer, Taylor Rapp, Jessie Bates, Tashaun Gipson Sr and Tyrann Mathieu. His PSC rating was high enough to land him as the 6th most productive DB in the NFL. If we considered only safetys, he ranked number 2 on the list, only behind Minkah Fitzpatrick.

During his most productive NFL season, he made 3 interceptions and was able to return 2 of them for touchdowns. His 145 interception return yards were 2nd most in the NFL, only behind Marcus Peters. He was one of only 5 players in the NFL who ended the season with more than 100 interception return yards. His 2 interception return touchdowns also ranked him tied with Stephon Gilmore for 2nd most in the league. He was named to the "PFF NFL Week 8 Team of the Week" during the 2019 season for his performance against the Houston Texans.

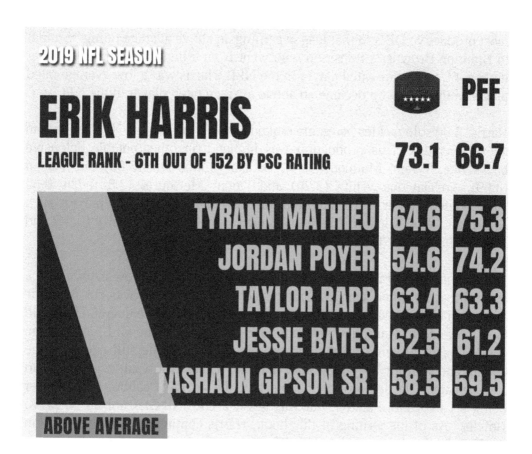

His most productive season in the NFL saw him improve on his best CFL numbers in every relevant metric. While his best season in the CFL saw him rated low average where he ended up as the 25th most productive DB in the league, he was able to transition to the NFL and end up as one of the top 10 most productive DB's in that league earning an above average rating. Similar to Brandon Browner's transition who went from a high average rated player in the CFL to an elite rated player in the NFL, Harris was a low average rated player in the CFL who became an above average rated player in the NFL.

Harris' 4.00 solo tackles per game ranked him 23rd best in the NFL rating him above average. This production was higher than other notable defensive backs like: Tyrann Mathieu (3.94), Ha Ha Clinton-Dix (3.88), Joe Haden (3.69), Tre'Davious White (3.20) and Devin McCourty (2.88). His 0.50 passes defended per game rated him high average and equal to players such as Adrian Amos, Ricardo Allen, and superior to Devin McCourty (0.44) and Ha Ha Clinton Dix (0.31).

After seeing what Erik Harris was capable of in the NFL, now imagine for a second that no other team was interested in him after he was cut from the Saints. Had the Raiders not taken a chance on him he more than likely would have returned to Hamilton and continued his career in the CFL; labelled an "NFL reject". Even after the Raiders picked him up, he still needed to be patient and wait for his opportunity that only came as a result of an injury to a teammate. He demonstrated himself to be an NFL calibre starter, after being a CFL calibre starter, but was never a CFL All-Star nor an NFL Pro Bowler. As of the writing of this book, Harris continues to ply his trade in the NFL having just completed his 7th season, now with the Atlanta Falcons.

Although it may be getting old at this point, perhaps you have started noticing a trend among all these scenarios.

"A player is who he is"

CAMERON WAKE

UNDRAFTED FREE AGENT

MIAMI DOLPHINS

"There are a lot of guys up there who could play the game, who could definitely make it down here, but a lot of guys AREN'T GETTING THE OPPORTUNITY"

CAMERON WAKE[81]

In my opinion, Cameron Wake is the ultimate modern day CFL to NFL success story. He played high level collegiate football at Penn State University, and was a three year starter. During his college career Wake recorded 191 tackles (118 solo), with 24 tackles for loss, 8.5 sacks, two forced fumbles, two fumble recoveries and one interception.[82] I will be comparing his 2005 NFL combine results with another notable linebacker from the same draft class; Shawne Merriman.

Cameron Wake	Shawne Merriman
Height:6'3"	Height: 6'4"
Weight: 236lbs	Weight: 272lbs
40 yard dash: 4.65	40 yard dash: 4.68
20 yard shuttle: 4.13	20 yard shuttle: 4.21
Vertical Jump: 45.5	Vertical Jump: 40.0
Broad jump: 10'10"	Broad jump: 10"1"
Bench press: 20	Bench press: 25
PSC Rating: 95.0	**PSC Rating: 96.9**

As is evident by his PSC rating, Wake's combine performance conclusively demonstrated that he had freakish explosion. His 45 1/2" vertical and 10'10" broad jump ranked him 2nd and 5th among all players tested at all positions; A trait that would later in his career be demonstrated on the field as one of the most explosive first steps in football. Wake was 0.03 seconds faster in the 40, 0.08 seconds faster in the 20 yard shuttle, jumped 5 1/2" higher in the vertical jump, and broad jumped 9" farther than Merriman. In the end, Merriman's 96.9 PSC Rating ended up only 1.9 points higher than Wake's 95.0, mainly due to being taller, heavier and benching 5 more reps of 225lbs. From an athleticism standpoint, both players were extremely comparable. Unfortunately for Wake, he only weighed 236lbs at the time, compared to Merriman's 272lbs. Wake's lack of prototypical outside linebacker or defensive end weight was likely enough to scare away all 32 NFL teams. Shawne Merriman ended up being drafted in the 1st round of the 2005 NFL draft, and Wake went undrafted.

He got a brief opportunity with the New York Giants in 2005 but was cut and after having no more NFL opportunities, ended up leaving football to work as a mortgage broker and personal trainer. They say a picture is worth a thousand words, and if that is true, I would say a video is worth a thousand pictures. I highly recommend watching a short video that Wake posted on his own YouTube channel which depicts a little snapshot of how driven and absolutely determined he was to excel.[83]

After watching his illustrious NFL career unfold over the following decade, it is unfathomable to consider that one of the greatest defensive players of his generation almost did not play professional football. He was a CFL All-Star turned potential NFL Hall of Famer, but today could just as easily be; Cameron Wake: experienced mortgage broker and financial planner. Believe it or not, there is a very thin line separating those two extremes.

What is most remarkable about Cameron's football journey, and not necessarily unique to Cameron but seen time and time again in the lives of many different players is that there were so many variables along the way that permitted his career trajectory, and multiple points along the way that could have ended his career before it even really began. Before he ever signed a contract and played a single professional snap, he attended the wrong university for his BC Lions tryout thus missing it completely. This fact alone could have ended his career before it even started, but he had the good fortune of still being invited to the BC Lions training camp as a result of his college game film; Thank you Wally Buono! Had he attended BC's training camp and not impressed immediately he would have been cut and that would likely have been the end of his pro career. Had he not cut out all distractions, focused on football, and played "lights out" in the CFL, he would likely have never been afforded another NFL opportunity, and would have either continued in the CFL or would have been cut, returning to the corporate world once again. Had he chosen a different NFL team to sign with, one that had a system that did not fit his skill set or that had big names ahead of him on the depth chart in their prime, he would likely have been cut; NFL career ended, back to the "bush league" in Canada. Had he signed with Miami a few seasons earlier when Joey Porter and Jason Taylor still had some good football left in them, Cameron would have been buried on the depth chart likely never to see any significant game time. Eventually cut and labelled "just not talented enough to play in the NFL".

In short, there were so many situations that Cameron (and virtually every professional player) had to overcome to get to where he did that his lack of initial success was more a product of his environment than his talent and ability.

Cameron Wake played in the CFL from 2007 to 2008, and later transitioned to the NFL where he played from 2009-2019. During that time he posted the following career statistics:

CFL	**NFL**
Games Played - 36	Games Played - 155
Solo Tackles - 131	Solo Tackles - 281
Tackles/Game - 3.64	Tackles/Game - 1.81
Sacks - 39	Sacks - 100.5
Sacks/Game - 1.08	Sacks/Game - 0.65
Forced Fumbles - 8	Forced Fumbles - 22

During his most productive CFL season he was rated elite and was the most productive front seven defender in the league. He recorded 3.39 solo tackles per game and 23 total sacks at a rate of 1.28 sacks per game in 2008. His play in the CFL technically wasn't comparable to any other player that season. His production rating of 95.4 was leaps and bounds above the next most productive pass rusher; team mate Aaron Hunt who's production rating was 55.2. As a matter of fact, Wake's dominance was such that it allowed the BC Lions defence to put up 68 sacks collectively; a full 23 sacks more than their next closest rival the Winnipeg Blue Bombers who managed 45 sacks as a team. As the expression goes, he was a one man wrecking crew. As a result he received the richest CFL to NFL contract in recent history, signing a four-year deal for $4.9 million with $1 million guaranteed when he went from the BC Lions to the Miami Dolphins in 2009.

If we were to compare Wake's most productive season (2010) to Shawne Merriman's most productive season (2006), we observe the following:

Cameron Wake	**Shawne Merriman**
GP: 16	GP: 12
Solo Tackles: 48	Solo Tackles: 49
Tackles/Game: 3.00	Tackles/Game: 4.08
Sacks: 14.0	Sacks: 17.0
Sacks/Game: 0.88	Sacks/Game: 1.41
Forced Fumbles: 3	Forced Fumbles: 4

While it is clear that Merriman's most productive single season was more productive than Wake's, especially if broken down on a per game basis, even still, the difference between them is far smaller than the casual fan would expect to see between a 1st round NFL draft pick and an undrafted CFL ex-pat. Over the course of their NFL careers Wake eventually overtook Merriman in virtually every relevant metric. Wake played 11 seasons to Merriman's 8, made 100 1/2 sacks to Merriman's 45 1/2, made 362 tackles to Merriman's 258, and had 22 forced fumbles to Merriman's 8.

Merriman's most productive pass rushing consecutive seasons were 2005-2007 where he recorded 39 1/2 sacks in a span of 42 games at a rate of 0.94 sacks per game. In contrast, Wake's most productive pass rushing consecutive seasons were 2010-2012 where over the course of 48 games he recorded 37 sacks at a rate of 0.77 sacks per game. Keep in mind that Wake was 28 and 29 years old over this period of time, in sharp contrast to Merriman having done it at 21 and 22 years of age; at roughly the same time that Wake was working a regular 9-5 job! Any way you choose to look at it, Cameron Wake was not a player who was vastly inferior to Shawne Merriman.

Wake's most productive seasons in the CFL and NFL were the 2008 and 2010 seasons respectively. The graphics on the following pages depict his statistics and league rankings for those seasons.

MOST PRODUCTIVE SEASON
CAMERON WAKE

★ ★ ★ ★ ★ ★ ★ ★ ★ ★ ★

YEAR	2008
GP	18
TACKLES	61
TCK/GM	3.39
SACKS	23.0
SCK/GM	1.28
FF	5
RANK	1ST

WAKE

91

95.4
PRODUCTION RATING

ELITE

MOST PRODUCTIVE SEASON
CAMERON WAKE

★★★★★★★★★★

YEAR	2010
GP	16
TACKLES	48
TCK/GM	3.00
SACKS	14.0
SCK/GM	0.88
FF	3
RANK	6TH

WAKE

91

86.1
PRODUCTION RATING

ABOVE AVERAGE

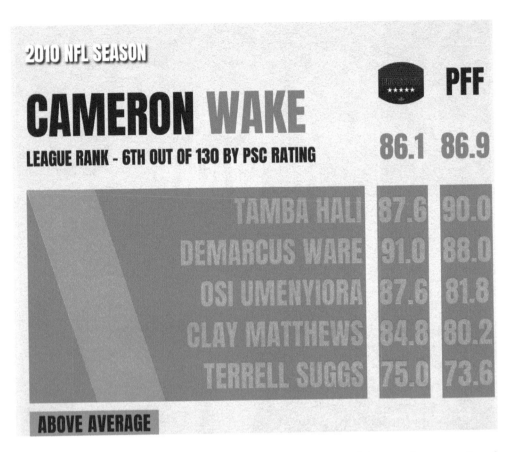

2010 NFL SEASON

CAMERON WAKE

LEAGUE RANK - 6TH OUT OF 130 BY PSC RATING

PFF

86.1 86.9

TAMBA HALI	87.6	90.0
DEMARCUS WARE	91.0	88.0
OSI UMENYIORA	87.6	81.8
CLAY MATTHEWS	84.8	80.2
TERRELL SUGGS	75.0	73.6

ABOVE AVERAGE

Wake's performance during the 2010 NFL season put him on the same level of production as players like Demarcus Ware, Tamba Hali, Clay Matthews, Terrell Suggs, and Osi Umenyiora. The chart above compares his PSC and PFF Overall Grade to theirs.

A 2010 article from Bleacher Report[84] had him ranked as the number 1 pass rusher in the NFL.

A Pro Football Focus article titled *"PFF All-Decade Top 101: The best NFL players from the 2010s"* ranked Wake as the 41st best player of the decade among all positions stating *"Wake was one of the most devastating speed-rushers the league has ever seen"*[85] Also according to PFF, on a list of players with the highest pressure percentage during the decade (2010-2019), Wake ended up second only to Von Miller and ahead of beasts like Aaron Donald and Joey Bosa.[86]

1. Von Miller – 17.0%
2. Cameron Wake – 16.4%
3. Aaron Donald – 15.8%
4. Joey Bosa – 15.7%

He was selected to the Pro Bowl 5 times, and voted to the NFL Top 100 player list 6 times. As of writing, he was one of only 60 players in NFL history to have registered over 100 career sacks. If we compare his sacks per game ratio to other players among these 60 most elite pass rushers, Wake's career 0.65 sacks per game ratio landed him tied for 30th – **ALL-TIME.** His NFL career sacks per game ratio of 0.65 ends up ahead of players such as Robert Mathis (0.64), Cameron Jordan (0.60), Julius Peppers (0.60), Jason Taylor (0.60), Dwight Freeney (0.58) and Terrell Suggs (0.57). Consider for a second that Wake began his NFL career at 27 years of age, in sharp contrast to many who start playing in the NFL after being drafted as young as 21-22. Had he been drafted in 2005, he would have played 5 professional seasons by age 27. In that case, had he been able to play at his demonstrated rate of production we can extrapolate that his career could have ended with 146 sacks, which would have ranked him in the top 10 ALL-TIME!

Although Wake's most productive season overall was the 2010 season, he reached double digit sacks 5 times in 10 seasons and had a career high 15 sacks during the 2012 season. He was never able to equal his CFL best 1.28 sacks per game ratio while in the NFL, however his 1.00 and 0.94 sacks per game ratios for the 2015 and 2012 seasons respectively came reasonably close and in fact were higher than his first CFL season where he recorded 16 sacks in 18 games at a rate of 0.89 sacks per game. Even with the knowledge that Wake was a part of the absolute upper echelon of all professional football, compare the best metrics of his career side by side, and we see that even still...

"A player is who he is"

NFL	CFL
Solo Tackles/Game Ratio: 3.00 (2010)	Solo Tackles/Game Ratio: 3.89 (2007)
Sacks: 15 (2012)	Sacks: 23 (2008)
Sacks per game: 1.00 (2015)	Sacks per game: 1.28 (2008)
Forced Fumbles: 5 (2016)	Forced Fumbles: 5 (2008)
Forced Fumbles/Game: 0.57 (2015)	Forced Fumbles/Game: 0.28 (2008)

Wake is a perfect example of one of those elite players that were in their own class of the NFL. He was one of those athletic freaks that I previously described who was in possession of the complete football pentagon. This was made clear by his play on either side of the border as Wake was a player that quite honestly tore the CFL apart and was virtually unstoppable in the process. The transition down to the NFL did not slow him down very much and as we just read, his name stands next to players like Von Miller over the course of a decade of work.

As we have discussed before, even a player like Wake who was one of the most elite of his generation could have never even played professional football! Just think about what would have happened if he hadn't been given an opportunity with the BC Lions? We would never have heard his name and would never have been privileged to watch such a force dominate offensive linemen across all of North America. He was able to "fit the mold" required for an NFL defensive end upon his arrival in the NFL, and gained weight from a CFL playing weight of 241 pounds to an NFL playing weight of 263 pounds, all while never losing that elite explosive first step quickness.

One can only imagine what Wake could have accomplished in the NFL had he been playing professional football since his draft year. However, the setbacks and roadblocks along the way definitely helped shape him not only into the player he ultimately became, but the man he became as well. Wake became an example of pure perseverance, and once again opened the eyes of the NFL to the elite talent that plays football in the CFL.

CASSIUS
VAUGHN

UNDRAFTED FREE AGENT

INDIANAPOLIS COLTS

CASSIUS VAUGHN

Cassius Vaughn played his collegiate football at Ole Miss in the SEC. Vaughn's final NCAA season with the Rebels in 2009 saw him make: 56 tackles (44 solo) with 2 interceptions for 31 interception return yards. This production was very comparable to fellow SEC alum; Alabama's Kareem Jackson. Jackson ended his 2009 season having made 49 tackles (30 solo) with 1 interception for 79 interception return yards. By the conclusion of Vaughn's NCAA career he had amassed 104 solo tackles, 1 sack, 1 forced fumble, along with 5 interceptions for 57 interception return yards. Contrast this production to Kareem Jackson's NCAA career which ended with 102 solo tackles, 0 sacks, 1 forced fumble, 5 interceptions for 164 interception return yards and we have to conclude that Cassius Vaughn was a productive player at the SEC level.

Cassius Vaughn	**Kareem Jackson**
Games Played - 40	Games Played - 33
Solo Tackles - 104	Solo Tackles - 102
Tackles/Game – 2.60	Tackles/Game – 3.09
Interceptions - 5	Interceptions - 5
Interceptions/Game – 0.13	Interceptions/Game – 0.15
Interception Return Yards - 57	Interception Return Yards - 164
Interception TD - 0	Interception TD - 0
Sacks - 1	Sacks - 0
Forced Fumbles - 1	Forced Fumbles – 1
PSC Rating – 81.5	**PSC Rating – 80.1**

Comparing their college careers side by side, it is obvious that both players were fairly equal from a production standpoint with Cassius Vaughn ending his NCAA career with a PSC rating of 81.5 compared to Kareem Jackson's NCAA career PSC rating of 80.1. There was essentially nothing separating these two athletes who both played against the same top competition in the SEC. Kareem Jackson was invited to the NFL Scouting combine where he ran a 4.48 40 yard dash, and Cassius Vaughn was limited to running the 40 at his Pro Day at Ole Miss where he ripped a blistering 4.34.

Despite playing productively in college, Vaughn went undrafted in the 2010 NFL Draft while Kareem Jackson was taken in the 1st round 20th overall. He was later signed as an undrafted free agent with the Denver Broncos and ended up playing in the NFL from 2010-2015, later transitioning to the CFL where he played from 2016 to 2018. During that time he posted the following career statistics:

NFL	**CFL**
Games Played - 68	Games Played - 33
Solo Tackles - 125	Solo Tackles - 82
Tackles/Game - 1.83	Tackles/Game - 2.48
Passes Defended - 25	Interceptions - 5
Passes Defended/Game - 0.36	Interceptions/Game - 0.15
Interceptions - 7	Interception Return Yards - 209
Interceptions/Game - 0.10	Interception TD - 1
Interception Return Yards - 137	Forced Fumbles – 1
Interception TD - 2	
Forced Fumbles - 2	

Vaughn was used sparingly in Denver his rookie season and only saw limited action on defence, mostly relegated to playing special teams. He showed flashes of elite potential on specials where he returned a kickoff 97 yards for a touchdown against the San Diego Chargers. This return was the third longest play in Broncos history and the second longest by an undrafted rookie in NFL history. However, it wasn't until he was traded to the Indianapolis Colts that he finally got an opportunity to play meaningful starting reps at corner.

Upon being acquired by his new team, Colts GM Ryan Grigson had this to say about him: *"Cassius is a young cornerback who brings game experience at his position, proven kickoff return ability and pure speed to the Colts. He's a player who can really run and when you turn on the film you instantly recognize his athletic ability and speed. He's a guy who has not hit his ceiling as a player yet and we saw some really encouraging things on tape that led us to the trade."*[87]

Vaughn ultimately started at corner in his first season in Indianapolis and ended up playing the most productive season of his NFL career in Colts blue and white. He was named AFC Player of the Week in week 14 for his defensive performance against the Tennessee Titans where he had 1 interception which he returned for a touchdown, 8 tackles and 3 passes defended.[88] Interestingly, with that interception Vaughn joined former Detroit Lions cornerback Alvin Hall as one of only two undrafted players in NFL history to return a kickoff and interception for a touchdown in their careers.

Vaughn's most productive seasons in the NFL and CFL were the 2012 and 2017 seasons respectively. The graphics on the following pages depict his statistics and league rankings for those seasons.

MOST PRODUCTIVE SEASON
CASSIUS VAUGHN

★★★★★★★★★★★

YEAR	2012
GP	16
TACKLES	58
TCK/GM	3.63
INT	1
INT/GM	0.06
INT TD	1
RANK	71ST

VAUGHN

32

47.3
PRODUCTION RATING

HIGH AVERAGE

MOST PRODUCTIVE SEASON
CASSIUS VAUGHN

★★★★★★★★★★★★

YEAR	2017
GP	16
TACKLES	32
TCK/GM	2.00
INT	5
INT/GM	0.31
INT TD	1
RANK	5TH

84.4
PRODUCTION RATING

ABOVE AVERAGE

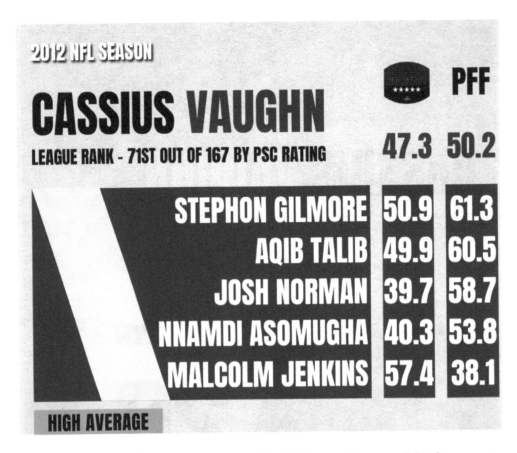

CASSIUS VAUGHN

LEAGUE RANK - 71ST OUT OF 167 BY PSC RATING

PFF

47.3 50.2

STEPHON GILMORE	50.9	61.3
AQIB TALIB	49.9	60.5
JOSH NORMAN	39.7	58.7
NNAMDI ASOMUGHA	40.3	53.8
MALCOLM JENKINS	57.4	38.1

HIGH AVERAGE

Vaughn's most productive season in the NFL saw him rated high average, ending the season as the 71st most productive DB out of 167 rated. His production was comparable to Malcolm Jenkins (35th), Stephon Gilmore (56th), Aqib Talib (59th), Nnamdi Asomugha (94th), and Josh Norman (97th).

Vaughn's PSC rating of 47.3 was average in this group of players. He allowed 66 receptions on 106 targets that season for an allowed catch rate of 62.2%. This rate was better than Josh Norman (67.5%), Malcolm Jenkins (67.4%), Nnamdi Asomugha (66.6%) and Aqib Talib (66.6%). The only player in this group with a better allowed catch rate was Stephon Gilmore at 56.3%.

Vaughn's 9 passes defended at a rate of 0.56 passes defended per game was on par with Earl Thomas III, and Champ Bailey. This production was superior to such players as: Prince Amukamara (0.54) and Josh Norman (0.44).

He spent two seasons with Indianapolis eventually signing a one year contract with the Detroit Lions before closing out his NFL career. He spent parts of 2015 with the Baltimore Ravens and San Diego Chargers. It was at that point, with no further NFL opportunities available that he signed with the Hamilton Tiger-Cats, playing parts of 9 games with the team before being released in early 2017.

Vaughn was subsequently signed by the Toronto Argonauts after his release from Hamilton. It was with the Argonauts that he was finally able to get real playing time on defence in the CFL and ultimately recorded the most productive season of his entire professional career.

Vaughn's performance for the 2017 CFL season was good enough to be rated above average. He ended the season as the 5th most productive DB out of 36 rated, behind Chris Randle (4th), TJ Heath (3rd), Richard Leonard (2nd), and Ed Gainey (1st). His 5 interceptions put him in a 4-way tie for 3rd best in the CFL with Ciante Evans, TJ Heath, and Chris Randle. His 0.31 interceptions per game was good for 4th best in the CFL only behind Richard Leonard (0.39), Mitchell White (0.50) and Ed Gainey (0.56).

The 2017 CFL season was not only the most productive of Vaughn's career, but it also culminated with his first professional championship victory. A victory that was won in no small part, thanks to Vaughn making a clutch fumble recovery and return for a touchdown. Vaughn's Toronto Argonauts were down 24-16 with only 4:57 left to play in the 4th quarter. Their opponents, the mighty Calgary Stampeders, had been the best team in the CFL that year and were in possession of the ball at the Argo 8 yard line facing a 1st and goal. Had Calgary managed to score a touchdown at that point they would have been up 31-16 and would have been able to essentially put the game to bed. But it was at that precise moment that Vaughn came up huge with a Grey Cup record 109 yard fumble recovery returned for a touchdown that allowed the Argos to tie the game and swung the game's momentum ultimately out of Calgary's reach.

Despite having the overall most productive season of his professional career while in the CFL, a closer look at his career best numbers in either league shows us that while his CFL career improved on the metrics recorded during his NFL career, even still, the change is not as dramatic as his most productive single seasons in each league would imply.

We can see his most productive individual metrics on the following page:

NFL	CFL
Solo Tackles – 58 (2012)	Solo Tackles – 32 (2017)
Tackles/Game – 3.63 (2012)	Tackles/Game – 3.00 (2018)
Interceptions – 3 (2013)	Interceptions – 5 (2017)
Interceptions/Game – 0.19 (2013)	Interceptions/Game – 0.31 (2017)
Interception Return Yards – 70 (2014)	Interception Return Yards – 209 (2017)
Interception TD – 1 (2012)	Interception TD – 1 (2017)
Forced Fumbles – 2 (2013)	Forced Fumbles – 1 (2018)

In the NFL his 3.63 solo tackles per game was higher than his CFL best 3.00 solo tackles per game recorded during the 2018 season, although very comparable. Similarly, his career best 5 interceptions at 0.31 interceptions per game recorded during his most productive CFL season was his best, but again, not worlds apart from his NFL best 3 interceptions at 0.19 interceptions per game during the 2013 NFL season.

Vaughn is an example of a player who was a high average rated NFL DB that was able to adapt to the CFL game, become an impact player, and ultimately play at an above average level as one of the best DB's in the league. Even still, through it all we can still see elements of the phrase in action:

"A player is who he is"

JUMAL
ROLLE

UNDRAFTED FREE AGENT

HOUSTON TEXANS

"CFL talent is REALLY COMPETITIVE. Relatively similar to NFL in skills positions"

JUMAL ROLLE[89]

Jumal Rolle was an NCAA division II standout at Catawba College. A Bleacher Report article from 2013 described him as follows: *"Jumal Rolle is a 5'11", 187 pound cornerback from Catawba College. In 2012, Rolle had 56 tackles to go with six interceptions, two fumble recoveries and 10 passes broken up. He has also blocked four punts. Rolle has been all over the field as a senior and the numbers show how good he has been. Rolle is an outstanding athlete with great coverage and ball skills. He is a natural play maker who can alter the game in many ways. Like most small-school prospects, there are going to be questions about the lack of quality competition that Rolle sees on a weekly basis"*[90]

Rolle's division II career proved he was an instinctive ball hawk, ending his time at Catawba with a total of 16 interceptions, an impressive number any way you slice it. He attended Wake Forest for his pro day where he recorded a 4.5 40 yard dash time, a 36" vertical jump, and bench pressed 225lbs a total of 17 reps.[91] Had Rolle been invited to the 2013 NFL combine, this is how he would have stacked up from an athleticism standpoint against top NCAA competition: Out of 36 participating DB's, his 4.5 40 yard dash time would have ranked him 18th, tied with LSU Corner Tyrann Mathieu. His 36" vertical jump would have ranked him 9th, tied with Alabama's Dee Milliner, and his 17 reps on the bench press would have ranked him tied for 2nd.

As a matter of fact, comparing Jumal Rolle and Tyrann Mathieu side by side, it quickly becomes evident who is the more athletic of the two.

Jumal Rolle	Tyrann Mathieu
Height:5'11"	Height:5'9"
Weight: 188	Weight: 186
40 yard dash: 4.50	40 yard dash: 4.50
Vertical Jump: 36"	Vertical Jump: 34"
Bench Press: 17	Bench Press: 4

Isn't the NFL supposed to be "bigger, faster, stronger"? Looking at these two spectacular athletes side by side, the only difference I can see is that one played with the letters "L-S-U" on the side of his helmet, and the other a "C" from the lowly second division. Rolle's Coach at Catawba, Chip Hester had this to say about Rolle: *"He's a legit prospect...We've had about 20 NFL teams come in and check him out. It's hard to find corners that have some size but can still move like Jumal moves. And he's really good running down on special teams. That's another big plus for him."*[92]

Not only did Jumal Rolle look the part, but he played the part as well. His on-field play was outstanding, and his demonstrated athleticism was on par with numerous players who ended up going in the early rounds of the NFL Draft, and who went on to enjoy lengthy and productive careers in the NFL. Sadly, the "lack of quality competition" Rolle played against in division II raised enough questions to have all 32 NFL teams decide he wasn't worth a draft pick. He signed with the Buffalo Bills as an undrafted free agent and spent the off season with the team, but was released prior to the start of the season. He then signed with and was released by the New Orleans Saints and Green Bay Packers, before ultimately getting his first playing time after signing with the Houston Texans.

Jumal Rolle played in the NFL from 2014-2015, and then in the CFL from 2018 -2022. During that time he posted the following career statistics:

NFL	CFL
Games Played - 19	Games Played - 65
Solo Tackles - 18	Solo Tackles - 150
Tackles/Game - 0.95	Tackles/Game - 2.30
Passes Defended - 4	Interceptions - 11
Passes Defended/Game - 0.21	Interceptions/Game - 0.17
Interceptions - 3	Interception Return Yards - 287
Interceptions/Game - 0.16	Interception TD - 2
Interception Return Yards - 25	Forced Fumbles – 0
Interception TD - 0	
Forced Fumbles – 0	

His best statistical seasons in the NFL and CFL were the 2014 and 2019 seasons respectively. The graphics on the following pages depict his statistics and league rankings for those seasons.

MOST PRODUCTIVE SEASON
JUMAL ROLLE

★★★★★★ ★★★★

YEAR	2014
GP	10
TACKLES	17
TCK/GM	1.70
INT	3
INT/GM	0.30
KD/GM	0.40
RANK	132ND

32.7
PRODUCTION RATING

LOW AVERAGE

MOST PRODUCTIVE SEASON
JUMAL ROLLE

★★★★★★★★★★★★

YEAR	2019
GP	18
TACKLES	32
TCK/GM	1.78
INT	5
INT/GM	0.28
KD/GM	0.39
RANK	10TH

ROLLE

25

55.0
PRODUCTION RATING

HIGH AVERAGE

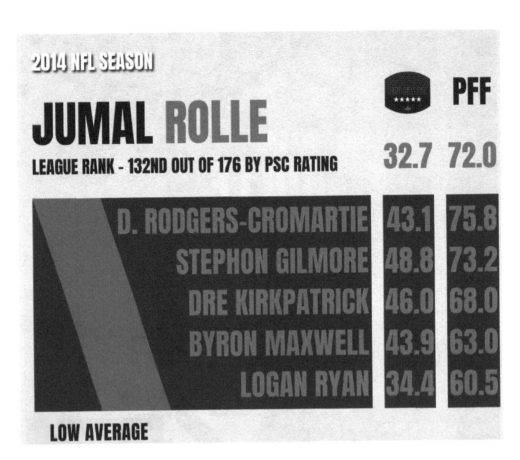

2014 NFL SEASON

JUMAL ROLLE

PFF

LEAGUE RANK - 132ND OUT OF 176 BY PSC RATING

32.7 72.0

D. RODGERS-CROMARTIE	43.1	75.8
STEPHON GILMORE	48.8	73.2
DRE KIRKPATRICK	46.0	68.0
BYRON MAXWELL	43.9	63.0
LOGAN RYAN	34.4	60.5

LOW AVERAGE

Rolle's play during the 2014 season earned him a PSC Rating of 32.7 which rated him low average as the 132nd most productive DB in the NFL out of 176. Although he was less productive overall than the above mentioned players by PSC Rating, his PFF overall grade actually compared very favourably to all the above mentioned players landing him 3rd highest in the group. Rolle's grade was higher than Dre Kirkpatrick, Byron Maxwell and Logan Ryan.

Rolle's 3 interceptions in 10 games represented an interception per game ratio of 0.30, which was rated above average and good for 14th best in the NFL. This ratio was higher than, but comparable to: Aqib Talib (17th, 0.27/gm), Charles Woodson (27th, 0.25/gm) and Richard Sherman (28th, 0.25/gm). Rolle's passes defended per game ratio of 0.40 ranked him 101st out of 176 and was comparable to: Micah Hyde (93rd, 0.44/gm), Ha Ha Clinton-Dix (121st 0.38/gm), and Tyrann Mathieu (137th, 0.31/gm).

If we once again compare Jumal Rolle to Tyrann Mathieu, this time evaluating their on-field performance for the 2014 NFL season we observe the following:

196

Jumal Rolle	**Tyrann Mathieu**
GP: 10	GP: 13
Solo Tackles: 17	Solo Tackles: 35
Tackle/Game: 1.70	Tackle/Game: 2.69
Passes Defended: 4	Passes Defended: 4
PD/Game: 0.40	PD/Game: 0.31
Interceptions: 3	Interceptions: 1
INT/Game: 0.30	INT/Game: 0.08
INT Return Yards: 25	INT Return Yards: 9
Allowed Catch Rate: 69.5%	Allowed Catch Rate: 72.4%
PFF Overall Grade: 72.0	PFF Overall Grade: 68.5
PSC Rating: 32.7	**PSC Rating: 26.1**
League Rank: 132nd out of 182 rated	League Rank: 150th out of 182 rated

Keep in mind that Tyrann Mathieu went on to become a 3 time First Team All-Pro, while Rolle went on to be released and eventually signed in the CFL. Two players who were equally athletic, with relatively comparable production over the small playing window observed above ultimately ended up with two very different outcomes. Based on the objective metrics we have observed, how can anyone logically conclude anything besides the fact Jumal Rolle was a highly talented cornerback that possessed elite athleticism and football intelligence? These are not opinions; they are facts, backed by data.

Rolle is an example of a player that was able to perform in the NFL despite his division II pedigree and very limited playing time. He showed obvious talent and ability during his short NFL career, but unfortunately despite showing that promise fell prey to the numbers game when he was released by Houston to make room for the team to sign QB Brandon Weeden. Upon his release from the Texans he signed with the Baltimore Ravens shortly thereafter and spent the 2015 season on the team's practice squad. He later suffered a torn achilles tendon and as a result was forced to miss the entire 2016 season. Sadly, he did not get another opportunity in the NFL after that.

While his play in the CFL during his most productive season saw a substantial improvement in PSC rating compared to his time in the NFL, (CFL PSC Rating of 55.0 vs NFL PSC Rating of 32.7) if we take a closer look at his metrics, we can see that Rolle's performance between both leagues was actually very comparable. His NFL tackles per game ratio of 1.70 is remarkably similar to his 1.78 tackles per game ratio in the CFL. His NFL interception per game ratio of 0.30 was also virtually identical to his CFL interception per game ratio of 0.28. Even his NFL passes defended per game ratio of 0.40 was a mirror image of his CFL best 0.39.

Just as Tyrann Mathieu improved over the course of his career, it would make sense that most players who are given lots of playing time will do the same, Jumal Rolle would have been no exception. Phillip Daniels; Defensive Line Coach for the Philadelphia Eagles made this insightful statement: *"I know a lot of guys go to the CFL because they are overlooked and you've heard success stories about them —years later they become stars."*[93]

Jumal Rolle was one of those players that against all odds was able to work toward CFL stardom, ultimately becoming an elite player. Make no mistake, had he continued to be provided opportunities in the NFL he would very likely have matured into a good to great player in that league. Unfortunately we will never know for sure, but there is one thing we do know:

"A player is who he is"

JONATHAN
NEWSOME

5TH ROUND NFL DRAFT PICK

INDIANAPOLIS COLTS

JONATHAN NEWSOME

Jonathan Newsome split his time in college playing between Ohio State and Ball State. He ended his 4 year college career with modest production, having made 134 total tackles (57 solo), 16.5 sacks, 1 forced fumble and 1 interception. His final college season in 2013 was his most productive. That season saw him make 64 total tackles (24 solo), 8.0 sacks, 1 forced fumble and 1 interception. I will be comparing his final college season and combine performance to another notable outside linebacker from the same draft class; Kyle Van Noy.

Jonathan Newsome	**Kyle Van Noy**
Games Played - 11	Games Played - 11
Total Tackles - 57	Solo Tackles - 55
Tackles/Game – 5.18	Tackles/Game – 5.00
Sacks – 8.0	Sacks – 4.0
Sack/Game – 0.73	Sack/Game – 0.36
Forced Fumbles – 1	Forced Fumbles – 0
PSC Rating – 89.6	**PSC Rating – 77.6**

Although Newsome's final college season was more productive than Van Noy's, their careers were not at all comparable as Van Noy had a far more productive college career in its entirety. Newsome's college career seemed to gain steam at the end which was likely the reason he was invited to attend the 2014 NFL Combine. At the combine Newsome performed at a below average level among 16 players classified as outside linebackers who completed all the required combine drills. Newsome's combine metrics ranked him as the 15th most productive outside linebacker in this group earning him a PSC rating of 87.2 in a group that averaged a rating of 90.1. As such, Newsome's production wasn't out of place. By comparison, Kyle Van Noy only out performed Newsome by 0.2 rating points after earning himself a PSC rating of 87.4 for his combine performance.

Newsome's pre-draft NFL scouting report listed his strengths as: *"Very good edge burst, has a long second step and attacks the edges with speed and leverage, flattens down the line. Good lateral pursuit, can get depth in coverage and spot drop, flashes explosive striking ability as a tackler"*. That same scouting report listed his weaknesses as: *"Strength-deficient and gets hammered in the box, thin-legged and narrow-based, too light to set the edge, limited cover skills. Is tight in the hips and not natural moving in reverse or coming out of breaks, immature early in college career."*[94]

Ultimately, Newsome was drafted by the Indianapolis Colts in the 5th round, 166th overall in the 2014 NFL draft, while Kyle Van Noy was drafted by the Detroit Lions in the 2nd round, 40th overall. All things considered, I would agree that their draft positions were fair relative to each other given their performances at the combine and in college.

Newsome's professional career in the NFL spanned from 2014 to 2015, and he later transitioned to the CFL from 2016-2019. His most productive NFL and CFL seasons were the 2014 and 2017 seasons respectively. The graphics on the following pages depict his performance during those seasons.

MOST PRODUCTIVE SEASON
JONATHAN NEWSOME

★★★★★★★ ★★

YEAR	2014
GP	16
TACKLES	21
TCK/GM	1.31
SACKS	6.5
SCK/GM	0.41
FF	3
RANK	62ND

NEWSOME

91

39.6
PRODUCTION RATING

HIGH AVERAGE

MOST PRODUCTIVE SEASON
JONATHAN NEWSOME

★★★★★★★★★★★

YEAR	2017
GP	10
TACKLES	14
TCK/GM	1.40
SACKS	4.0
SCK/GM	0.40
FF	1
RANK	36TH

NEWSOME

43

42.8
PRODUCTION RATING

LOW AVERAGE

JONATHAN NEWSOME

PFF

LEAGUE RANK - 62ND OUT OF 145 BY PSC RATING

39.6 65.3

CLIFF AVRIL	30.7	68.1
CAMERON JORDAN	43.1	66.7
MELVIN INGRAM III	33.5	66.6
DEMARCUS WARE	47.1	66.4
WHITNEY MERCILUS	38.6	64.0

HIGH AVERAGE

Newsome's production during the 2014 NFL season was rated high average. He ended up as the 62nd most productive front seven defender. His production was comparable to Demarcus Ware (35th), Cameron Jordan (52nd), Whitney Mercilus (67th), Melvin Ingram III (89th), and Cliff Avril (103rd) by PSC rating.

Newsome's strengths were on full display during his rookie season in 2014, which ended up being his most productive in the NFL. He was named by PFF as the '2015 Colts' PFF Secret Superstar' after having ranked 12th in the NFL out of all 3-4 outside linebackers in pass rush productivity.[95]

During that first season in the NFL he showed flashes of brilliance recording the second highest sack total of any rookie DE/OLB in the game, proving his production during his final couple of college seasons was no fluke and would translate well to the pro game. Newsome's very first start in the NFL saw him make 8 tackles, 2 sacks and a forced fumble which won him an AFC Defensive Player of the Week honour. Newsome's 1.45% sack per snap percentage was comparable to elite players such as Terrell Suggs (1.44%), Cameron Wake (1.40%) and only slightly behind Von Miller (1.58%)[96]

Newsome's 6.5 sacks in 16 games represented a 0.41 sack per game ratio, which was 54th best out of 145 rated. Here's how that ratio compared to the following notable players.

32nd – Calais Campbell – 0.50 per game (7 sacks in 14 games)
43rd – Julius Peppers – 0.44 per game (7 sacks in 16 games)
46th – Trent Cole – 0.43 per game (6.5 sacks in 15 games)
56th – Olivier Vernon – 0.41 per game (6.5 sacks in 16 games)
63rd – Tamba Hali – 0.38 per game (6.0 sacks in 16 games)
120th – Dwight Freeney – 0.22 per game (3.5 sacks in 16 games)

By comparison, the top three sack per game ratios in the NFL that season were:

1st – Justin Houston – 1.38 per game (22 sacks in 16 games)
2nd – J.J. Watt – 1.28 per game (20.5 sacks in 16 games)
3rd – Elvis Dumervil – 1.06 per game (17 sacks in 16 games)

Maybe even more impressive than his sack per game ratio was his forced fumbles per game ratio of 0.19. This production put him on par with Jason Pierre-Paul, Cameron Wake, Junior Galette and Jerry Hughes; all highly disruptive players, but again still lagged behind NFL leaders Ryan Kerrigan (0.31), Robert Quinn (0.31) and Jamie Collins Sr. (0.27).

Despite his extremely promising first season, the Colts decided to sign Trent Cole and Kendall Langford to bolster their defensive line. Those signings coupled with a still productive Robert Mathis saw Newsome's production significantly decline during his second season. In 2016 he ran into some off-season trouble and was arrested for possession of marijuana, which prompted the Colts to release him shortly thereafter. Unfortunately, despite his physical gifts and highly promising rookie season he did not receive another opportunity in the NFL.

Once he transitioned to the CFL, it is remarkable to note how comparable his pass rush metrics were to his NFL metrics. In 10 games played during the 2017 CFL season, his 0.40 sacks per game ratio was virtually identical to his NFL output, and ranked 19th best in the league. His pass rush productivity in the CFL was comparable to:

15th – Willie Jefferson – 0.44 per game (8 sacks in 18 games)
17th – Craig Roh – 0.44 per game (7 sacks in 16 games)
18th – Almondo Sewell – 0.41 per game (7 sacks in 17 games)

By comparison, the three highest sack per game ratios in the CFL that season were:

1st – Ja'Gared Davis – 0.90 per game (9 sacks in 10 games)
2nd – Victor Butler – 0.83 per game (10 sacks in 12 games)
3rd – Charleston Hughes – 0.79 per game (11 sacks in 14 games)

Newsome was undoubtedly a talented but troubled player. He was yet another example of a player who had remarkably consistent production between both leagues. He ended up mid pack in the NFL and similarly ended up mid pack in the CFL. A highly talented player that was drafted into the NFL and produced in a manner that began to demonstrate how elite he could be, ended up plying his trade in the CFL and producing at a very similar level, despite doing it against supposedly inferior competition.

If we compare his career NFL and CFL metrics side by side, the consistency is clearly visible.

NFL	CFL
Games Played – 30	Games Played – 50
Solo Tackles – 31	Solo Tackles – 64
Tackles/Game – 1.03	Tackles/Game – 1.28
Sacks – 7.5	Sacks – 11.0
Sacks/Game – 0.25	Sacks/Game – 0.22
Forced Fumbles – 5	Forced Fumbles – 2
FF/Game – 0.16	FF/Game – 0.04

Yet again, the slogan is proven true:

"A player is who he is"

TROY SMITH

5TH ROUND NFL DRAFT PICK

SAN FRANCISCO 49ERS

TROY SMITH

Make no mistake about it, Troy Smith was not some "scrub" division III player, but a big-time major college phenomenon. All one has to do is watch highlights from his college film to see that he was an absolute star at the college level. He took over the reins as the starting quarterback of the Ohio State Buckeyes midway through the 2004 season and never looked back. He ended his college career with 420 completions on 670 attempts, at a 62.7% completion rate, with 5,720 passing yards, 54 touchdowns and 13 interceptions. All these numbers added up to a quarterback rating of 108.7 (calculated according to the professional game's formula). Over his career he added another 1,154 yards rushing on 290 attempts at a rate of 4.0 yards per carry with 14 rushing touchdowns.

Smith's final season at Ohio State was one to remember as he had 203 completions on 311 attempts with a completion rate of 65.3%. Add to those numbers 30 passing touchdowns to only 6 interceptions and we get a quarterback rating of 114.7 (pro formula). His performance that season was so good that he went on to ultimately win the Heisman Trophy, which for those that do not know is awarded annually to the most outstanding player in all of college football; certainly no small accomplishment. In addition, he received the following accolades for his performance in the 2006 college football season:

2006 Consensus All American
2006 Sporting News College Football Player of the Year
2006 Fiesta Bowl MVP
2006 Walter Camp Award
2006 Davey O'Brien Award
2006 Buckeyes MVP
2006 Associated Press Player of the Year

He was ranked number 1 on a list of "Big TEN players of the decade" (2000-2009) by Adam Rittenberg, a Senior Writer at ESPN.[97] During his time at Ohio State he was throwing passes to Brian Hartline and Ted Ginn Jr., who themselves enjoyed 7 and 14 season NFL careers respectively. Hartline with 2 back to back 1000 yard seasons with the Miami Dolphins in 2012 and 2013, and Ginn Jr. who over his lengthy career racked up 15,751 all purpose yards. If there was ever a player with a winning pedigree from a major college program who had the talent and all the intangibles to be a star at the pro level, it was Troy Smith.

He was drafted by the Baltimore Ravens in the 5th round of the 2007 NFL draft, 174th overall. He spent 3 seasons with the Ravens but only played sparingly. He was eventually released at which point he signed with the San Francisco 49ers in 2010 where he ended up playing the most productive season of his NFL career. Unfortunately for Troy, despite all the accolades and success he enjoyed at the collegiate level, it just did not translate into lengthy success at the professional level; NFL or later CFL.

Smith played in the NFL from 2007 to 2010 and later transitioned to the CFL for the 2013 and 2014 seasons. The graphics on the following pages depict his statistics and league rankings for his most productive seasons in the NFL and CFL; 2010 and 2013 respectively.

MOST PRODUCTIVE SEASON
TROY SMITH

★★★★★★★★★★★

YEAR	2010
GP	6
COMP	73
ATT	145
YARDS	1176
TD/INT	5/4
QBR	77.8
RANK	37TH

SMITH

1

53.3
PRODUCTION RATING

LOW AVERAGE

MOST PRODUCTIVE SEASON
TROY SMITH

★★★★★★★★★

YEAR	2013
GP	6
COMP	60
ATT	114
YARDS	884
TD/INT	9/5
QBR	86.3
RANK	15TH

SMITH

1

52.1
PRODUCTION RATING

LOW AVERAGE

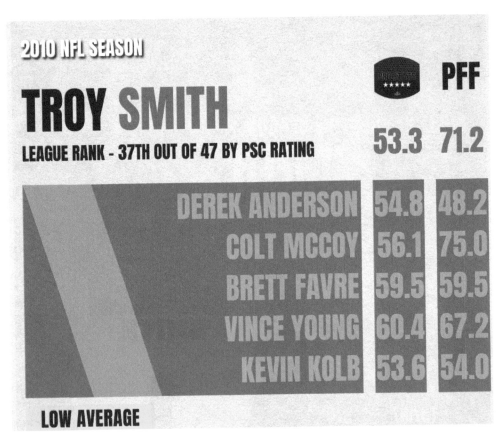

TROY SMITH

LEAGUE RANK - 37TH OUT OF 47 BY PSC RATING

PFF

53.3 71.2

DEREK ANDERSON	54.8	48.2
COLT MCCOY	56.1	75.0
BRETT FAVRE	59.5	59.5
VINCE YOUNG	60.4	67.2
KEVIN KOLB	53.6	54.0

LOW AVERAGE

Troy Smith's performance during his most productive season in the NFL was comparable to Derek Anderson, Colt McCoy, Brett Favre, Vince Young and Kevin Kolb.

Note that of the 6 players we just finished comparing, Troy Smith's NFL career was by far the shortest at only 4 seasons. Vince Young (1ˢᵗ round pick) and Kevin Kolb (2ⁿᵈ round pick) enjoyed 6 year careers, Colt McCoy (3ʳᵈ round pick) continues playing and has thus far enjoyed a 12 year career, and Derek Anderson (6ᵗʰ round pick) played for 13 seasons. Although Smith's final season in the NFL was by far his most productive, no other team was willing to take a chance on him, not even by offering him a backup position which in my opinion was a role he was MORE than qualified to hold.

But that in a nutshell is the NFL; <u>Not For Long.</u> And not just the NFL, but all of professional football for that matter. Smith's 49ers missed the playoffs, fired then Head Coach Mike Singletary and brought in Jim Harbaugh to replace him. With the regime change in San Francisco also came the inevitable roster casualties that so often accompany such a rebuild and Smith became one of them.

During his most productive NFL season his completion percentage was an abysmal 50.3%, rated below average. This ranked him third worst in the entire NFL out of all 47 quarterbacks rated. As a matter of fact, his completion percentage was only better than Tim Tebow (50.0%) and John Skelton (47.6%). These numbers were a far cry from NFL leaders Tony Romo (69.5%), Drew Brees (68.1%) and Peyton Manning (66.3%).

Upon transitioning to the CFL where many would expect him to excel, or at least improve significantly due to the wider field, wider throwing windows and "inferior competition", we observed him to be much the same player he had been in the NFL. His best season completion percentages improved slightly from 50.3% in the NFL to 52.6% in the CFL, although was still rated below average. Despite the small improvement, his CFL completion percentage ranked him second last in the league, only better than Jonathan Crompton (51.7%). Definitely nowhere near CFL leaders Ricky Ray (77.2%) and Bo Levi Mitchell (69.6%).

In the NFL Smith's QBR of 77.8 was rated low average, miles behind league leaders Tom Brady (111.0), Philip Rivers (101.8) and Aaron Rodgers (101.2). During his best CFL season his QBR of 86.3 was similarly low average, also far behind league leaders Ricky Ray (126.4) and Bo Levi Mitchell (111.2).

What we observe from Troy's play on either side of the border was that his production and level of play in the NFL was comparable to a typical NFL backup. Upon transitioning to the CFL, rather than tearing it up as a player with NFL experience and an elite college pedigree, he very similarly produced at a rate comparable to a CFL back up. In fact, his PSC rating of 52.1 in the CFL had him rated as low average and was comparable to Drew Tate (60.1), Thomas DeMarco (53.3), Buck Pierce (47.2), Tanner Marsh (45.9), and Justin Goltz (40.1), all players that were CFL calibre backups, and none of which had experienced the high level of play and success at the college level that he had.

In an interview while with Montreal, Troy was asked "Do you think it takes people some time to realize there is some really good ball played (in the CFL)?" To which he replied: *"Yeah, and I mean it's the dictionary version of just being ignorant and not knowing. You turn on the TV, you come up here and you watch the game and you'll see guys, excuse my language, busting their ass every play."*[98] Troy Smith learned about the quality of play in the CFL first hand. His most relevant point is the simple fact that people are just ignorant of the facts and do not understand that...**"A player is who he is"**

TRE
MASON

3RD ROUND NFL DRAFT PICK

ST. LOUIS RAMS

TRE MASON

Tre Mason played high level college football for the Auburn Tigers in the SEC. Let's begin by listing some of his accomplishments as a collegiate player: Heisman Trophy finalist (2013), SEC champion (2013), SEC Championship Game MVP (2013), SEC Offensive Player of the Year (2013), Second-team All-American (2013), and First-team All-SEC (2013).

During his final season of college football, he finished with 317 carries for 1,816 rushing yards at a rate of 5.7 yards per carry with an astonishing 23 touchdowns. With this incredible season performance he broke Bo Jackson's school record of 1,786 yards which had been set in 1985. His exceptional yardage total still stands as the 5th highest single season rushing yards total in SEC history, only behind Derrick Henry (2,219 yards), Leonard Fournette (1,953 yards), Herschel Walker (1,891 yards), and Darren McFadden (1,830 yards). Those 23 rushing touchdowns? Still tied for 3rd highest in a single season in the SEC, only behind Derrick Henry (28) and Najee Harris (26). As far as rushing prowess in the SEC goes, Tre Mason was one of the best to ever do it.

In the 2013 SEC Championship game against the Missouri Tigers, he set the SEC rushing record with 46 carries for 304 yards at a rate of 6.6 yards per carry, with 4 touchdowns. Digest that for a moment. A reasonable output for a full season, accomplished in one single game at what is essentially the highest level of collegiate football in America! For context, during the 2013 NCAA season, Alabama's then 3rd string running back Derrick Henry ended his season with 36 carries for 382 yards with 3 touchdowns. Mason's performance was a highly impressive accomplishment any way one looks at it. As a matter of fact, taking a quick look at his performances against SEC opposition that season it quickly becomes apparent that even the most elite football programs in the country were unable to slow him down:

1. Versus Texas A&M – 27 carries for 178 yards at 6.6 YPC with 1 TD.
2. Versus Arkansas – 32 carries for 168 yards at 5.3 YPC with 4 TD.
3. Versus Alabama – 29 carries for 164 yards at 5.7 YPC with 1 TD.
4. Versus LSU – 26 carries for 132 yards at 5.1 YPC with 2 TD.
5. Versus Tennessee – 20 carries for 117 yards at 5.9 YPC with 3 TD.
6. Versus Georgia – 27 carries for 115 yards at 4.3 YPC with 1 TD.
7. Versus Ole Miss - 21 carries for 77 yards at 3.7 YPC with 1 TD.

In the BCS National Championship game versus the Florida State Seminoles, although his Tigers lost the game, Mason's production was once again dominant; 34 carries for 195 yards at 5.7 YPC with 1 TD. The numbers and performances speak for themselves. Tre Mason was an unbelievable talent, and one of the most prolific running backs in all of college football, with record breaking, award winning dominance over the best of the best in the SEC.

Mason decided to forgo his senior season at Auburn and declared for the 2014 NFL Draft. His college coach had this to say about him: *"The [NFL] is getting one of the tougher individuals in all of college football. He can run between the tackles. He has great courage. He played his best games in the biggest games, and he's a good receiver out of the backfield, also."*[99]

A pre-draft article in Bleacher Report[100] listed some of his strengths as:

- Possesses a low center of gravity and excellent balance. Bouncing off would-be tacklers and gaining yards after contact.
- Elusive and slippery runner, makes defenders miss in the hole and in space. Utilizes a jump-cut, sidesteps defenders and breaks lazy tackles.
- Strong and compactly built
- Very effective between the tackles due to combination of patience, vision, agility and power.
- Finished his college career playing the best football of his career. Gouged some of the nation's best defences in his final games.

The article listed some of his weaknesses as:

- Ball security is a huge concern. Fumbled eight times in the last two seasons, or approximately once per 65 touches.
- Lacks proper pass-protection technique. Does not sustain blocks and is often overpowered.
- Shows little effort when it comes to blocking. Does not work to pick up blocks in space.
- Will likely be seen as a candidate for a committee, at least right away. Does not offer much on third down at this point and will need to improve as both a blocker and receiver.

Mason was ultimately selected by the St. Louis Rams in the 3rd round (75th overall) in the 2014 NFL draft. He made the 53 man roster out of training camp and had an immediate impact as the leading rusher on the team his rookie season. As the featured back who was now receiving pro level coaching, he seemed to improve on fumbles as he only had 2 that season at a rate of one fumble every 90 carries. This was definitely not a good number when compared to the best players in the league, but was at the very least trending in the right direction.

Despite the very promising rookie season, for whatever reason the Rams decided to draft another running back; Todd Gurley in the 1st round, 10th overall in the 2015 NFL Draft. This obviously posed problems for Mason to remain as the featured back. In the end, Mason was relegated to playing second fiddle to Gurley for the 2015 season and as a result Mason's second season in the NFL took a nose dive in terms of his on-field production. Sadly, right around that time he also began having serious off-field issues with his mental health. After the 2015 season, Mason did not contact his teammates or coaches during the off season at all. At one point he was even apprehended by police due to concerns for his mental health after his mother called police reporting that her son was "acting unusual and making irrational statements."[101] He did not play at all during the 2016 season and was eventually released by the Rams in early 2017, not signing with any other NFL teams after that.

Mason's NFL career lasted two seasons where he played from 2014-2015, and he later transitioned to the CFL for the 2018 season. His best statistical seasons in the NFL and CFL were the 2014 and 2018 seasons respectively. The graphics on the following pages depict his statistics and league rankings for those seasons.

MOST PRODUCTIVE SEASON
TRE MASON

★★★★★★★★★★★★★

YEAR	2014
GP	12
CARRIES	179
YARDS	765
YPC AVG	4.3
RUSH TD	4
LONG	89
RANK	17TH

MASON

27

55.8
PRODUCTION RATING

HIGH AVERAGE

MOST PRODUCTIVE SEASON
TRE MASON

★★★★★★★★★

★★★

YEAR	2018
GP	18
CARRIES	160
YARDS	809
YPC AVG	5.1
RUSH TD	3
LONG	42
RANK	7TH

MASON

10

58.4
PRODUCTION RATING

HIGH AVERAGE

TRE MASON

LEAGUE RANK - 17TH OUT OF 89 BY PSC RATING

PFF

55.8 65.8

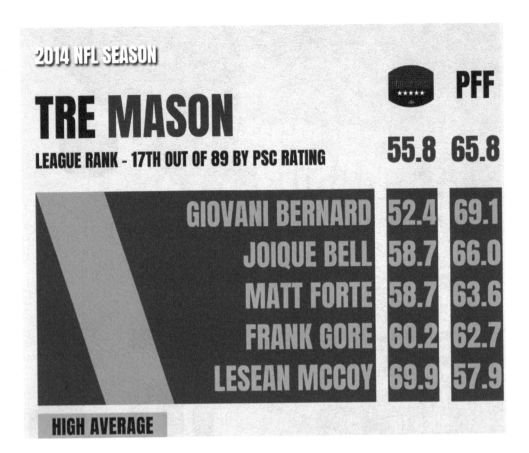

GIOVANI BERNARD	52.4	69.1
JOIQUE BELL	58.7	66.0
MATT FORTE	58.7	63.6
FRANK GORE	60.2	62.7
LESEAN MCCOY	69.9	57.9

HIGH AVERAGE

During his most productive season in the NFL, Tre Mason turned in a performance comparable to Giovani Bernard, Joique Bell, Matt Forte, Frank Gore and LeSean McCoy. Had he played the entire slate of 16 games that season and continued at the same rate of production, he would have ended the season with 238 carries for 1,020 rushing yards and 5 touchdowns, which would have earned him a PSC rating of 62.0. This production would have been good enough for 12th best in the NFL and would have been rated above average. He was nominated to the NFL All-Rookie Team for his performance by the Pro Football Writers of America.

Out of the 37 running backs to have over 500 yards rushing that season, Mason's 63.8 yards per game ranked him 15th. His 4.3 yards per carry average ranked him 16th. He scored a touchdown every 44.8 carries, which was low average but still better than LeSean McCoy (62.4), Frank Gore (63.8) and Andre Ellington (67.0). His longest play of 89 yards was tied for 4th best in the NFL. Although his issues with fumbles were not yet resolved, as he still fumbled roughly once every 90 carries, this low average ratio was still better than some big names in Jonathan Stewart (88), Eddie Lacy (82), Jeremy Hill (56), and Jamaal Charles (52).

If we compare his most productive NFL and CFL seasons side by side we see:

NFL	CFL
Games Played - 12	Games Played - 18
Carries - 179	Carries - 160
Carries/Game - 14.9	Carries/Game - 8.9
Yards - 765	Yards - 809
Yards/Game - 63.8	Yards/Game - 44.9
Rushing Average - 4.3	Rushing Average - 5.1
TD - 4	TD - 3
Carries/Touchdown – 44.8	Carries/Touchdown - 53.3
Long – 89	Long – 42
PSC Rating - 55.8 (High Average)	**PSC Rating - 58.4 (High Average)**

While his overall carries were comparable, we can see that his carries per game dropped dramatically from his NFL 14.9 carries per game, rated above average, to his CFL 8.9 carries per game, rated low average. This discrepancy is easy to explain as the CFL rushes far less than its southern counterpart, so it is not at all surprising. Following the same trend, his yards per game average drops from 63.8 in the NFL rated high average, to 44.9 in the CFL rated low average. His touchdown per game ratio in the NFL of 0.33 was rated high average vs 0.17 in the CFL rated low average. His carries per touchdown ratio stayed comparable at 44.8 in the NFL rated low average vs 53.3 in the CFL, also rated low average. In short, Mason was remarkably consistent with his performance between leagues.

With Mason we find a player who could be described as a high potential pro prospect. His college resume spoke for itself with record setting performances, awards, and recognition. A player of this calibre would be expected to be a productive professional in the NFL, which he proved to be during his playing time there. His fall in the NFL had much more to do with team politics and his mental health issues than his talent or ability.

Mason is a player that "Dave; the NFL ONLY fan" would quite obviously expect to completely dominate the game in Canada. Remember, Dave believes that an NCAA team would whip a CFL team. If Tre Mason was able to tear up the Alabama, LSU and Georgia defences, just imagine what he would do against the defences in the CFL. An elite player with SEC award winning pedigree and proven, above average NFL performance? 2000+ yards rushing in the CFL for sure. But unfortunately for Dave, yet again it is not what we find. Mason was given comparable playing time in both leagues and lo and behold, put up fairly comparable performances. He was a high average performing running back in the NFL, and became a high average performing running back in the CFL as well.

In Mason, we find a player who puts up similar production to a 28 year old Matt Forte while he was in the NFL, then transitions to the CFL and puts up similar production to Jeremiah Johnson and James Wilder Jr. My belief based on the numbers is that this phenomenon does not speak to any weakness in Mason's game, but yet again speaks to the quality of players in the CFL such as Johnson and Wilder Jr. who were in fact elite athletes that were among the best in the world, but constantly devalued because of the league they played in and the size of their paychecks.

As with the players we have already seen, yet again we find that

"A player is who he is"

JALEN
COLLINS

2ND ROUND NFL DRAFT PICK

ATLANTA FALCONS

JALEN COLLINS

Jalen Collins played his college football at LSU in the SEC. Although he only started 10 games at cornerback, he took snaps in a total of 39 games over three years in Baton Rouge and ended his college career having recorded 95 total tackles, 17 passes defended, with 3 interceptions. He decided to forgo his final year of college eligibility and entered the 2015 NFL Draft. Collins was invited to the 2015 NFL Combine where he performed well, running the 40 yard dash in 4.48 seconds (12th out of 33), putting up a vertical jump of 36" (17th out of 33), and a broad jump of 10'4" (15th out of 33).

He was projected by many to be a 1st round talent, and was expected to be drafted in the mid to late 1st round of the 2015 NFL Draft. NFL Draft analyst Lance Zierlein had this to say about Collins: *"Immensely talented cornerback who brings the entire triangle (height, weight, speed) with him. Still learning technique and how to sink his feet with his eyes, but the instincts and athleticism to make plays on the ball both short and deep are what set him apart. Collins is a work in progress, but his physical and play traits create a very high ceiling if he continues to learn to play the position."*[102]

NFL Analyst Bucky Brooks evaluated him as follows: *"Physically, he has all the tools and traits that you look for in a blue chip cornerback. He's long, he's rangy, he's athletic. Obviously he's fast...The big thing about Jalen Collins is when you get him on the field. This is a guy that excels in press coverage, does a great job putting his hands on people...when you're looking at a corner, you want a guy that can do multiple things, can employ multiple techniques, Jalen Collins can do all those things, plus he brings ball skills to the table...I'm OK taking him in the 1st round because if it works out you're talking about an All-Star that your hitting on."*[103]

Ultimately, Collins slid down to the 2nd round and was drafted by the Atlanta Falcons with the 42nd overall pick. His fall to the 2nd round had likely been related to reports that Collins had failed multiple drug tests during the course of his time with the Tigers. Unfortunately for Collins, his issues with substance abuse followed him into the pros where he was suspended 4 times for a total of 28 games. He was suspended the first 4 games of the 2016 season, 10 games to start the 2017 season, followed by another 4 games to end the 2017 season, with the final suspension being another 10 games to start the 2018 season.[104]

Upon completing his final suspension he was signed to the Indianapolis Colts' practice squad at the end of 2018, but was ultimately released by the team a year later. He then spent a brief period in the XFL during 2019, was released in early 2020, and spent the remainder of the year out of football altogether. Then in October of 2021 he signed with the Toronto Argonauts where he once again was able to play meaningful football.

Collin's most productive seasons in the NFL and CFL came during the 2016 and 2021 seasons respectively. The graphics on the following pages depict Collins' performance for those most productive seasons.

MOST PRODUCTIVE SEASON
JALEN COLLINS

★★★★★☆★★★★

YEAR	2016
GP	8
TACKLES	28
TCK/GM	3.50
INT	2
INT/GM	0.25
KD/GM	1.25
RANK	76TH

COLLINS

32

43.9
PRODUCTION RATING

HIGH AVERAGE

MOST PRODUCTIVE SEASON
JALEN COLLINS

★★★★★★★★★★★★

YEAR	2021
GP	5
TACKLES	12
TCK/GM	2.40
INT	2
INT/GM	0.40
KD/GM	0.80
RANK	26TH

COLLINS

7

42.0
PRODUCTION RATING

HIGH AVERAGE

JALEN COLLINS

PFF

LEAGUE RANK - 76TH OUT OF 172 BY PSC RATING

43.9 74.9

PATRICK PETERSON	42.7	79.8
RICHARD SHERMAN	58.2	78.7
JALEN RAMSEY	68.4	72.8
DARRELLE REVIS	37.8	63.8
XAVIEN HOWARD	27.7	57.4

HIGH AVERAGE

During his most productive season in the NFL, Collins was ranked the 76th most productive defensive back in the league out of 172 defensive backs rated. His PSC Rating of 43.9 was higher than Patrick Peterson, Darrelle Revis and Xavien Howard. Although Richard Sherman and Jalen Ramsey had more productive seasons overall, as evidenced by their higher PSC Ratings of 58.2 and 68.4 respectively, Collins' PFF overall grade was very comparable to any of the above mentioned players.

Collins' 3.50 solo tackles per game ratio was rated high average, and higher than any of the above players except Xavien Howard (4.14). His 0.25 Interceptions per game was rated above average, tied with Richard Sherman, and higher than Patrick Peterson (0.19), Jalen Ramsey (0.13), and Darrelle Revis (0.07). Even more impressively his 10 passes defended in only 8 games represented a passes defended per game ratio of 1.25 which was rated elite, tying him with Casey Hayward for 4th best in the NFL and only behind Brent Grimes (1.50), Dominique Rodgers-Cromartie (1.40) and Marcus Peters (1.33).

Collins' allowed catch percentage of 56.0% was better than Darrelle Revis (66.7%), Patrick Peterson (60.6%), Stephon Gilmore (60.3%), Xavien Howard (59.2%) and Marcus Peters (58.6%) according to PFF.

If we were to extrapolate his performance to a full slate of 16 games he could have ended up with 56 solo tackles, 20 passes defended with 4 interceptions. This would have added up to a PSC rating of 66.7 which would have ranked him in the top 20 DB's in the NFL and would have been rated above average.

Collins' most productive season culminated in a post season run with the Falcons that went all the way to the Superbowl. He played in the NFC divisional round vs Seattle, the NFC Championship round vs Green Bay, and ultimately in the Superbowl vs New England. During those 3 games he made 16 solo tackles at a rate of 5.33 solo tackles per game, with a staggering 10 solo tackles in the Superbowl alone. He forced and recovered 1 fumble, and added 2 passes defended at a rate of 0.66 per game for a highly productive post season that ended with the now infamous Superbowl LI, which saw Atlanta squander a 21-3 half time lead to lose in overtime 34-28.

Collins obviously had a troubled NFL career, primarily hampered by substance abuse issues. Despite missing as much time as he did and losing out on valuable game reps to improve his play, he showed flashes of elite potential.

He signed with the Argonauts late in the 2021 season and only appeared in 5 regular season games, but when we look closely at his play we can also see the same flashes of elite potential he showed in the NFL. His 2.40 solo tackles per game ratio was rated high average. His elite coverage skills really begin to shine however when examining his interceptions and pass knockdown metrics. In only 5 games played he managed 2 interceptions at a rate of 0.40 per game rated above average. This rate was good enough for 3rd best in the league among eligible defensive backs, equal to Nafees Lyon and only behind Brandin Dandridge (0.50), and Cariel Brooks (0.42). His 0.80 pass knockdowns per game were best in the league, rated him elite and ahead of Jumal Rolle (0.79), Monshadrik Hunter (0.71) Tyquwan Glass (0.71) and Garry Peters (0.64).

His sample size of games played in the CFL was quite small, but even still he was able to take advantage of the opportunity and proved that he still had the ability to play at an elite level. If we were to extrapolate his rate of production to the entire slate of the 14 games played during the 2021 CFL season Collins could have ended up with: 34 solo tackles, 6 interceptions, and 11 pass knockdowns. This performance would have been good enough to rank him as the 6th most productive defensive back in the league, rating him above average, with the most interceptions, and tied for the most pass knockdowns. He had higher tackles and passes defended per game ratios in the NFL, and a higher interception per game ratio in the CFL. His PSC rating in the CFL of 42.0 was rated high average, and was very comparable to his NFL best of 43.9 which rated him high average as well.

Sometimes it seems that the more things change, the more they stay the same.

"**A player is who he is**"

TRENT
RICHARDSON

1ST ROUND NFL DRAFT PICK

CLEVELAND BROWNS

TRENT RICHARDSON

Tuscaloosa; The home town of the University of Alabama. This is the place where top flight NFL talent is forged in the fires of the SEC, winning national championship after national championship. Alabama is not only one of the best, most decorated college football programs in the United States, it is arguably the closest thing to pro football one can find among the NCAA ranks. Alabama was the birthplace of talents such as Derrick Henry, Shaun Alexander, Mark Ingram Jr and Eddie Lacy. Trent Richardson was similarly a product of this talent factory.

Richardson had been a 5 star prospect coming out of high school and had been considered the number 2 running back prospect in the nation. He committed to Alabama and played 3 solid seasons racking up a total of 3,130 rushing yards on 540 carries at 5.8 yards per carry average with 35 rushing touchdowns. His final season at 'Bama saw him rush for 1,679 yards on 283 carries at 5.9 yards per carry average and scoring 21 touchdowns.

When his college career came to a close, he had received the following accolades: 2× BCS National Champion (2009, 2011), Unanimous All-American (2011), Doak Walker Award (2011), Heisman Trophy Finalist (2011), SEC Offensive Player of the Year (2011), 2× First-team All-SEC (2010, 2011), SEC Champion (2009), SEC All-Freshman Team (2009).

Richardson was selected in the first round of the 2012 NFL draft (3rd overall) and his most productive season, his rookie season, was 2012 where he rushed for 950 yards on 267 carries at 3.6 yards per carry with 11 touchdowns.

Below you will see his NFL career totals.

NFL

Games Played: 46
Carries: 614
Carries/Game: 13.3
Yards: 2,032
Yards/Game: 44.2
Rushing Average: 3.3
TD: 17
Carries/Touchdown: 36.1
Long: 32

*Note: Richardson's career CFL stats are equal to his most productive season.

MOST PRODUCTIVE SEASON
TRENT RICHARDSON

YEAR	2012
GP	15
CARRIES	267
YARDS	950
YPC AVG	3.6
RUSH TD	11
LONG	32
RANK	14TH

RICHARDSON
33

57.8
PRODUCTION RATING

ABOVE AVERAGE

MOST PRODUCTIVE SEASON
TRENT RICHARDSON

★★★★★★★ ★★★

YEAR	2017
GP	4
CARRIES	48
YARDS	259
YPC AVG	5.4
RUSH TD	2
LONG	38
RANK	11TH

RICHARDSON

33

49.8
PRODUCTION RATING

HIGH AVERAGE

TRENT RICHARDSON

PFF

LEAGUE RANK - 14TH OUT OF 93 BY PSC RATING

57.8 72.5

FRANK GORE	64.1	72.1
DEMARCO MURRAY	47.2	70.2
MATT FORTE	57.1	67.6
REGGIE BUSH	57.5	65.2
DARREN MCFADDEN	46.8	52.7

ABOVE AVERAGE

During his most productive season in the NFL, Richardson was ranked the 14th most productive running back, and produced comparably to Frank Gore (10th), Reggie Bush (15th), Matt Forte (16th), DeMarco Murray (23rd), and Darren McFadden (24th) by PSC rating. His PFF overall grade of 72.5 was actually highest in the above mentioned group of players. His 11 rushing touchdowns had him in a 3-way tie for 4th most in the NFL, and his 0.73 touchdowns per game was good enough for 5th best. Richardson scored a touchdown on average every 24.3 carries, which ranked 19th best in the league. This carries per touchdown ratio was better than, but comparable to Alfred Morris (25.8), Ray Rice (28.6), Marshawn Lynch (28.6), Adrian Peterson (29.0), and Doug Martin (29.0). His yards per carry average was among the lowest in the league at 3.6, however despite being low, it was still comparable to Darren McFadden (3.3), Michael Turner (3.6), Mikel Leshoure (3.7), Shonn Greene (3.9), and BenJarvus Green-Ellis (3.9).

His rookie season was by far his most productive in the NFL. He would eventually play two more seasons with Cleveland and Indianapolis respectively, carrying the ball 347 more times for 1,082 yards at 3.1 yards per carry with 6 more touchdowns. Unfortunately for Richardson, neither his pedigree, high level college experience, or his high NFL draft pick status could save him from all the negative outside influences he was plagued by. From injury troubles to off-field issues with family, Richardson never fully became the player he had the potential to be.

In a Bleacher Report article, Richardson's former high school coach and mentor Derrick Boyd stated *"He didn't realize the NFL required a whole bunch of time; I'm sure he's aware of that now."* That same article quoted Richardson as saying *"I was young-minded. I didn't know how to handle it on a professional team."*[105] Richardson had come from an environment in Tuscaloosa, where he did not have to worry about anything. He was told when to eat, when to sleep, when to practice etc. Upon graduating to the professional ranks, where he would be responsible for himself and his own time management, he found it extremely difficult to dedicate the necessary time and effort to working on his craft. Having friends and family always around wasn't an environment that was necessarily conducive to becoming a better player and putting in the work required to be a true pro.

Although his transition to the CFL was short lived and only provided a small sample size; away from all the distractions of the NFL and the rock star lifestyle many players live on a daily basis, Richardson began to show glimpses of the dominant running back that had tore up SEC defences just a few years earlier.

In the CFL during his most productive season, Richardson ended the season with a PSC rating of 49.8, rated high average as the 11th most productive running back overall. His performance in the CFL was comparable to teammate Cameron Marshall (63.4 - 9th), Terry Williams (60.6 - 10th), Mossis Madu (45.6 - 13th), and Brandon Rutley (44.8 - 15th) by PSC rating.

As it stands, his lone CFL season despite being respectable, especially if broken down on a per game basis was still not able to exceed the production of other lesser known players such as, for example, Alex Green; himself a former 2011 NFL draft pick of the Green Bay Packers (3rd round, 96th overall) who ranked 8th in the CFL by PSC rating during the 2017 season.

Alex Green	**Trent Richardson**
Games Played: 6	Games Played: 4
Carries: 79	Carries: 48
Carries/Game: 13.2	Carries/Game: 12.0
Yards: 447	Yards: 259
Yards/Game: 74.5	Yards/Game: 64.8
Rushing Average: 5.7	Rushing Average: 5.4
TD: 5	TD: 2
TD/Gm: 0.83	TD/Gm: 0.50
Carries/Touchdown: 15.8	Carries/Touchdown: 24.0
Long: 26	Long: 38

You may be saying 'he only played 4 games in the CFL, that is not an adequate sample size', and fair enough! Would him having played more games have helped paint a better picture? Of course! The bigger the sample, the more accurate the results. However even despite the small sample size when we look at his performance a little closer we can quickly find the similarities between his NFL and CFL production when comparing his positional rates of production.

17.8 carries per game in the NFL (10th highest) Above Average
12.0 carries per game in the CFL (5th highest) High Average

63.3 yards per game in the NFL (22nd highest) High Average
64.8 yards per game in the CFL (3rd highest) Above Average

0.73 touchdowns per game in the NFL (6th highest) Above Average
0.50 touchdowns per game in the CFL (6th highest) High Average

24.3 carries per touchdown in the NFL (19th highest) High Average
24.0 carries per touchdown in the CFL (9th highest) High Average

Longest NFL play 32 yards (43rd best) High Average
Longest CFL play 38 yards (11th best) High Average

3.6 yards per carry average in the NFL (81st best) Below Average
5.4 yards per carry average in the CFL (15th best) Low Average

His most productive single games in either league during his most productive seasons were also not significantly different:

NFL vs Bengals	**CFL vs Alouettes**
Carries: 19	Carries: 20
Yards: 109	Yards: 127
Rushing Average: 5.7	Rushing Average: 6.4
TD: 1	TD: 2
Long: 32	Long: 38

His career best single game metrics in either league were also similar.

NFL Career Best	**CFL Career Best**
Carries: 29 vs Steelers	Carries: 20 vs Alouettes
Yards: 122 vs Chargers	Yards: 127 vs Alouettes
Rushing Average: 5.9 vs Broncos	Rushing Average: 6.4 vs Alouettes
TD: 2 vs Redskins	TD: 2 vs Alouettes
Long: 32 vs Bengals	Long: 38 vs Alouettes

The reality is, Trent Richardson had all the talent in the world. His "failure" as an NFL running back and his lack of tangible success at the CFL level did not have anything to do with a lack of talent or ability. The more one studies his life and career, the quicker one realizes that Richardson like many others, was a victim of circumstances. He fell prey to immaturity, injuries, and getting caught up with numerous distractions from friends and family and as a result never lived up to his full potential.

Had he been focused and determined to be great from day one of his pro career, we likely would never have seen him in the CFL at all. He had all the conditions necessary to be a perennial All-Pro. Similarly, had he continued his CFL career past one single season and had reported for training camp on time and in shape the following year, he could have been a player that re-wrote the CFL record books during the following few seasons.

Success, or lack thereof is multifaceted. As they say "hard work beats talent, until talent works hard." A fitting slogan for Richardson and others like him. Even still, when examining Richardson's performance on either side of the border in detail, yet again we can see elements of:

"**A player is who he is**"

JOHNNY MANZIEL

1ST ROUND NFL DRAFT PICK

CLEVELAND BROWNS

"It's not the NFL, it's the CFL, it's different. You expect to do well... Then you come up here and it's not what you expected... THIS GAME HUMBLES YOU."

JOHNNY MANZIEL[106]

Johnny Manziel has been called one of the most electrifying college football players to ever play the game, earning him the nickname "Johnny Football". In just two seasons as a starter for Texas A&M, he threw for over 7,800 yards and 63 touchdowns, all while rushing for 2,169 yards and 30 rushing touchdowns. His performances were good enough to earn him a Heisman Trophy, making him the first freshman to ever accomplish the feat. He not only put up incredible stats, he did so playing against the best possible college competition in the SEC. Despite losing close games to Alabama and Auburn during his senior season, against them he still managed 56 of 77 (72.7% completion rate), 918 yards with 9 touchdowns and 4 interceptions for a QBR of 129.7 (pro formula). He also added 146 yards rushing on 32 attempts with a touchdown. He ended his college career with the following stats:

Attempts: 863
Completions: 595
Completion %: 68.9
Yards: 7,820
Touchdowns: 63
Interceptions: 22
QBR: 111.0 (pro formula)
Rushing Attempts: 345
Rushing Yards: 2,169
YPC: 6.3
Rushing TD: 30

Yardbarker.com ranked him number 22 on their list of top 50 college quarterbacks of all-time.[107] Saturdayblitz.com had him ranked number 21 on their list of the top 30 college quarterbacks of all-time.[108] Love him or hate him, there can be no denying that Johnny Manziel was a highly decorated star of epic proportions during his time in College Station. His accolades speak for themselves:

Heisman Trophy (2012)
Davey O'Brien Award (2012)
Manning Award (2012)
Associated Press Player of the Year (2012)
Sporting News Player of the Year (2012)
SEC Offensive Player of the Year (2012)
Consensus All-American (2012)
2× First-team All-SEC (2012, 2013)

He was so impressive in fact, that Cleveland traded up in the first round to draft him 22nd overall in the 2014 NFL Draft. Despite a white hot college career and the great fanfare that followed him into the NFL, the years and seasons that followed were tumultuous to say the least. His most productive seasons in the NFL and later the CFL were the 2015 and 2018 seasons respectively.

The graphics on the following pages depict his statistical production for those seasons.

MOST PRODUCTIVE SEASON
JOHNNY MANZIEL

★★★★★★★★★★★★

YEAR	2015
GP	9
COMP	129
ATT	223
YARDS	1500
TD/INT	7/5
QBR	79.4
RANK	35TH

MANZIEL

2

53.4
PRODUCTION RATING

LOW AVERAGE

PRO STATS
★★★★★

MOST PRODUCTIVE SEASON
JOHNNY MANZIEL
★★★★★★★★★

PRO STATS
★★★★★

YEAR	2018
GP	8
COMP	106
ATT	165
YARDS	1290
TD/INT	5/7
QBR	80.6
RANK	14TH

MANZIEL

2

51.1
PRODUCTION RATING

LOW AVERAGE

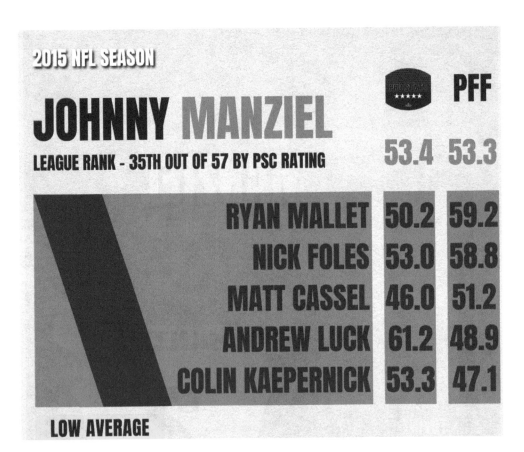

2015 NFL SEASON

JOHNNY MANZIEL

LEAGUE RANK - 35TH OUT OF 57 BY PSC RATING

PFF

53.4 53.3

RYAN MALLET	50.2	59.2
NICK FOLES	53.0	58.8
MATT CASSEL	46.0	51.2
ANDREW LUCK	61.2	48.9
COLIN KAEPERNICK	53.3	47.1

LOW AVERAGE

During his most productive NFL season Manziel was ranked the 35th most productive quarterback, earning a low average PSC rating of 53.4. He produced at a level comparable to Andrew Luck (29th), Colin Kaepernick (36th), Nick Foles (37th), Ryan Mallett (42nd), and Matt Cassel (45th). While all these players at one point or another were NFL starters, most of them (with the exception of Andrew Luck) could be best described as players on the fringe of being regular, consistent starters. Their play putting them somewhere between starting and backup calibre.

Understanding that mobility was an aspect of Manziel's game that he was well known for in college, I compared his rushing ability with the top 15 rushing quarterbacks in the NFL for the 2015 season. When the results were tabulated, Manziel ended up 10th out of 15 quarterbacks evaluated. His 39.6 PSC rating was rated high average and was comparable to Ryan Fitzpatrick (39.8 PSC Rating – 9th), Blaine Gabbert (38.7 PSC Rating - 11th), and Colin Kaepernick (38.3 PSC Rating – 12th). Manziel's 25.6 rushing yards per game was good for 7th best, and his yards per carry average of 6.2 was good for second, only behind Marcus Mariota's 7.4.

When he transitioned to the CFL, Manziel's performance similarly earned him a low average PSC rating of 51.1, ranking him as the 14th most productive quarterback in the league. His level of production was comparable to James Franklin (59.0 – 9th), Jonathon Jennings (58.0 - 10th), Chris Streveler (54.7 - 12th), and Antonio Pipkin (46.8 - 17th).

An uncannily similar dynamic was uncovered as I performed my evaluation. All the quarterbacks in the CFL that Manziel most compared to from a production standpoint were players that were basically on the fringe of being regular, consistent starters. Players that lingered somewhere between a QB1 and QB2, exactly the same dynamic that existed in the NFL.

His rushing performance in the CFL earned him a high average PSC rating of 41.9 which ranked him as the 7th most productive QB in the league out of 20 evaluated. This rating was comparable to Jonathon Jennings (40.9 - 8th). Manziel's 26.9 rushing yards per game was good for 4th best, rated high average and his yards per carry average of 7.4 was good for third, rated above average, and only behind Vernon Adams Jr's 7.6, and Jeremiah Masoli's 7.5.

These statistics were once again eerily similar to his production in the NFL. One would be inclined to believe that if anything, his rushing performance should have significantly improved due to the one yard neutral zone and wider field in Canada, but it is just not what the numbers demonstrated.

NFL	CFL
Rushing Attempts: 37	Rushing Attempts: 29
Attempts/Game: 4.1	Attempts/Game: 3.6
Yards: 230	Yards: 215
Yards/Carry Average: 6.2	Yards/Carry Average: 7.4
Yards/Game: 25.6	Yards/Game: 26.9
Touchdowns: 0	Touchdowns: 0

Here's an in-depth look at how his P.R.O.P. in the NFL compared to his P.R.O.P. in the CFL.

14.3 completions per game in the NFL rated low average
13.3 completions per game in the CFL rated high average

24.8 attempts per game in the NFL rated low average
20.6 attempts per game in the CFL rated low average

166.7 passing yards per game in the NFL rated low average
161.3 passing yards per game in the CFL rated high average

79.4 QBR in the NFL rated low average
80.6 QBR in the CFL rated low average

25.6 rushing yards per game in the NFL rated above average
26.9 rushing yards per game in the CFL rated high average

6.2 rushing yards per carry in the NFL rated above average
7.4 rushing yards per carry in the CFL rated above average

Just like Troy Smith before him, Johnny Manziel was a Heisman Trophy winning college quarterback who despite having a ton of talent was not able to translate a stellar college career at the highest level into any substantial success at the professional level. His play in either pro league was more comparable to each leagues' backup quarterbacks than starters.

In fairness to Manziel and Troy Smith, the quarterback position is one of the hardest positions in sport. Having played for two different CFL teams within the same season and having to learn two different playbooks in such a short period of time would be difficult for even the most experienced pro. Manziel is a player that had a sky high potential but much like Trent Richardson, allowed his off-field issues to get the better of him. Those issues ended up being a true impediment to him ever reaching the potential his talent could have carried him to.

As we have seen above, when looking at Johnny Manziel's NFL and CFL metrics side by side once again it quickly becomes evident that:

"A player is who he is"

SHANE
RAY

1ST ROUND NFL DRAFT PICK

DENVER BRONCOS

"I can't say that I would just come out here and run through guys, that's not what's going on...
I APPRECIATE THE COMPETITION"

Shane Ray played his college football for the Missouri Tigers in the SEC. In 33 games played at Mizzou, he made 120 total tackles, 82 solo, 19 sacks and 1 forced fumble. His career P.R.O.P. while in college was 3.63 tackles per game and 0.57 sacks per game. His most productive college season was the 2014 season where in 12 games played he put up 65 tackles (47 solo) with 14.5 sacks and 22.5 tackles for loss. His most productive college season saw him put up a P.R.O.P. of 5.41 total tackles per game, (3.91 solo tackles per game), 1.20 sacks per game, and 1.88 tackles for loss per game. His 14.5 sacks were good enough to rank him 3rd in the entire NCAA and broke a record held by Michael Sam and Aldon Smith for most sacks during a season in the SEC. All of this ultimately earned him unanimous All-American selection, First team All-SEC, and SEC Defensive Player of the Year accolades. As far as college pass rushers went, Shane Ray was a proven elite talent.

His stellar college production was backed up by a pro day/NFL combine performance that saw him put up a 4.68 40 yard dash, 21 reps of 225lbs on the bench press, a 33" vertical jump, a 4.58 second 20 yard shuttle and a 7.60 second 3-cone drill. I will be comparing his college production and his combine/pro day metrics to another well known NFL pass rusher from the same draft class; Frank Clark.

Shane Ray	**Frank Clark**
GP: 33	GP: 33
Total Tackles: 120	Total Tackles: 117
Solo Tackles: 82	Solo Tackles: 67
Solo/Gm: 2.48	Solo/Gm: 2.03
Assisted Tackles: 38	Assisted Tackles: 50
Sacks: 19	Sacks: 11
Sacks/Gm: 0.58	Sacks/Gm: 0.33
FF:1	FF: 1
PSC Rating: 96.6	**PSC Rating: 82.4**

Shane Ray	**Frank Clark**
Height: 6'3"	Height: 6'3"
Weight: 245	Weight: 271
40 Yard: 4.68	40 Yard: 4.66
Vertical: 33.0"	Vertical: 38.5
Bench: 21	Bench: 19
Broad Jump: 10'0"	Broad Jump: 9'10"
3 Cone: 7.60	3 Cone: 7.08
Shuttle: 4.58	Shuttle: 4.05
PSC Rating: 93.9	**PSC Rating: 98.4**

Combining their scores for both their college production as well as their combine metrics we arrive at a final PSC rating of 95.3 for Shane Ray and 90.4 for Frank Clark. Both had productive college careers, with Ray having the edge, and both were highly athletic, with Clark having the edge. Shane Ray's prospect grade according to NFL scouts rated him as a potential Pro Bowl Talent. As per NFL Analyst Lance Zierlein, Ray's NFL draft bio read as follows:

"It's hard to find many weaknesses for Ray. He pursues the quarterback and the ball like it's his last snap. An alpha male packaged in an explosive frame, Ray has the traits and skills to be a dominant pass rusher and potential Pro Bowler. He also has the athleticism and strength to play in any defensive front."[110]

He had been projected by some to be a top 10 pick in the 1st round, but ultimately fell to the end of the 1st where he was drafted by the Denver Broncos at 23rd overall. The fall likely having been related to him being cited for possession of Marijuana just days before the draft.

Ray became a Superbowl Champion his first season with the Broncos, coming off the bench in Superbowl 50 to make 2 solo tackles and a QB hit. He ended his rookie NFL season with modest production as a rotational player: 20 total tackles, 15 solo, and 4 sacks at a P.R.O.P. of 1.43 total tackles per game, 1.07 solo tackles per game, and 0.29 sacks per game. His sophomore season was his most productive in the NFL, however he soon began running into injury troubles after numerous injuries to his wrist. He spent a total of 4 seasons with the Denver Broncos, but at that point was most likely deemed to be "injury prone" after 3 wrist surgeries completed, and requiring a 4th. The team ultimately decided he wasn't worth the risk of picking up his 5th year option which would have cost them $9.2 million, and be guaranteed for injury.[111]

He signed with the Baltimore Ravens for the 2019-20 NFL season, however he was released during final roster cuts. He spent 2020 out of football but he ultimately found his way to the CFL signing a contract with the Toronto Argonauts for the 2021 season. His first season in Canada saw very modest production as a rotational player on Toronto's defensive line. He ended the season having played in only 5 games making 4 solo tackles at a rate of 0.80 solo tackles per game. In the Eastern Semi-Final against the Tiger-Cats he recorded 1 solo tackle and made his first CFL sack in a losing effort.

His most productive CFL season to date was his sophomore season; 2022. The graphics below depict his statistics for his most productive NFL and CFL seasons; 2016 and 2022 respectively.

MOST PRODUCTIVE SEASON
SHANE RAY

YEAR	2016
GP	16
TACKLES	33
TCK/GM	2.06
SACKS	8.0
SCK/GM	0.50
FF	1
RANK	39TH

RAY

56

56.5
PRODUCTION RATING

HIGH AVERAGE

MOST PRODUCTIVE SEASON
SHANE RAY

★★★★★★★★★★★

YEAR	2022
GP	13
TACKLES	13
TCK/GM	1.00
SACKS	6.0
SCK/GM	0.46
FF	2
RANK	22ND

RAY
56

42.1
PRODUCTION RATING

HIGH AVERAGE

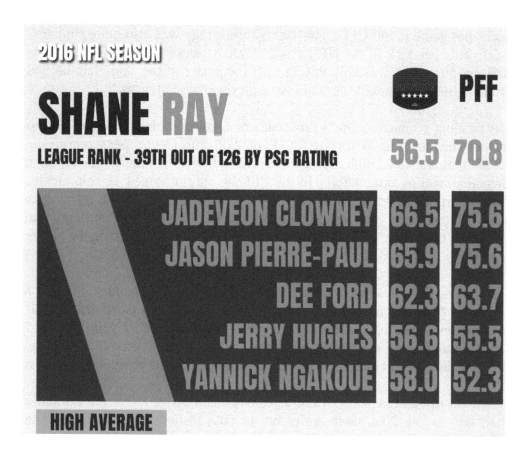

SHANE RAY

LEAGUE RANK - 39TH OUT OF 126 BY PSC RATING

PFF

56.5 70.8

JADEVEON CLOWNEY	66.5	75.6
JASON PIERRE-PAUL	65.9	75.6
DEE FORD	62.3	63.7
JERRY HUGHES	56.6	55.5
YANNICK NGAKOUE	58.0	52.3

HIGH AVERAGE

During his most productive NFL season, Ray put up production similar to Jadeveon Clowney, Jason Pierre-Paul, Dee Ford, Jerry Hughes and Yannick Ngakoue. Out of 126 pass rushers evaluated he earned a high average PSC rating of 56.5 which ranked him 39th in the league. His 8.0 QB sacks on the season ranked him 26th in the league and rated him high average. His P.R.O.P. of 0.50 sacks per game ranked 31st also rating him high average. This P.R.O.P. was higher than notable pass rushers Whitney Mercilus, Cameron Jordan, and Julius Peppers. While his statistical production was 2nd lowest in the group above, his PFF overall grade was above average and only slightly behind Clowney and Pierre-Paul.

Upon his transition to the CFL, once he found a starting role for Toronto during his most productive season he earned a high average PSC rating of 42.1 which ranked 22nd in the league. His 6.0 sacks were good for 15th in the league rated high average, and his P.R.O.P. of 0.46 sacks per game ranked 7th in the CFL, rated above average.

It is interesting to note that Ray's pass rushing P.R.O.P. was virtually identical between both leagues; 0.50 sacks per game in the NFL and 0.46

sacks per game in the CFL. His sack yard average was also quite similar; -5.50 yards per sack in the NFL vs -5.17 yards per sack in the CFL. In the CFL he proved he was still able to rush the passer at the same rate he had while in the NFL, making similar losses for opposing offences.

His tackling production was a different story however. He managed 33 solo tackles for the Broncos for a P.R.O.P. of 2.06 solo tackles per game in the NFL. This was rated high average and ranked him 40th in the league for edge defender tackling production. In the CFL he only managed 13 solo tackles for the Argonauts for a P.R.O.P. of 1.00 solo tackles per game. This was rated low average, and ranked him 30th in the league. The attributes he displayed in either league were similar; he was far better at rushing the passer than stopping the run.

As always, the naysayers could try to cherry pick an argument for Ray's similar production between leagues: *"**He is old and washed up, so his production north of the border actually proves the CFL's inferiority**."* Does it though? As previously mentioned, Ray was 29 years old during his most productive CFL season. Is that really too old for the position?

Based on my assessments, while a pass rusher's prime years are normally their mid to late 20's, there are plenty of pass rushers who continue to be productive well into their mid 30's and beyond. A quick look at this season's most productive NFL pass rush P.R.O.P. to date reveals numerous players still putting up above average pass rush production well past 30.

Justin Houston – 33 – 0.82 sacks per game
J.J. Watt – 33 – 0.73 sacks per game
Von Miller – 33 – 0.67 sacks per game
Jerry Hughes – 34 – 0.57 sacks per game
Khalil Mack – 31 – 0.50 sacks per game

Ray is yet another example of a player that "Dave; the NFL ONLY fan" would expect to tear the CFL apart. He played college ball at the highest possible level, won All-American, First Team All-SEC, Defensive Player of the Year, was a 1st Round NFL Draft pick, and proved he could put up solid NFL production when he was healthy. Add to all that the fact that during his most productive CFL season he was still just 29 years old and you have a set of circumstances which could reasonably lead to believing Ray was going to absolutely dominate the "inferior competition" in the CFL.

Whether one wants to admit it or not, Ray falling out of favour in the NFL was the result of a business decision that Denver made because of his injury troubles, and not truly indicative of his talent or lack thereof. If the team that drafted you has determined you are not worth the financial risk, the chances of getting signed by another team are slim to nil. That is not unexpected, it is just the reality of the NFL business.

Thankfully, the numbers do not preoccupy themselves with such things. Politics and business strategy aside, whether in the NFL or CFL, once again this book's slogan repeats itself:

"A player is who he is"

CHRIS MATTHEWS

UNDRAFTED FREE AGENT

SEATTLE SEAHAWKS

*Big time PLAYERS
Make big time PLAYS
in big time GAMES*

CHRIS MATTHEWS

No doubt you have heard the expression "big time players, make big time plays, in big time games". This expression was most notably made famous based on the utterances of former NFL player Santana Moss. He made the statement after the Orange Bowl in 2000 where his #7 ranked Miami Hurricanes defeated the #1 ranked Florida State Seminoles. The expression means that the best sports superstars are the ones who are able to dominate by making the biggest plays in the biggest games on the biggest stage. Despite the fact that Chris Matthews did not enjoy a lengthy NFL career, when his number was called in the biggest game of his life and on the biggest stage in football, he proved he was one of those big time players who could make big time plays in those big time games.

Before we get into his life as a professional, let's examine his college career. Chris Matthews' NCAA career consisted of two seasons at the University of Kentucky, which competes in the NCAA division I's FBS; in the much vaunted South Eastern Conference (SEC). Below you will find his college stats which are compared to fellow SEC alumni Julio Jones.

Chris Matthews	**Julio Jones**
Season: 2	Seasons: 3
GP: 26	GP: 40
Receptions: 93	Receptions: 179
Rec/Gm: 3.6	Rec/Gm: 4.5
Rec/Season: 46.5	Rec/Season: 59.7
Yards: 1,279	Yards: 2,653
Yards per game: 49.2	Yards per game: 66.3
Yards/Season: 639.5	Yards/Season: 884.3
Average per reception: 13.8	Average per reception: 14.8
Touchdowns: 12	Touchdowns: 15
Touchdowns/Game: 0.46	Touchdowns/Game: 0.38
Touchdowns/Season: 6.0	Touchdowns/Season: 5.0
PSC Rating: 75.8	**PSC Rating: 97.2**

As is evident from the PSC rating difference, overall Julio Jones had a far more productive college career than Matthews. The only metrics where Matthews comes within 10% of Jones is career average per reception, and his touchdown statistics which were actually better than Jones' on a per game and per season basis. One of the reasons for the large discrepancy in their ratings can in part be attributed to the fact that Julio Jones played 3 seasons in college, while Chris Matthews only played 2.

During the 2010 NCAA season, which was either player's final college season, Mathews and Jones actually had very comparable production. Jones still ultimately ended up with the more productive season overall thanks to a couple of monster games against Auburn and Tennessee, however Matthews' production was nothing to scoff at. He put up 177 receiving yards on 12 receptions with 1 touchdown against the South Carolina Gamecocks, 114 receiving yards on only 6 receptions with 2 touchdowns against the Florida Gators, 85 receiving yards on 4 receptions against the Tennessee Volunteers, and 83 receiving yards on 4 receptions against the Georgia Bulldogs. This was elite production against some of the best teams in the entire NCAA.

Chris Matthews	Julio Jones
GP: 13	GP: 13
Rec: 61	Rec: 78
Rec/Gm: 4.7	Rec/Gm: 6.0
Yards: 925	Yards: 1,133
Rec AVG: 15.2	Rec AVG: 14.5
Yds/Gm: 71.2	Yds/Gm: 87.2
TD: 9	TD: 7
TD/Gm: 0.69	TD/Gm: 0.54
PSC Rating: 89.0	PSC Rating: 94.6

At 6'5", 218lbs he was a beast of a receiver; virtually the same size as Julio Jones (Jones being two pounds heavier and 2 inches shorter).

Here's how Matthews' pro day numbers compared to Jones' combine numbers.

Chris Matthews	Julio Jones
40 yard dash: 4.57	40 yard dash: 4.39
20 yard shuttle: 4.29	20 yard shuttle: 4.25
Three cone drill: 6.90	Three cone drill: 6.66
Vertical Jump: 33-1/2"	Vertical Jump: 42"
Broad Jump: 9'10"	Broad Jump: 11'7"
PSC Rating: 91.2	PSC Rating: 100.0

Comparing Matthews and Jones side by side, it becomes evident that just as Jones had a more productive college career, he was also clearly the more athletic of the two, although the difference between them athletically is significantly smaller than their PSC rating disparity for college production. Jones recorded better test results in every single metric, earning himself a perfect PSC rating of 100.0, but looking closely at Matthews' numbers demonstrates that while he definitely had nowhere near the explosion of a

Julio Jones, he did have the size and decent speed to go along with it. When all was said and done, Matthews' PSC rating of 91.2 for his athleticism only represented a difference of 8.8 points. If we were to combine their ratings for college production and athleticism we find Chris Matthews' final overall PSC rating is **83.5** compared to **98.6** for Julio Jones. This represents a 15.1 rating point drop.

Let me be clear, this comparison was never intended to be fair right from the start. I was comparing Chris Matthews to Julio Jones; a player who was considered to be a once in a generation type receiver coming out of college. Julio's prospect grade of 7.50 indicated that NFL scouts believed he would be a perennial All-Pro, and in his case they were correct. He went on to become one of the best receivers in NFL history recording seven 1000+ yard seasons on his way to over 13,000 receiving yards as of the time of writing, landing him squarely into the top 20 (16th) most productive NFL receivers of all-time.

Just as we have seen in other similar comparisons, if we were to think of Julio Jones as being virtual football perfection at the receiver position, any way you slice it a player that is 84.7% of that perfect player is a pretty amazing player on his own merits! A 99 overall rating in Madden means you are likely the best in the game at your position, but what about a player rated at 84 overall? Would they be some kind of amateur that plays beer league football on the weekends? Definitely not! While they might not be a WR1 (depending on the team), they are definitely WR2 or WR3 material; and without a doubt at least more than worthy to be a starter in the NFL from a talent standpoint.

Matthews put up some elite production against some of the best teams in the entire NCAA during his college career, and proved he had the athleticism required to play in the pros. Despite all this, after Matthews completed his NCAA career he went undrafted in the 2011 NFL draft. He subsequently signed an undrafted free agent contract with the Cleveland Browns, attended training camp with the team, but was ultimately a final cut at the end of camp and was released. With no further NFL opportunities, Matthews signed with the Iowa Barnstormers of the Arena Football League where he played during the 2012 AFL season. He later signed with the Winnipeg Blue Bombers and ended up not only making the team, but winning the CFL's most outstanding rookie award in 2012 after playing 18 games, making 81 receptions on 143 targets for 1,192 yards and 7 touchdowns. His excellent rookie season was followed up by a sophomore slump as injuries limited him to only 5 games played in 2013.

During his time in the CFL his most productive single game came during the 2012 regular season against the Edmonton Eskimos where he had 7 receptions for 171 yards at an average of 24.4 yards per reception with 1 touchdown. Matthews' Blue Bombers lost the game 42-10, but it was by far the most productive single game of his career in the CFL. During that game he was the most productive receiver and earned an elite production rating of 94.4. Although it was not the biggest or most important game he would ever play in, and his team ended up being soundly defeated by their opponents, his play demonstrated he was a play maker capable of taking over a game at the professional level.

In the football world there can be little doubt that the Superbowl is by far the biggest game on the biggest stage of football anywhere on the planet. According to a CNN article[112], the big game has averaged 107.3 million viewers during the past 6 years. The Superbowl is the culmination of the NFL season and is more than just a football game; it is a social event that attracts viewers from all walks of life and from all over the world. While there are certainly many true blue football fans who watch each and every year (like yours truly), the Superbowl is unique in that a large percentage of viewers are people who know little to nothing about football. Thousands of Super Bowl parties around the world see millions of people gather to watch the spectacle that includes elaborate half time shows, commercials that cost advertisers upwards of 5 million dollars for a 30 second slot[113], and the biggest stars of the NFL season competing for a championship. This is the very stage that Chris Matthews proved the expression true, and proved that he was in fact capable of being a big-time player.

During the 2015 NFL season Chris Matthews had been a member of the Seattle Seahawks. He had been a practice roster player for the majority of the season who was finally activated to the 53 man roster in December of that year and saw action in 3 games, mostly on special teams, recording only 1 special teams tackle. He did not get any reps on offence during that time. It wasn't until the NFC Championship game that he finally had an opportunity to make an impact. Seattle was trailing 19-14 with only 2:09 on the clock in the 4th quarter.

With the Seahawks' season on the line, Head Coach Pete Carol made a gutsy play call to attempt an onside kick and that is where the world was first introduced to Chris Matthews. In what was likely the most high stress and high profile game of his life, Matthews was able to make a big play and recovered the onside kick for Seattle. As a result of his clutch play, Seattle was able to eventually win the game that would allow them to advance to the

Superbowl. With the season on the line, Matthews proved the moment was not too big for him and he rose to the occasion making his first big time play in a big time game at the NFL level. If that were the only action he ever got in the NFL, while certainly impressive, it would not be evidence that he was a big-time player; only that he was able to perform under pressure and be in the right place at the right time for a single play. Fortunately for Matthews, this clutch play was only the beginning of his magical post season run.

Pete Caroll chose wide receivers; Doug Baldwin, Jermaine Kearse and Ricardo Lockette to start in the Superbowl. Although not chosen to start the game, Matthews was on the active roster and was in fact used at wide receiver. The combination of size, speed, and good hands that Matthews possessed became a nightmare match up that would ultimately result in Matthews nearly being named Superbowl MVP. Matthews saw his first action late in the second quarter when at 4:19 he made the first catch of his NFL career; a 44 yard reception with Kyle Arrington in coverage. Then with 0:02 left in the second quarter he made an 11 yard reception for his first touchdown, with Logan Ryan in coverage. At 13:48 of the third quarter he again made a big reception for 45 yards, with Kyle Arrington in coverage. With his aforementioned size and speed he was proving to be too much to handle for Ryan and Arrington. As a result, Patriots Head Coach Bill Belichick was forced to make a change. In a fitting turn of events, he assigned him the one player he knew could handle Matthews with his own combination of size and speed; former CFL'er Brandon Browner. With Browner now covering Matthews, he was kept in check for the remainder of the game. Matthews' final reception of the game was a short 9 yard reception with Browner in coverage. Matthews was targeted deep one last time late in the 4th quarter, however the pass was incomplete as Browner had him in tight coverage. If the Seahawks had gone on to win the game, Matthews could very well have been voted an improbable Superbowl MVP. However, with Seattle down by 4, with 26 seconds left on the clock in the 4th quarter, facing a second and goal from the 2 yard line, Caroll famously called a pass play which was intercepted on the goal line by New England sealing their victory.

Superbowl XLIX will be most remembered for that goal line interception. However, before that play took over the headlines and the history books, Chris Matthews completed the most productive NFL game of his career, recording 4 receptions on 5 targets for 109 yards at an average of 27.3 yards per reception with 1 touchdown. The very same attributes we observed during his stint in the CFL could be seen in his play during Superbowl XLIX where his above average production rating of 84.1 was good for second most productive receiver in the game, ending ahead of such notable players as Rob

Gronkowski, Danny Amendola, Ricardo Lockette, Doug Baldwin, and as I already mentioned, nearly winning him Superbowl MVP.

There are a couple of stats that stand out from both of his most productive games which were similar. Firstly, his above average receiving percentage 70% in the CFL vs. 80% in the NFL, and his average yards per reception of 24.4 in the CFL vs. 27.3 in the NFL. These two metrics demonstrate he had great hands and was a deep threat. He was not only able to put up team leading/MVP worthy performances in the CFL against supposedly inferior competition, but he was able to demonstrate his big play ability against the most elite team the NFL had seen in recent history in the New England Patriots.

And after all of that, what was Chris Matthews' reward for showing his coaches and the entire world he was a big-time player? He was offered a spot back on Seattle's practice squad for the following season; an offer he politely declined. In an article in Sports Illustrated Matthews advised *"I felt like I was too far ahead for that. I didn't want to go back to that life."*[114] Personally I believe that by that point he had more than earned an opportunity to start somewhere but as I have mentioned before, the NFL is a fickle business. Matthews signed with the Baltimore Ravens for the following season but eventually ran into injury trouble, and ultimately ended up being released and returned north to the CFL.

Whether it was playing against the Eskimos in Winnipeg in front of 30,000 fans, or against the Patriots in front of millions around the world, Matthews proved he was one of the rare players who had the ability to make big-time plays, in big-time games.

MOST PRODUCTIVE GAME

CHRIS MATTEWS

★★★★★★★ ★★

YEAR	2013
GP	1
REC	7
TARGETS	10
YARDS	171
AVERAGE	24.4
TD	1
RANK	1ST

MATTHEWS

13

94.4
PRODUCTION RATING

ELITE

MOST PRODUCTIVE GAME
CHRIS MATTHEWS

★★★★★★★★★★★★

YEAR	2015
GP	1
REC	4
TARGETS	5
YARDS	109
AVERAGE	27.3
TD	1
RANK	2ND

MATTHEWS

13

84.1
PRODUCTION RATING

ABOVE AVERAGE

CONCLUSION AND FINAL THOUGHTS

The concept for this book arose as a result of all the hate and shade I have seen thrown the CFL's way over the years. It began long before I even really knew anything about the CFL or football for that matter. I am a person who stands vehemently against criticizing others without walking a mile in their shoes. There are haters for virtually everything and everyone in life. The advent of the internet and social media has provided a platform where keyboard warriors can anonymously hate on and criticize virtually anyone or anything they want. It is so easy to jump to conclusions about someone or something without really knowing anything about the matter. Today, people can watch a short clip of a video online or hear a few sentences of someone speaking and instantly draw conclusions and pass judgments on those things despite not being able to see the big picture. The lack of critical thinking in this world has become a true pandemic. It is so much easier to go with the flow, believe what others believe, and not ruffle anyone's feathers that that is exactly what most people end up doing to get through life with the least amount of resistance possible.

The comparisons I detailed in this book were structured on objective metrics; think of them like grades in school. A grade in school is an objective way of determining how much or how little a student knows, or for lack of a better phrase "how good a student is". While they may not tell the entire story, at the very least grades provide us some objective metrics to be able to compare one student to another. I am a firm believer that most things in life can be boiled down to the numbers. This book arose in an attempt to add some objectivity to a situation that the average Joe has historically looked at only subjectively.

People look at the players in the CFL and immediately jump to the conclusion that because they are not in the NFL, they are obviously "not talented enough" to play there. If they were, they would be there right? This overly simplistic thinking is anchored on a couple of erroneous presuppositions; namely that talent evaluators responsible for signing players in the NFL are perfect in their assessments, infallible in their decision making, and have an unlimited number of roster spots available.

The truth is, every industry pays people to evaluate talent. They seek out candidates to do a job, review the applications, and ultimately choose whomever they think will be the best fit for the company. This however does not indicate in any way that the rejected candidates would be <u>unable</u> to do the job, especially with a vast talent pool to draw from.

Think about your own workplace, and I have no doubt you can quickly bring to mind numerous individuals that probably have no business being there, yet there they are. Does their presence mean that the candidates they beat out for the job were conclusively unable to do that job? Not likely. I wrote this book in an attempt to provide more context to a situation that is multifaceted and complex.

What I have always hated was hearing people make completely ridiculous statements about the CFL and its players, knowing full well that those people knew virtually nothing about football; although they would claim otherwise. I do not actually know a CFL hater named Dave, but I have met "Mark; the NFL ONLY fan", "Roger; the NFL ONLY fan", and many other people who live with varying degrees of dislike or even all-out hate for the only professional all-Canadian team league that has been around in one way or another for over 100 years! It is cool to hate on the CFL! It is so cool in fact that the haters go out of their way to publicly express their disdain for the CFL every opportunity they get. Almost as if they believe they somehow gain credibility by publicly expressing they do not watch "bush league" football. They are such superior sports fans, and superior people that they do not sully themselves by watching sub-par, inferior sports.

Let me leave something perfectly clear: When people watch NFL football, I believe they are watching an excellent product! It is a product that has only gotten better and better over the years as the NFL has transitioned to a more wide open passing game. I happen to be an NFL fan, and as a matter of fact was an NFL fan **BEFORE** I was a CFL fan. With a few exceptions, the NFL contains the most elite football players in the world, and at no point did I ever state otherwise. However, as I mentioned earlier in this book not all players in the NFL are created equal. People may wish to think otherwise, but the reality is there is only one Julio Jones. There is only one Aaron Donald. For every team like the Kansas City Chiefs there is an equal and opposite New York Jets. In other words, in contrast to all the amazing teams down south, there is also a lot of bad football that is played in the NFL.

Those that truly believe the NFL and CFL are galaxies apart in terms of talent are simply victims of two things; Firstly, ignorance of the CFL game, and secondly, falling prey to the marketing and hype machine that is the NFL. The NFL is likely the world's best marketed sports league. In fact, their marketing is so good that players in the NFL are made to appear larger than life when in reality the majority of them are absolutely comparable to most players in the CFL.

People who watched Delvin Breaux patrolling the Ticats' secondary may have scoffed at the "inferior" players that were playing our uniquely Canadian brand of football. Yet anyone who actually had their eyes and mind open would see a player who when afforded an opportunity to do so, became a year one starter in the NFL and objectively graded better than Stephon Gilmore and Darrelle Revis! Please note, I am not giving my opinion that I think or feel that Breaux was better than those players, I am stating a fact based on analytics. The numbers **SHOW** that Breaux played better than those two corners during the 2015 season. Would anyone dare make the statement that Stephon Gilmore or Darrelle Revis were "bush league players"? Of course not! Not only were they not bush league players, they were among the best in the game, and in my opinion, among the best of all time! The fact that Delvin Breaux could transition to the NFL and immediately produce and grade similarly to All-Pro's like Gilmore and Revis is a true testament to how incredibly talented many CFL players actually are! Although I do not understand why, for some reason it seems to hurt some people's feelings to have to acknowledge that many CFL players are actually highly talented elite players, but it is the truth!

When "bush-leaguer" Jerrell Freeman dominated the CFL in Saskatchewan out of a division III school, to some it may have been evidence that the CFL was such bad football that a division III player could be the best in the league. But what about when that same Jerrell Freeman ended the 2016 season with the highest tackle per game ratio in the NFL? What was the excuse then? How about when he graded as the 3rd best front seven defender in the entire league, was he a "bush-leaguer" then too? When the data showed that Freeman's name was in the same conversation as players like Luke Kuechly and Khalil Mack by performance; which one was it? Were Kuechly and Mack bush league players too? Or was Freeman actually among the game's elite? The reality is, you cannot have it both ways.

How can all this be? What's the explanation? The explanation is, the CFL is high level football. Period. It is a higher level than the NCAA, it is certainly a much higher level than Texas high school football, and with the exception of a relatively small percentage of the NFL's absolute best players; it is a notch below, but still a comparable level to the NFL.

If you will permit me to make one last comparison to the soccer world, I find that the hate many Canadians have for the CFL would be akin to people in Spain hating La Liga. Akin to people in Germany hating the Bundesliga. Akin to people in Italy hating Serie A, just because their league is not the English Premier League. As they always do however, the naysayers would likely have something to say about this: *"That comparison is stupid, it is totally not the same thing. La Liga has Real Madrid and Barcelona, Bundesliga has Bayern Munich and Borussia Dortmund, Serie A has Juventus, Napoli, and AC+Inter Milan, all elite teams."* While this statement is accurate; those teams do play in those leagues, are we just going to pretend that those teams do not play against teams like Elche CF, Cadiz CF, VfL Bochum, FC Schalke 04, Spezia, and US Cremonese? As always, it is just a cherry picked rebuttal the likes of which naysayers will always make no matter what contrasting information is presented.

The fact is, as of the writing of this chapter, the most up-to-date average squad value of teams in the English Premier League is now 521 million euros. If we compare this number to the same average squad values from Bundesliga (240.6 million), La Liga (239 million), and Serie A (231.5 million), once again, we objectively determined that these three "secondary" leagues are only 46.1%, 45.8% and 44.4% of what the Premier League is respectively. They are <u>clearly</u> not the "best of the best", so why not just shut them down, right?

Can you imagine people in Berlin, Mallorca or Genoa rejecting their teams in favour of supporting Manchester City? Supporting a team from hundreds or even thousands of miles away in a foreign country, representing a city they have likely never seen? I sure can't. Being of Portuguese descent myself, I cannot fathom people in Portugal not supporting Benfica, Porto, Sporting or any of the other teams in the Primeira Liga, simply because they are not in the Premier League. We love our teams as we should! As a matter of fact, Portuguese Primeira Liga might be minuscule compared to the Premier League in terms of finances, but the Premier League can thank the Primeira Liga for developing Cristiano Ronaldo, Bruno Fernandes, João Moutinho, Diogo Jota, Ruben Dias, Bernardo Silva and so many others.

Some of you who managed to get through this whole book may still think this project proves nothing. The analytics prove nothing, the statistical comparisons prove nothing, heck, even the player and coach quotes also prove nothing. You may even think *"They are just being nice. They would never tell the truth about how bad CFL football really is."* Funny enough, if one looks at the global sports picture we can find so many examples of players that transition to other leagues in their respective sports and in fact do make honest statements that describe how they believe one league compares to the other, even if it does not necessarily paint the lesser league in a positive light. In fact, some of the quotes from CFL players and coaches you have read in this very book are examples of this!

One of Europe's most famous soccer players; Zlatan Ibrahimovic had this to say about the level of play in North American Major League Soccer during his stint with the Los Angeles Galaxy: *"MLS is not the level of Europe, to be honest. Before, I played with players either on my level or close to it which makes the game connect easier. Here, I am like a Ferrari among Fiats.* [115] In addition he also stated *"I can only compare what is here with where I've been. It's a big difference, but I think MLS is growing, it's in the right direction."* [116] From his statement, there can be no doubt that he considered the level of play in Major League Soccer much lower than the leagues he played in in Europe; Premier League, La Liga, Serie A and Ligue 1.

Very similarly, Frederico Bernardeschi made this statement about the level of play he encountered after signing with Toronto FC in MLS:

"I didn't expect this kind of intensity. This is a different type of football, which still has some growing to do, but great strides have been made. It is still lacking a little, but physically the athletes are at a good level. I think that tactically they are not yet at Italian levels, but I believe that athletically, watching Premier League matches and having played against Premier League teams, this football resembles the English one." [117] Frederico made it clear that the physicality of Major League Soccer was more intense than he was initially expecting. Just like Zlatan however, he also made it clear that tactically, from a football quality standpoint, MLS still lags behind soccer in Europe, Italian Serie A more specifically.

Ruben Dias, a defender who transitioned from Benfica in the Portuguese Primeira Liga to Manchester City in the English Premier League had this to say when asked 'how different did he find the Premier League to what he was used to' (in Portugal): *"Obviously it's just one match still, but the intensity, the pitch (field), the quality of the pitch as well, it's another league. It's the top league. It's the top."* [118] Dias clearly indicates that there is a noticeable difference in the intensity of the EPL over his league in Portugal. He further indicates that the quality of the pitch, in other words the facilities etc are better in England compared to Portugal. Honest statements that are not derogatory in nature but simply citing differences encountered.

Former German Footballer Lothar Matthaus compares the English Premier League to his country's top flight Bundesliga and was quoted as saying: *"You can play in the first four or five clubs in the Bundesliga and have the same quality as the Premier League."* [119] This statement makes it clear that he believes that while the Bundesliga possesses 4-5 teams (out of 18 total) that are on par with teams in the Premier League, the majority by inference, are not. Interestingly, I believe this statement is actually supported by my analysis of average team values where the data shows that only 4 Bundesliga teams are valued close to or above the Premier League average squad value of 516 million euros.

Moving a little closer to home, Toronto Argonauts rookie offensive lineman Dylan Giffen had this to say during his first training camp about the level of play in the CFL, after coming out of the University of Western Ontario in U-Sports. *"Physically, the speed is insane. These guys are so fast, and there are so many guys who came up here (from the NFL) and brought all of that skill with them. They are such amazing pass rushers. The speed of the game is what I'm trying to learn and catch up to the most."*[120] In making this statement, he was clearly admitting the speed, and by inference the level of play he experienced in U-Sports was significantly lower than what he was experiencing in the CFL.

CFL Global Defensive End Thiadric Hansen had this to say when comparing the level of play he experienced in the CFL vs what he had experienced in the GFL (German Football League): *"It's super fast (in the CFL), way more physical than I was used to in Europe. It was really an eye opener. It's different here. The speed is way different, also the individual guys are way better. They are more sound in their technique. They are physical and they know their technique, that's really the big big difference."*[121] In making this statement, Thiadric made it exceedingly clear that the play in the CFL was much more physical, much faster, with much more talented players than he played against in the GFL.

While all these examples clearly make distinctions between the noted leagues, does that for example mean that Major League Soccer, Portuguese Primeira Liga, German Bundesliga, U-Sports and GFL are all bush league and not worth watching? OF COURSE NOT! That is the point of this whole book!

There is nothing inherently insulting about admitting something one has experienced just isn't as difficult as something else they've experienced. I believe players are being honest when they say that the CFL is a very high level of football, and similarly honest when they state there is in fact a small gap between the NFL and CFL from a talent and intensity standpoint, and a humongous gap in finances, both in favour of the NFL. I have yet to find one single player who has experienced the play in both leagues that made a statement to the effect that the CFL is "bush league" football; they could not say that because it would not be true if they did!

If I had to summarize this whole book into one single paragraph, this is what I would say:

'From a talent perspective? Any CFL team would beat any college team. An average CFL team would play respectably against an average NFL team; they may not win, but they would not be destroyed. A team of CFL All-Stars would be in the top half of the NFL. A team of NFL All-Pros would beat any CFL team, including a team of CFL All-Stars.'

The conclusion I arrived at after an enormous amount of analysis is this: The difference between the NFL and CFL from a talent perspective is basically just the relatively small number of NFL All-Pro calibre players.

Former Toronto Argonauts and journeyman NFL quarterback McLeod Bethel-Thompson explains it like this: *"There's a top 20 percent of the NFL that are freak daddies, no doubt. The Aaron Donald's of the world, freak daddies, right? And there's the middle 60 percent just like us — I was there, just like me — and there's a bottom 20 percent where it's like, bruh, you would get cut from a CFL team."*[122] It is interesting to note, that just like numerous examples we have seen previously, McLeod also alludes to the CFL being approximately 80% of what the NFL is from a talent standpoint.

Rennie Curran, a former University of Georgia and Tennessee Titans linebacker summed it up nicely when he was asked to compare the talent level between the NFL and CFL. *"I'd say it's definitely neck and neck. I mean, you got a lot of guys who play in the CFL who played on NFL rosters and who performed extremely well. And that was one of the things that really was surprising to me was coming from playing in the NFL with the Tennessee Titans and then going up to the CFL, was just how many guys that were up there that were more than good enough to play on NFL rosters. And maybe it was a case where they didn't get an opportunity, maybe they got hurt or had some type of trouble they ran into, but ultimately the talent was there. You see it even now a lot of guys are going back and forth between the NFL and the CFL and it was good quality football."*[123]

Chris Streveler, former Blue Bombers back up quarterback, now a back up with the New York Jets said it this way: *"You see a lot of guys up there that have success, that come down to the NFL and continue to have success...If you take out the top 3 to 5% of NFL players, that's exactly what the CFL is. There's so many players out there that are good enough to be in the NFL, for one reason or another they're just not. And so, a lot of them are up there."*[124]

I will end with one of my favourite quotes ever that came from former NFL tight end Luke Willson. Luke played a total of 8 seasons in the NFL after having been drafted in the 5th round of the 2013 NFL draft by Seattle. His rookie season he played in, and won Superbowl XLVIII with the Seahawks. He described a comical scenario during an NFL off season where he had trained with a CFL linebacker who was previously unknown to him named...Adam Bighill.

"There's a guy that I trained with in the offseason one year, you played against him: Adam Bighill. Oh, man, this dude was dominant. Dominant.

He's like, 'Hey, do you want to do some one-on-ones? He's a linebacker and I could run pretty good, so I remember looking at him like, 'Bro, get the f*** out of here. You want to do one-on-ones? I'm about to roast you, my guy. You're a linebacker, no one on the planet Earth would want to do this.

This guy was glued to me! And then I'm like, okay, I'm just gonna run by him but he was fast as f***. I'm like, 'This guy does it all' and it was very confusing to me how not only he wasn't in the NFL, he was not starting in the NFL.

At that point when I was training with Rob, I'd seen a lot of NFL linebackers in my life and Adam Bighill athletically — and I'm assuming he was also cerebral — was up there with the best of them."[125]

The quotes could go on, and on, and on...

Every single player quote I have provided in this book leads us to the understanding that the CFL is good quality football, played by high level athletes. These are not statements from beer bellied fans who watch some football on TV and think they know what they are talking about. These are not my opinions, but the testimonies of players; elite athletes who have played at some of the highest levels in the United States that are saying these things. When Cris Carter says *"Any CFL team could beat the University of Alabama"* he means what he says and knows what he's talking about. A Pro Football Hall of Famer who made 1,101 receptions for almost 14,000 receiving yards and scored 130 touchdowns in the NFL likely knows a thing or two about football. The fact that "Dave; the NFL ONLY fan" can hear statements like these yet can still hold onto the belief that the CFL is on par with American high school football reveals an arrogant bias that just will not let them see the truth.

TSN's Farhan Lalji once told me on Twitter: *"Small piece of advice: Don't empower the haters by letting them infuriate you or by reacting. You don't need their validation to love this game"*. And you know what? He is absolutely right! We do not need the hater's validation to love this game. The reality is, if "Dave; the NFL ONLY fan" managed to get through this entire book, they would likely still not believe a single word I wrote. They have an unbelievable ability to ignore the numbers, ignore the analytics, ignore the player testimonies, and ignore the other issues we examined because the truth is just too hard of a pill to swallow for them. The cognitive dissonance is just too uncomfortable. In the end, the "Daves" will most likely return to their safe place. To the one statement that will make them feel like all is once again right in the world:

"If they were good enough...They'd be in the NFL"

Even though the "Daves" of the world will continue to recite their mantra, likely for the rest of their lives, most of you who finished this book have allowed yourselves to follow the evidence to see where it led. As such, you should now have a much more robust understanding of the quality of play that is found in the Canadian Football League. Hopefully this has given you a greater appreciation for the highly talented, elite athletes who ply their football trade in the great white north, and beyond!

SUPPLEMENTAL DATA

Player composition of "mini league" teams

	Player	Position	Market Value	League	Team
1	Nabil Fekir	CAM	40,000,000	La Liga	Real Betis
2	João Palhinha	CDM	28,000,000	Premier League	Fulham FC
3	Aleksandar Mitrović	CF	28,000,000	Premier League	Fulham FC
4	Axel Disasi	CB	25,000,000	Ligue 1	Monaco
5	Yunus Musah	CM	25,000,000	La Liga	Valencia
6	Gabriel Barbosa	CF	22,000,000	Brasileirão	Flamengo
7	Mattia Zaccagni	LW	22,000,000	Italian Serie A	Lazio
8	Ismaïla Sarr	RW	22,000,000	English Championship	Watford
9	Alejandro Grimaldo	LB	20,000,000	Liga Portugal	Benfica
10	Brennan Johnson	CF	20,000,000	Premier League	Nottingham Forest
11	Maxence Lacroix	CB	20,000,000	Bundesliga	Wolfsburg
12	Moussa Niakhate	CB	18,000,000	Premier League	Nottingham Forest
13	Ritsu Doan	RW	15,000,000	Bundesliga	Freiburg
14	Manuel Lazzari	RB	15,000,000	Italian Serie A	Lazio
15	Alassane Plea	LW	15,000,000	Bundesliga	Monchengladbach
16	Ugurcan Cakir	GK	14,000,000	Turkish SuperLig	Trabzonspor
17	Julian Draxler	LW	12,000,000	Liga Portugal	Benfica
18	Junior Firpo	LB	12,000,000	Premier League	Leeds United
19	João Mário	RB	12,000,000	Liga Portugal	Porto
20	Gelson Martins	RW	10,000,000	Ligue 1	Monaco
21	Bright Osayi-Samuel	RB	9,000,000	Turkish SuperLig	Fenerbahce
22	Anthony Lopes	GK	9,000,000	Ligue 1	Lyon
23	Matheus Reis	LB	8,000,000	Liga Portugal	Sporting CP
24	Adam Marusic	RB	7,500,000	Italian Serie A	Lazio
25	Ezgjan Alioski	LB	6,500,000	Turkish SuperLig	Fenerbahce
26	Julen Agirrezabala	GK	5,000,000	La Liga	Athletic Bilbao

TEAM 1 TOTAL   440,000,000
AVERAGE/PLAYER   16,923,077

SUPPLEMENTAL DATA

	Player	Position	Market Value	League	Team
1	Edson Álvarez	CDM	35,000,000	Eredivisie	Ajax
2	Diogo Costa	GK	35,000,000	Liga Portugal	Porto
3	Orkun Kökcü	CM	27,000,000	Eredivisie	Feyenoord
4	Mattéo Guendouzi	CM	25,000,000	Ligue 1	Marseille
5	Arnaud Kalimuendo	CF	25,000,000	Ligue 1	Stade Rennais
6	Gonçalo Inácio	CB	23,000,000	Liga Portugal	Sporting CP
7	Pepê	LW	22,000,000	Liga Portugal	Porto
8	Philipp Lienhart	CB	20,000,000	Bundesliga	Freiburg
9	Wissam Ben Yedder	CF	20,000,000	Ligue 1	Monaco
10	Ramy Bensebaini	LB	20,000,000	Bundesliga	Monchengladbach
11	Taiwo Awoniyi	CF	20,000,000	Premier League	Nottingham Forest
12	Francisco Trincão	RW	20,000,000	Liga Portugal	Sporting CP
13	Chancel Mbemba	CB	17,000,000	Ligue 1	Marseille
14	Álex Berenguer	LW	15,000,000	La Liga	Athletic Bilbao
15	Jonathan Clauss	RB	15,000,000	Ligue 1	Marseille
16	Tecatito	RW	14,000,000	La Liga	Sevilla
17	Altay Bayindir	GK	13,000,000	Turkish SuperLig	Fenerbahce
18	Owen Wijndal	LB	12,000,000	Eredivisie	Ajax
19	Gabriel Veron	LW	12,000,000	Liga Portugal	Porto
20	Gonzalo Montiel	RB	12,000,000	La Liga	Sevilla
21	Ansgar Knauff	RW	10,000,000	Bundesliga	Eintracht Frankfurt
22	Kiliann Sildillia	RB	9,000,000	Bundesliga	Freiburg
23	Kevin Trapp	GK	8,500,000	Bundesliga	Eintracht Frankfurt
24	Melvin Bard	LB	8,000,000	Ligue 1	Nice
25	Kenny Tete	RB	7,000,000	Premier League	Fulham FC
26	Bjorn Meijer	LB	6,500,000	Belgian League	FC Brugge

TEAM 2 TOTAL	451,000,000
AVERAGE/PLAYER	17,346,154

SUPPLEMENTAL DATA

	Player	Position	Market Value	League	Team
1	Ibrahim Sangaré	CDM	35,000,000	Eredivisie	PSV Eindhoven
2	Martin Terrier	LW	35,000,000	Ligue 1	Stade Rennais
3	Manu Koné	CM	25,000,000	Bundesliga	Monchengladbach
4	Danilo	CDM	25,000,000	Premier League	Nottingham Forest
5	Borja Iglesias	CF	25,000,000	La Liga	Real Betis
6	Giorgi Mamardashvili	GK	25,000,000	La Liga	Valencia
7	Angeliño	LB	20,000,000	Bundesliga	1910 Hoffenheim
8	Matthias Ginter	CB	20,000,000	Bundesliga	Freiburg
9	Pascal Struijk	CB	20,000,000	Premier League	Leeds United
10	Jonathan Bamba	LW	20,000,000	Ligue 1	Lille
11	Breel Embolo	CF	20,000,000	Ligue 1	Monaco
12	Dominic Solanke	CF	18,000,000	Premier League	Bournemouth
13	Jeremy Doku	RW	18,000,000	Ligue 1	Stade Rennais
14	Marcos Senesi	CB	17,000,000	Premier League	Bournemouth
15	Noa Lang	LW	15,000,000	Belgian League	FC Brugge
16	Héctor Bellerín	RB	15,000,000	Liga Portugal	Sporting CP
17	Erik Lamela	RW	14,000,000	La Liga	Sevilla
18	Justin Bijlow	GK	13,000,000	Eredivisie	Feyenoord
19	Javi Galán	LB	12,000,000	La Liga	Celta Vigo
20	Joe Scally	RB	12,000,000	Bundesliga	Monchengladbach
21	Dango Ouattara	RW	10,000,000	Premier League	Bournemouth
22	Alexander Bah	RB	8,000,000	Liga Portugal	Benfica
23	Luís Maximiano	GK	8,000,000	Italian Serie A	Lazio
24	Kevin Mbabu	RB	7,000,000	Premier League	Fulham FC
25	Ismail Jakobs	LB	7,000,000	Ligue 1	Monaco
26	Borna Barisic	LB	6,500,000	Scottish Premiership	Rangers

TEAM 3 TOTAL	450,500,000	
AVERAGE/PLAYER	17,326,923	

SUPPLEMENTAL DATA

	Player	Position	Market Value	League	Team
1	Gonçalo Guedes	LW	32,000,000	Liga Portugal	Benfica
2	Brenden Aaronson	CAM	30,000,000	Premier League	Leeds United
3	Unai Simón	GK	25,000,000	La Liga	Athletic Bilbao
4	Maxence Caqueret	CM	25,000,000	Ligue 1	Lyon
5	Morgan Gibbs-White	CAM	25,000,000	Premier League	Nottingham Forest
6	Noah Okafor	CF	25,000,000	Austrian Bundesliga	Red Bull Salzburg
7	Marcus Edwards	RW	25,000,000	Liga Portugal	Sporting CP
8	Renan Lodi	LB	20,000,000	Premier League	Nottingham Forest
9	David Ca o	CB	20,000,000	Liga Portugal	Porto
10	Mehdi Taremi	CF	20,000,000	Liga Portugal	Porto
11	Arthur Theate	CB	20,000,000	Ligue 1	Stade Rennais
12	Manor Solomon	LW	18,000,000	Premier League	Fulham FC
13	Moussa Dembélé	CF	18,000,000	Ligue 1	Lyon
14	Harry Wilson	RW	17,000,000	Premier League	Fulham FC
15	Malo Gusto	RB	15,000,000	Ligue 1	Lyon
16	Oumar Solet	CB	15,000,000	Austrian Bundesliga	Red Bull Salzburg
17	David Brooks	RW	14,000,000	Premier League	Bournemouth
18	Justin Kluivert	LW	14,000,000	La Liga	Valencia
19	Ferdi Kadioglu	RB	12,000,000	Turkish SuperLig	Fenerbahce
20	Pau López	GK	12,000,000	Ligue 1	Marseille
21	Zaidu	LB	10,000,000	Liga Portugal	Porto
22	Devyne Rensch	RB	8,000,000	Eredivisie	Ajax
23	Koen Casteels	GK	8,000,000	Bundesliga	Wolfsburg
24	Jordan Teze	RB	7,000,000	Eredivisie	PSV Eindhoven
25	Cristiano Biraghi	LB	6,500,000	Italian Serie A	Fiorentina
26	Philipp Max	LB	6,000,000	Bundesliga	Eintracht Frankfurt

TEAM 4 TOTAL	447,500,000	
AVERAGE/PLAYER	17,211,538	

SUPPLEMENTAL DATA

	Player	Position	Market Value	League	Team
1	Jonathan David	CF	45,000,000	Ligue 1	Lille
2	Daichi Kamada	CAM	30,000,000	Bundesliga	Eintracht Frankfurt
3	Pedro Gonçalves	LW	30,000,000	Liga Portugal	Sporting CP
4	Iñaki Williams	CF	25,000,000	La Liga	Athletic Bilbao
5	Nico Williams	RW	25,000,000	La Liga	Athletic Bilbao
6	Mohamed Camara	CDM	25,000,000	Ligue 1	Monaco
7	Aleksandr Golovin	CAM	22,000,000	Ligue 1	Monaco
8	Dean Henderson	GK	22,000,000	Premier League	Nottingham Forest
9	Nikola Milenković	CB	20,000,000	Italian Serie A	Fiorentina
10	Benjamin Sesko	CF	20,000,000	Austrian Bundesliga	Red Bull Salzburg
11	Robin Koch	CB	18,000,000	Premier League	Leeds United
12	Nuno Tavares	LB	18,000,000	Ligue 1	Marseille
13	Lucas Ocampos	LW	18,000,000	La Liga	Sevilla
14	Cengiz Ünder	RW	17,000,000	Ligue 1	Marseille
15	António Silva	CB	15,000,000	Liga Portugal	Benfica
16	Armand Laurienté	LW	14,000,000	Italian Serie A	US Sassuolo
17	Thierry Correia	RB	14,000,000	La Liga	Valencia
18	Krépin Diatta	RW	13,000,000	Ligue 1	Monaco
19	Lutsharel Geertruida	RB	12,000,000	Eredivisie	Feyenoord
20	Walter Benítez	GK	12,000,000	Eredivisie	PSV Eindhoven
21	Antonee Robinson	LB	10,000,000	Premier League	Fulham FC
22	Matheuzinho	RB	8,000,000	Brasileirão	Flamengo
23	Brice Samba	GK	8,000,000	Ligue 1	RC Lens
24	Mert Müldür	RB	7,000,000	Italian Serie A	US Sassuolo
25	Luca Netz	LB	6,500,000	Bundesliga	Monchengladbach
26	Matías Viña	LB	6,000,000	Premier League	Bournemouth

TEAM 5 TOTAL	460,500,000
AVERAGE/PLAYER	17,711,538

SUPPLEMENTAL DATA

	Player	Position	Market Value	League	Team
1	Amine Gouiri	CF	38,000,000	Ligue 1	Stade Rennais
2	Seko Fofana	CM	30,000,000	Ligue 1	RC Lens
3	Steven Bergwijn	LW	27,000,000	Eredivisie	Ajax
4	Enes Ünal	CF	25,000,000	La Liga	Getafe
5	Hugo Guillamón	CDM	25,000,000	La Liga	Valencia
6	Malcom	RW	24,000,000	Russian Premier League	Zenit St. Petersburg
7	Hamed Junior Traorè	CAM	22,000,000	Premier League	Bournemouth
8	Illan Meslier	GK	22,000,000	Premier League	Leeds United
9	Nico Elvedi	CB	20,000,000	Bundesliga	Monchengladbach
10	Andrea Pinamonti	CF	20,000,000	Italian Serie A	US Sassuolo
11	Calvin Bassey	CB	18,000,000	Eredivisie	Ajax
12	Vanderson	RB	18,000,000	Ligue 1	Monaco
13	Sofiane Diop	LW	18,000,000	Ligue 1	Nice
14	Daniel James	RW	16,000,000	Premier League	Fulham FC
15	Douglas Santos	LB	16,000,000	Russian Premier League	Zenit St. Petersburg
16	Morato	CB	15,000,000	Liga Portugal	Benfica
17	Diego Rossi	LW	14,000,000	Turkish SuperLig	Fenerbahce
18	Youcef Atal	RB	14,000,000	Ligue 1	Nice
19	Jonas Hofmann	RW	13,000,000	Bundesliga	Monchengladbach
20	Christian Günter	LB	10,000,000	Bundesliga	Freiburg
21	Ruben Aguilar	RB	10,000,000	Ligue 1	Monaco
22	Alexander Nübel	GK	10,000,000	Ligue 1	Monaco
23	Clinton Mata	RB	7,000,000	Belgian League	FC Brugge
24	Ivan Provedel	GK	7,000,000	Italian Serie A	Lazio
25	Paulo Otávio	LB	6,500,000	Bundesliga	Wolfsburg
26	Mauro Júnior	LB	6,000,000	Eredivisie	PSV Eindhoven

TEAM 6 TOTAL	451,500,000	
AVERAGE/PLAYER	17,365,385	

SUPPLEMENTAL DATA

	Player	Position	Market Value	League	Team
1	José Gayà	LB	40,000,000	La Liga	Valencia
2	Randal Kolo Muani	CF	37,000,000	Bundesliga	Eintracht Frankfurt
3	Otávio	RM	30,000,000	Liga Portugal	Porto
4	Sofyan Amrabat	CDM	25,000,000	Italian Serie A	Fiorentina
5	Jack Harrison	LW	25,000,000	Premier League	Leeds United
6	Rafa Silva	CF	23,000,000	Liga Portugal	Benfica
7	Domenico Berardi	RW	23,000,000	Italian Serie A	US Sassuolo
8	Djibril Sow	CM	22,000,000	Bundesliga	Eintracht Frankfurt
9	Pedro	CF	20,000,000	Brasileirão	Flamengo
10	Strahinja Pavlovic	CB	20,000,000	Austrian Bundesliga	Red Bull Salzburg
11	Alessio Romagnoli	CB	18,000,000	Italian Serie A	Lazio
12	Neco Williams	RB	18,000,000	Premier League	Nottingham Forest
13	Odysseas Vlachodimos	GK	16,000,000	Liga Portugal	Benfica
14	Jonathan Ikoné	RW	16,000,000	Italian Serie A	Fiorentina
15	Samuel Lino	LW	16,000,000	La Liga	Valencia
16	Tuta	CB	15,000,000	Bundesliga	Eintracht Frankfurt
17	Adrien Truffert	LB	15,000,000	Ligue 1	Stade Rennais
18	Stephane Singo	RB	14,000,000	Italian Serie A	FC Torino
19	Ryan Kent	LW	14,000,000	Scottish Premiership	Rangers
20	Tajon Buchanan	RW	12,000,000	Belgian League	FC Brugge
21	Gerónimo Rulli	GK	10,000,000	Eredivisie	Ajax
22	Amar Dedic	RB	10,000,000	Austrian Bundesliga	Red Bull Salzburg
23	Luca Pellegrini	LB	9,000,000	Italian Serie A	Lazio
24	Jonas Omlin	GK	7,000,000	Bundesliga	Monchengladbach
25	Valentino Lazaro	RB	6,500,000	Italian Serie A	FC Torino
26	Ayrton Lucas	LB	6,000,000	Brasileirão	Flamengo

TEAM 7 TOTAL		467,500,000		
AVERAGE/PLAYER		17,980,769		

SUPPLEMENTAL DATA

	Player	Position	Market Value	League	Team
1	Jurrien Timber	CB	45,000,000	Eredivisie	Ajax
2	Marcus Thuram	CF	32,000,000	Bundesliga	Monchengladbach
3	Jesper Lindström	CAM	28,000,000	Bundesliga	Eintracht Frankfurt
4	Khéphren Thuram	CDM	25,000,000	Ligue 1	Nice
5	Nicolás González	LW	23,000,000	Italian Serie A	Fiorentina
6	Ciro Immobile	CF	23,000,000	Italian Serie A	Lazio
7	David Neres	RW	22,000,000	Liga Portugal	Benfica
8	Destiny Udogie	LB	22,000,000	Italian Serie A	Udinese
9	Davide Frattesi	CM	22,000,000	Italian Serie A	US Sassuolo
10	Jean-Clair Todibo	CB	20,000,000	Ligue 1	Nice
11	Endrick	CF	20,000,000	Brasileirão	Palmeiras
12	Tosin Adarabioyo	CB	18,000,000	Premier League	Fulham FC
13	Dodô	RB	17,000,000	Italian Serie A	Fiorentina
14	Felipe Anderson	RW	15,000,000	Italian Serie A	Lazio
15	Galeno	LW	15,000,000	Liga Portugal	Porto
16	Rui Silva	GK	15,000,000	La Liga	Real Betis
17	Alex Telles	LB	14,000,000	La Liga	Sevilla
18	Kerem Aktürkoglu	LW	13,000,000	Turkish SuperLig	Galatasaray
19	Ridle Baku	RB	13,000,000	Bundesliga	Wolfsburg
20	Timothy Weah	RW	12,000,000	Ligue 1	Lille
21	Bernd Leno	GK	10,000,000	Premier League	Fulham FC
22	James Tavernier	RB	10,000,000	Scottish Premiership	Rangers
23	Nicolás Tagliafico	LB	9,000,000	Ligue 1	Lyon
24	Mark Flekken	GK	7,000,000	Bundesliga	Freiburg
25	Sacha Boey	RB	6,500,000	Turkish SuperLig	Galatasaray
26	Ridvan Yilmaz	LB	6,000,000	Scottish Premiership	Rangers

TEAM 8 TOTAL 462,500,000
AVERAGE/PLAYER 17,788,462

SUPPLEMENTAL DATA

	Player	Position	Market Value	League	Team
1	Sergej Milinković-Savić	CM	60,000,000	Italian Serie A	Lazio
2	Evan Ndicka	CB	32,000,000	Bundesliga	Eintracht Frankfurt
3	Gonçalo Ramos	CF	30,000,000	Liga Portugal	Benfica
4	Guido Rodríguez	CDM	28,000,000	La Liga	Real Betis
5	Youssouf Fofana	CM	25,000,000	Ligue 1	Monaco
6	Luis Sinisterra	LW	22,000,000	Premier League	Leeds United
7	Nicolas Pépé	RW	22,000,000	Ligue 1	Nice
8	Evanilson	CF	22,000,000	Liga Portugal	Porto
9	Castello Lukeba	CB	20,000,000	Ligue 1	Lyon
10	Caio Henrique	LB	20,000,000	Ligue 1	Monaco
11	João Pedro	CF	20,000,000	English Championship	Watford
12	Iñigo Martínez	CB	18,000,000	La Liga	Athletic Bilbao
13	Rasmus Kristensen	RB	15,000,000	Premier League	Leeds United
14	Luiz Henrique	RW	15,000,000	La Liga	Real Betis
15	Juanmi	LW	15,000,000	La Liga	Real Betis
16	Bono	GK	15,000,000	La Liga	Sevilla
17	Marcos Acuña	LB	14,000,000	La Liga	Sevilla
18	Djed Spence	RB	13,000,000	Ligue 1	Stade Rennais
19	Roland Sallai	RW	12,000,000	Bundesliga	Freiburg
20	Karl Toko Ekambi	LW	12,000,000	Ligue 1	Stade Rennais
21	David Soria	GK	10,000,000	La Liga	Getafe
22	Hamari Traore	RB	10,000,000	Ligue 1	Stade Rennais
23	Abner	LB	8,000,000	La Liga	Real Betis
24	Gilberto	RB	6,000,000	Liga Portugal	Benfica
25	Hassane Kamara	LB	6,000,000	English Championship	Watford
26	Marko Dmitrović	GK	5,000,000	La Liga	Sevilla

TEAM 9 TOTAL	475,000,000	
AVERAGE/PLAYER	18,269,231	

SUPPLEMENTAL DATA

	Player	Position	Market Value	League	Team
1	Sergej Milinković-Savić	CM	60,000,000	Italian Serie A	Lazio
2	Nabil Fekir	CAM	40,000,000	La Liga	Real Betis
3	Edson Álvarez	CDM	35,000,000	Eredivisie	Ajax
4	Jurrien Timber	CB	45,000,000	Eredivisie	Ajax
5	Evan Ndicka	CB	32,000,000	Bundesliga	Eintracht Frankfurt
6	Axel Disasi	CB	25,000,000	Ligue 1	Monaco
7	José Gayà	LB	40,000,000	La Liga	Valencia
8	Destiny Udogie	LB	22,000,000	Italian Serie A	Udinese
9	Caio Henrique	LB	20,000,000	Ligue 1	Monaco
10	Vanderson	RB	18,000,000	Ligue 1	Monaco
11	Neco Williams	RB	18,000,000	Premier League	Nottingham Forest
12	Dodô	RB	17,000,000	Italian Serie A	Fiorentina
13	Jonathan David	CF	45,000,000	Ligue 1	Lille
14	Amine Gouiri	CF	38,000,000	Ligue 1	Stade Rennais
15	Randal Kolo Muani	CF	37,000,000	Bundesliga	Eintracht Frankfurt
16	Marcus Edwards	RW	25,000,000	Liga Portugal	Sporting CP
17	Nico Williams	RW	25,000,000	La Liga	Athletic Bilbao
18	Malcom	RW	24,000,000	Russian Premier League	Zenit St. Petersburg
19	Martin Terrier	LW	35,000,000	Ligue 1	Stade Rennais
20	Gonçalo Guedes	LW	32,000,000	Liga Portugal	Benfica
21	Pedro Gonçalves	LW	30,000,000	Liga Portugal	Sporting CP
22	Diogo Costa	GK	35,000,000	Liga Portugal	Porto
23	Giorgi Mamardashvili	GK	25,000,000	La Liga	Valencia
24	Unai Simón	GK	25,000,000	La Liga	Athletic Bilbao
25	Ibrahim Sangaré	CDM	35,000,000	Eredivisie	PSV Eindhoven
26	Marcus Thuram	CF	32,000,000	Bundesliga	Monchengladbach

MINI LEAGUE ALL STARS

TEAM TOTAL	815,000,000
AVERAGE/PLAYER	31,346,154

SUPPLEMENTAL DATA

NFL Salary Cap Information – from "Overthecap.com"

2023 - NFL league wide average salary:
$3,141,820 (All players at all positions)

NFL league wide median annual salary = **$1,062,762**

NFL league wide average guaranteed salary = **$1,436,092**
Total number of players = **2,474**

Group A – Players earning over 1 million/season

Total number of players = **1,425 (57.6%)**
Average annual salary = **$4,823,052**
Average annual guaranteed money = **$2,475,841**

Group B – Players earning under 1 million/season

Total number of players = **1,049 (42.4%)**
Average annual salary = **$857,973**
Average annual guaranteed money = $23,659

INDEX

1 https://www.si.com/2014/06/24/cfl-doug-flutie-grey-cup-canadian-football-league
2 https://www.pff.com/grades
3 https://www.youtube.com/watch?v=jGJyCxYMmeo
4 https://www.youtube.com/watch?v=6S7fUTqsASQ
5 https://www.statista.com/statistics/193457/total-league-revenue-of-the-nfl-since-2005/
6 https://www.youtube.com/watch?v=w9nmDTY4eVM
7 https://www.youtube.com/watch?v=_R943_HUSpg
8 https://jzmedia.ca/all-2/
9 https://www.youtube.com/watch?v=WVAq1Qw7oRE
10 https://www.usatoday.com/videos/sports/2017/10/26/marshawn-lynch-returns-his-high-school-run-over-teenagers/107030918/
11 http://www.sportyinsider.com/20-biggest-nfl-draft-busts-of-all-time/13/
12 https://www.thesportster.com/football/top-15-biggest-draft-busts-in-miami-dolphins-history/
13 When comparing Williams only to his teammates; Avery and Johnson, he was rated the highest of the 3 of them. However once we added the other top backs, many of which set new bars in the relevant metrics, we observe that in the league wide comparison Avery ends up higher rated than Williams. This is because each player's performance is being compared to the top output for a particular metric.
14 http://sports.espn.go.com/nfl/news/story?id=2462506
15 https://www.argonauts.ca/2018/07/17/argonauts-practice-s-j-green-july-17-2018/ at 0:37
16 http://bleacherreport.com/articles/2776989
17 To be eligible, leagues must be the top tier in their respective country and have a total market value of a minimum of 20 million euros as of the time of writing.
18 Market value reflects the combined transfer value of all players on the squad. All market value data from https://www.transfermarkt.com/
19 https://www.uefa.com/nationalassociations/uefarankings/country/#/yr/2023
20 https://www.youtube.com/watch?v=J-qU7AH1GzM
21 https://www.si.com/nfl/2014/06/23/marc-trestman-canada-week-guest-monday-morning-qb
22 http://www.ncaa.org/about/resources/research/football-probability-competing-beyond-high-school
23 https://www.youtube.com/watch?v=COfOxTgpBVEU at 0:22 and 3:14
24 https://www.cbc.ca/news/canada/manitoba/former-blue-bomber-chris-matthews-toast-of-super-bowl-xlix-1.2940857 starting at 1:54
25 7:55 of One Bills Live Podcast dated 8/12: Andrew Catalon & Cynthia Frelund preview Bills-Colts, The Maddy Awards from Bills camp, OBL Friday fan..."
26 https://www.columbian.com/news/2010/oct/15/baylor-drops-player-charged-with-pot-possession/
27 https://open.spotify.com/episode/6KCxGgnwXba5ycHbi5eBcX?si=G7INfA_MT6OgcqeoZZxkOQ&dl_branch=1 Move the Sticks Podcast – Episode 693 – 23:16
28 PFF NFL podcast episode: "OL Masterminds, building an offensive line and freaks of nature with Geoff Schwartz" at 32:04
29 https://www.youtube.com/watch?v=Tn3Cr7bEO48 starting at 6:08
30 http://www.colts.com/news/article-1/THE-WACO-KID/adcc2fd3-53d6-4e1d-99d5-fad0886e8406
31 https://www.argonauts.ca/2012/07/08/veteran-qb-theismann-has-fond-memories-of-71-argos/
32 Hamilton VS Toronto TSN/ESPN2 Broadcast 12:25 of 2nd quarter. 2016-06-23
33 https://nationalpost.com/sports/nfl/unplugged-theismann-on-the-cfl-nfl-and-mark-trestman?r
34 http://articles.latimes.com/1994-10-30/sports/sp-56556_1_doug-flutie
35 http://www.youtube.com/watch?v=Ud2uVG0JDjU from 0:59
36 http://slam.canoe.ca/Slam/Football/CFL/Toronto/2009/08/21/10547576-sun.html?cid=rsssportscfl
37 https://www.nfl.com/prospects/aaron-donald/3200444f-4e13-4977-da01-4e2f082de38b
38 http://slam.canoe.ca/Slam/Columnists/Busby/2010/02/17/pf-12912216.html
39 3down Nation podcast - March 24, 2020 – 26:27 - Adam Bighill droppin' knowledge about the business and politics in the NFL
40 http://www.tsn.ca/duron-carter-s-journey-to-the-nfl-1.283518

41 https://calgarysun.com/sports/football/cfl/calgary-stampeders/former-teammate-jones-thinks-mitchell-can-turn-nfl-heads

42 https://3downnation.com/2020/06/24/eskimos-head-coach-scott-milanovich-ricky-ray-and-anthony-calvillo-couldve-started-in-the-nfl/

43 Double Blue Podcast - Episode 13 – 25:56

44 http://3downnation.com/2018/01/26/victor-butler-argonauts-holding-hostage/

45 https://www.seccountry.com/sec/there-are-42-former-sec-players-playing-in-the-cfl-where-they-feel-wanted

46 http://www.herald-dispatch.com/sports/x988040988/Jennings-now-a-Montreal-Alouette

47 http://www.chargers.com/multimedia/videos/Inman-and-Law-From-CFL-to-San-Diego/8d067049-fb71-4188-9217-35f44bab7797

48 http://www.cfl.ca/thewaggle - Episode 3: Carter's Bump & Lemon's CFL Tour Continues – 37:31 of podcast

49 https://www.seccountry.com/sec/there-are-42-former-sec-players-playing-in-the-cfl-where-they-feel-wanted

50 https://3downnation.com/2020/11/13/3downnation-podcast-undrafted-derrick-moncrief-achieves-nfl-dream-through-canada/ 3DownNation Podcast - "Undrafted to NFL dream through Canada; Derrick Moncrief - 45:30 to 46:38

51 https://www.youtube.com/watch?v=OU5tl0FRrTw – 6:47, 8:04

52 http://www.cbc.ca/sports/football/opinion/2012/09/adjusting-to-cfl-life-can-be-tough-on-americans.html

53 http://torontosun.com/sports/football/cfl/toronto-argonauts/argonauts-jonathan-dowling-standing-tall-in-secondary

54 https://www.palmbeachpost.com/sports/20190905/miami-dolphins-lb-sam-eguavoen-closing-in-on-nfl-debut-says-lsquoirsquom-no-rookiersquo

55 https://3downnation.com/2021/02/24/you-guys-are-so-full-of-it-super-bowl-champion-db-will-blackmon-provides-glimpse-into-chris-jones-led-riders

56 https://www.riderville.com/2017/10/12/rakim-cox-gets-eyes-opened-cfl/

57 https://www.sportingnews.com/ca/soccer/news/where-will-bruno-fernandes-fit-in-at-manchester-united/hu4ucfdbdeah1unfbwj2p6jy6

58 https://www.miamidolphins.com/news/sam-eguavoen-enjoying-life-in-the-nfl-playing-for-dolphins

59 Although Breaux attended LSU, he did not actually play in a single game in college due to health concerns.

60 https://www.bakersfield.com/sports/bvarsity/west-high-graduate-reintroduces-himself-to-cfl-in-more-ways-than-one/article_c678b0da-de4e-11e8-ade3-d7918f138ffc.html

61 Personally provided quote – reached out via Twitter DM.

62 Personally provided quote – reached out via Twitter DM.

63 Minimum 5 returns.

64 https://www.seattletimes.com/sports/seahawks/former-cfl-stars-brandon-browner-cameron-wake-meet-again-sunday/

65 https://www.si.com/more-sports/2012/09/19/andrew-hawkins

66 https://twitter.com/ChicagoBears/status/899044116331339777

67 https://cruathletics.com/services/download_file.ashx?file_location=https://s3.us-east-2.amazonaws.com/sidearm.nextgen.sites/cruathletics.com/stats/football/2004/pdf/cume.pdf

https://cruathletics.com/services/download_file.ashx?file_location=https://s3.us-east-2.amazonaws.com/sidearm.nextgen.sites/cruathletics.com/stats/football/2005/pdf/cume.pdf

https://cruathletics.com/services/download_file.ashx?file_location=https://s3.us-east-2.amazonaws.com/sidearm.nextgen.sites/cruathletics.com/stats/football/2006/pdf/cume.pdf

https://cruathletics.com/services/download_file.ashx?file_location=https://s3.us-east-2.amazonaws.com/sidearm.nextgen.sites/cruathletics.com/stats/football/2007/pdf/cume.pdf

68 https://www.d3football.com/columns/around-the-region/south/2012/Freeman-makes-a-big-leap

69 http://www.chargers.com/news/article-1/Can-WR-Dontrelle-Inmans-Success-Carry-Over/b02b3345-0ab9-4229-b0c9-0af8350ba87d

70 Personally provided quote. Reached out and received answer on Twitter via DM

71 https://web.archive.org/web/20160207000723/http://whodatdish.com/2016/01/29/new-orleans-saints-fans-vote-delvin-breaux-defensive-mvp/

72 https://www.pff.com/news/pro-top-101-nfl-players-from-2015-nos-76-101

73 https://bleacherreport.com/articles/2623992-br-nfl-1000-ranking-the-top-101-cornerbacks-from-2015

74 www.palmbeachpost.com/news/sports/football/miami...marcus-thigpen...-/nTBzm/

75 Minimum 10 punt returns on the season.

76 https://www.cfl.ca/2020/04/19/singleton-calgary-just-embraced-loved 27:56 of The Waggle Ep 206

77 https://3downnation.com/2016/04/16/15832/

78 https://www.cfl.ca/2020/04/19/singleton-calgary-just-embraced-loved 28:04 of The Waggle Ep 206

79 https://www.cfl.ca/2020/04/19/singleton-calgary-just-embraced-loved 22:42 of The Waggle Ep 206

80 https://www.youtube.com/watch?v=r3Mi6pjeD4E 5:35-6:08

81 http://profootballtalk.nbcsports.com/2012/11/22/brandon-browner-cameron-wake-meet-in-match-up-of-cfl-success-stories/

82 https://gopsusports.com/news/2005/2/22/Derek_Wake_Participating_In_NFL_Scouting_Combine.aspx

83 https://www.youtube.com/watch?v=iOgh4geg4UU

84   https://bleacherreport.com/articles/548384-nfl-power-rankings-julius-peppers-jared-allen-and-2010s-25-best-pass-rushers#:~:text=%20NFL%20Power%20Rankings:%20Julius%20Peppers,%20Jared%20Allen,,back%20at%20top%20leading%20a%20Falcons...%20More

85 https://www.pff.com/news/nfl-pff-all-decade-top-101-best-nfl-players-2010s

86 https://twitter.com/PFF/status/1260276337979330560

87 https://www.colts.com/news/colts-trade-for-cassius-vaughn-7387913

88 https://profootballtalk.nbcsports.com/2012/12/12/cassius-vaughn-wins-afc-defensive-player-of-week-honors/

89 Personally provided quote – reached out and received response via DM on Instagram.

90 https://bleacherreport.com/articles/1466317-2013-nfl-draft-5-potential-late-rounders-that-could-become-stars

91 http://gocatawbaindians.com/article.asp?articleID=5653&mo=4

92 https://www.salisburypost.com/2012/10/17/college-football-catawbas-charest-rolle-determined-to-finish-strong/

93 *https://www.cfl.ca/davaris-daniels-making-every-step-count/*

94 https://www.nfl.com/prospects/jonathan-newsome/32004e45-5757-6048-e623-13a87a59a590

95 https://www.pff.com/news/secret-superstars-indianapolis-colts

96 https://horseshoeheroes.com/2014/12/17/jonathan-newsome-premier-pass-rushing-prowess/

97 https://www.espn.com/blog/bigten/post/_/id/9387/big-ten-players-of-the-decade

98 http://en.montrealalouettes.com/video/index/id/99245

99 https://www.espn.com/nfl/draft2014/story/_/id/10269223/2014-nfl-draft-tre-mason-auburn-tigers-forgoing-final-year-eligibility

100 https://bleacherreport.com/articles/1959508-tre-mason-nfl-draft-2014-highlights-scouting-report-more

101 https://www.foxsports.com/stories/nfl/police-rams-tre-mason-admitted-to-hospital-after-behaving-erratically

102 https://www.nbcsports.com/chicago/chicago-bears/nfl-draft-profile-lsu-cb-jalen-collins

103 https://www.youtube.com/watch?v=1F5wHVbDXfo

104 https://www.nola.com/archive/article_5e2b63e1-a4ed-5b45-be2d-021494830f20.html

105 https://bleacherreport.com/articles/2749275

106 https://www.cbssports.com/nfl/news/johnny-manziel-has-disastrous-cfl-debut-including-a-nightmarish-first-half/
107 https://www.yardbarker.com/college_football/articles/the_50_best_college_quarterbacks_of_all_time/s1__27528233#slide_22
108 https://saturdayblitz.com/2021/03/27/30-best-college-football-quarterbacks-of-all-time/11/
109 https://3downnation.com/2021/08/05/shane-ray-warns-nfl-players-who-sign-in-the-cfl-i-definitely-dont-think-you-should-take-it-as-high-school-football/
110 https://www.nfl.com/prospects/shane-ray/32005241-5942-7102-1e06-2662a8cf1a91
111 https://www.9news.com/article/sports/broncos-decline-fifth-year-92-million-option-on-shane-ray/73-548202055
112 https://www.cnn.com/2020/02/03/media/super-bowl-2020-ratings/index.html
113 https://www.statista.com/statistics/217134/total-advertisement-revenue-of-super-bowls/
114 https://www.si.com/nfl/2017/01/31/chris-matthews-seahawks-patriots-super-bowl-xlix
115 https://www.mirror.co.uk/sport/football/news/zlatan-ibrahimovic-hits-out-mls-18366017
116 https://youtu.be/v8gU34nvUeM at 2:18
117 https://gianlucadimarzio.com/it/bernardeschi-juventus-napoli-intervista-news-28-giugno-2022
    https://football-italia.net/bernardeschi-on-mls-tempo-juventus-regrets-and-napoli-links/amp/
118 https://www.youtube.com/watch?v=NzRtxellRvQ starting from 0:26
119 https://www.straitstimes.com/sport/football/football-bundesliga-is-of-the-same-quality-as-premier-league-says-german-great
120 https://www.argonauts.ca/2021/07/21/288925/
121 https://www.facebook.com/GermanFootballLeague/videos/interview-mit-thiadric-hansen/338183370190913/
122 https://3downnation.com/2022/11/17/it-starts-from-the-top-guy-argos-mcleod-bethel-thompson-takes-aim-at-cfl-commissioner-randy-ambrosie-for-negative-league-narratives/
123 https://www.youtube.com/watch?v=wfrB9-opTAs starting at 2:14
124 https://twitter.com/Wpg_BlueBombers/status/1645429362739777536?s=20
125 https://youtu.be/GoC7_7W9uqY from 28:10

Made in the USA
Monee, IL
07 May 2024

58063218R00168